CUTTHROAT

Editor in Chief...Pamela Uschuk
Associate Editors...Terry Acevedo
Karen Brennan
Bill Wetzel
Fiction Editor...Beth Alvarado
Poetry Editor...William Pitt Root
Online Fiction Editor...William Luvaas
Managing Editor..Andrew Allport
Assistant Fiction Editor...Julie Jacobson
Assistant Poetry Editor...Howie Faerstein
Assistant to the Editor..Susan Foster
Design Editor..Alexandra Cogswell
Editorial Assistants...Whitney Judd
Deborah Brandon
Interns..Tom Hallberg
Brigette Lewis
Stacey Allen Mills
Caitlin Vestal

CONTRIBUTING EDITORS: Sandra Alcosser, Charles Baxter, Frank Bergon, Red Bird, Janet Burroway, Robert Olen Butler, Ram Devineni, Rick DeMarinis, Joy Harjo, Richard Jackson, Marilyn Kallet, Richard Katrovas, Zelda Lockhart, Demetria Martinez, John McNally, Jane Mead, Dennis Sampson, Rebecca Seiferle, Luis Alberto Urrea and Lyrae van Clief-Stefanon.

Send submissions, subscription payments and inquiries to:
CUTTHROAT, A JOURNAL OF THE ARTS,
P.O. Box 2124,
Durango, Colorado 81302.

ph: 970-903-7914
email: cutthroatmag@gmail.com

Make checks payable to:
Raven's Word Writers Center or Cutthroat, A Journal of the Arts

Subscriptions are $25 per two issues or $15 for a single issue.
We are self-funded so all Donations gratefully accepted.

CUTTHROAT

CUTTHROAT THANKS

Website Design..Laura Prendergast
Pamela Uschuk
Cover Layout...Alexandra Cogswell
Pamela Uschuk
Magazine Layout..Alexandra Cogswell
Pamela Uschuk
Logo Design..Lynn McFadden Watt
Front Cover Art..Val Uschuk
The Guardian
Sculpture
concrete, found wood and metal, ceramics
Back Cover Art...Val Uschuk
Election Results
Sculpture
concrete, found wood and metal, ceramics

AND THANK YOU TO:

Alexandra Cogswell for her expertise in designing our cover and our magazine. Howie Faerstein and William Pitt Root proofreading. Doug Anderson, Howie Faerstein, Marilyn Kallet, Charlotte Lowe, Tim Rien, William Pitt Root and Pamela Uschuk, readers for our contests.

Val Uschuk for her sculptures used on our covers.
Photo credit: Val Uschuk and Pam Uschuk

Special thank you to Peggy Shumaker, Mariana Aitches, Marvin Bell, Dr. Dick and Gay Grossman, Joy Harjo, Lhotse and Kady Hawk, Marilyn Kallet, Willie Jame King, Jeffrey Levine, William Luvaas, Elise Paschen, William Pitt Root and Pamela Uschuk who donated at the Gold Level or far more to help fund this collection.

Our heartfelt gratitude to Susan Sheid for her generous donation of money and time to arrange a reading space for contributors in Washington, D.C. Thank you to Doug Anderson, Nickole Brown, Howie Faerstein, Willie James King, William Luvaas, Megan McNamer, Connie Post and Jesse Waters for setting up readings around the country.

We also thank our subscribers around the world.

Cutthroat, A Journal of the Arts presents...

Truth To Power:

Writers Respond To The Rhetoric Of Hate and Fear

*"Our lives begin to end the day we become silent
about things that matter."*
-Martin Luther King

Table Of Contents

Elmaz Abinader

Try This

Try

    Turn on the faucet--
    the water runs brown
    a smell that is acrid, it
    reminds you of flowers
    left in a vase too long--
    a toxicity you did not know
    flowers or water could have

Live free

    Without healthcare while the cancer
    in your stomach pushes you tight
    as a drum; clutch the script from the doctor
    for the eight-hundred dollar drug.
    Drink hot water, remember your
    grandmother's poultice, the smell of her hands,
    the rub that eased your cough.

Walk home

    Your hair wet from ball, hood up
    hungry and too thin for your clothes--
    the yelling behind you is indistinct;
    shrug on, block out the chamber click--
    say something as you fall gravel bits
    between the questions.

Read

    until the electricity is extinguished
    for good. Position their study table
    to catch the light from the street.
    Supply them with flashlights till
    the batteries are gone, and then
    candles that eventually melt
    into the plastic table covering

Wait
> Hold the picture until it imprints his face
> on your hand; someone will come soon
> to open the wall for a few minutes.
> You worry if your son will recognize you--
> if a hug can wrap him in the story
> of his ancestors, forgotten languages
> the music and swirl of your womb.

Trek new roads
> From your stone house not far from the school
> to a mountain path, hauling clothes and medicine
> pulling your children behind you, too shocked to cry--
> hungry and aching, they whimper. You slip
> your fingers into their mouths and they suck
> your skin to parchment

Sleep in a new position
> The one with your arm wrapped
> around your head, blocking
> the growl of jets, bedtime
> monsters. Leave one eye
> open, on the door, which could
> crash in, and disappear the tender
> bodies snuggled beside you

Sit
> With your mother's dead body
> for three days. The streets are not
> cleared, the piles grow. The smell
> is nothing when the air is charred
> and the buildings are embers.
> You do not bury her; you are
> entombed together.

Tend

> Run toward the fire, not away.
> Place what you believe on the pyre
> Stir in what you know and have lived
> Pull out the bones to build new
> cities. Tend the embers--plunge in
> one hand, cover it with ash. As it cools
> follow the cracks in your palm.

Samuel Ace

This is all that remains of the ghost

This is all that remains of the ghost it's my father who is dead I need more of his leg his arm his earth I need more of his moss his clouds his rain falling through the half decomposed skin onto the sand then into the wall that is the floor that is the wall no window inside the concrete box where I live my body slides through the drain my teeth beaten from my mouth and dissolved into the scum of my cold skin in the no breath naked in the box I can no longer see my killing that tulip the bringer of bringers of veils my blindness in the box almost complete I see nothing not even a word not even a house not even my dog my horse my foot not even your face or your fingers not even a fog I still know the keys but one word always means another cold means begins stool means voltage rope means silver they've all been switched if someone could just figure out the code it might make sense but they change the meanings then change them again then again until they are all scrambled I no longer remember my dreams but I do remember a well-dressed boy in a tuxedo who sits on a rocking lion he stomps furious into the lion's ribs the boy says taxi not lion he says run fast taxi his swift ride up the tower where he lives his father's mane and his mother's main of moated white certainty

I can no longer see my killing that tulip it's my father who is dead I need more of his leg his arm his earth more of his moss his clouds his rain

Jack Agüeros

Psalm for Distribution

Lord,
on 8th Street
between 6th Avenue and Broadway
there are enough shoe stores
with enough shoes
to make me wonder
why there are shoeless people
on the earth.

Lord,
You have to fire the Angel
in charge of distribution.

Andrew Allport

The Practical Use of Air Arms

Some of us took the position
it was impossible to fight in air. Some took
the position of wings, rapid and hectic

our broken hands arguing against the use
of force. Some of us were born lethal, special
in our small, light-moving bodies.

Some of us saw the playground diminish
in size, restricted in the name of self.
Games that once relied upon elaborate signals

were replaced by twin trenches, and by sheer repeated
battering—by bow, by catapult, we learned to live
close to the earth, and score each sparrow's heart

with a bullet. We were disproportionate,
like a man following pigeons on a bicycle.
Some challenged the state distinctions

between part and principle, how its rose-shaped
logic seemed to advance a system of conflict
between belligerent leaders and unmanned Author,

who authorized all aerial measures. The individual,
such as he is, shall be employed in conformity
with applicable calibers, recited the law.

Let us imagine thirty men, desperately bent.
Let us imagine the poison heart of future infancy.
Let me be clear as our domestic sky, said some

prayers, sent by ballista to parents the clouds resembled,
and while some saw in the planes a third brother,
some suggested targets: they were dealt new hands.

*note: the source texts of this poem are *The Command of the Air* by Giulio
Douhet, translated by Dino Ferrari; and a speech given by Harold Koh, the Legal
Adviser to the US Department of State, clarifying the legality of preemptive drone
strikes.

Beth Alvarado

Thanksgiving, 2016

When my daughter was thirty-six weeks pregnant with twins, she checked into the hospital to deliver even though she was not in labor. Her husband called me in the afternoon and left a message that I should come from work right away: they had decided to do a C-section. I tried to drive carefully. The message didn't say that this was an emergency C-section, but I'd been called out of class and the hospital was an hour away.

I should probably mention that this was the day before Trump was elected. I had recently moved to Oregon from Arizona and so the heavy November sky above the forest seemed out of a fairytale. The narrow winding roads were possibly slick with black ice. I was afraid deer might leap in front of my car or a semi veer into my lane.

I was worried about the C-section. Just the day before, the doctor had said both boys were head-down; she thought they could try a vaginal birth. The other doctor on-call was great, she said, at reaching up into the uterus and pulling out the second baby. Even breech. I did not like to imagine this happening to my daughter, but neither did I like thinking about a C-section.

That day, as I got into the car to drive to the hospital, everyone thought Hillary would win. Some predicted by a landslide. Some were buying champagne. I was not so sure. Disembodied heads, like Trump's—male, blustery, bullying, blind— had been hanging over my landscape for decades. Limbaugh, Gingrich, Cheney, to name a few, now Ryan and Pence, all men who called themselves "pro-life" although they would take food out of the mouths of the poor, health care away from children, and pensions away from the elderly.

When I got to the hospital, my daughter was still in her room, waiting. Her husband was sitting in a chair next to her bed. She explained to me that baby A was still head-down, but baby B was transverse and so the current doctor on call had said, "Call me a wimp, but I'd feel better doing a C-section." My daughter, who was a nurse and who'd reconciled herself to having these children however she could, agreed. "Nothing about this pregnancy," she told him, "has gone as planned."

When they came for my daughter, she stood up and walked out of the room, one hand closing the hospital gown behind her. My daughter is tall and strong and when her hair is down, it hangs to her waist in dark waves. About half way through her pregnancy, I began thinking of her as an Aztec goddess, although I'd never seen an Aztec goddess. Her body looked nothing like I remembered mine, so wide and soft mine was, I carried low, blue veins showing through the skin. She carried the babies out front, her belly round and hard, her legs long and slim, her breasts full. She looked much more like her father's sisters, I thought, although I didn't remember ever having seen them naked. I should remember what this is like, I'd tell myself, my daughter's body, pregnant.

That day in the hospital, just before she rounded the corner towards the delivery room, I realized that I'd imagined her on a gurney; I'd imagined kissing her forehead as they wheeled her out. Instead, she was walking away from me. I said, "I love you. I'll see you soon." She gave a small wave with her hand. "Love you."

We have this thing where we tell ourselves: it is nothing. A small operation, that's all. A procedure.

I waited. There was something about the election on the TV in the room, but I had muted it.

I remembered when my first grandson was born at only 31 weeks; he had to live in a plexiglass crib in the NICU for six more weeks—until just about the age of these babies, gestationally speaking. When my son had gone to the NICU with the baby, I'd stayed with his wife while they surgically removed the placenta, which had attached itself to her uterine wall with scar tissue. This condition, known as placenta accreta, without intervention, can result in the death of the mother. I didn't know this in the moment, but I felt it. She was in danger.

Now, in this hospital, the day before the election, my daughter was the only one I was worried about. I didn't even know the babies yet.

Of course, I hadn't known my daughter when she was first born, nor my son. They'd been small strangers, their appearance in my arms mysterious even though I'd been present at the moments of their births. I remember gazing at them and wondering who they were. I remember hoping I would love them.

I didn't know, then, that giving birth to them would make me essential, would attach me to this world as if with scar tissue. Even when their father died and some part of me longed to go with him, I would have to stay here. In so many fairytales, the mother abandons her children, usually through death, and that's why I had to drive so carefully. My children were not ready to be orphaned, even though they were both adults.

As I sat in the room, waiting for my daughter, the irony of my fears did not escape me. I was watching the muted television news, I was aware of what was *not* being shown: *not* the children actually being orphaned or killed in Aleppo, *not* the families of refugees in flimsy yellow boats on the Mediterranean seas, *not* the child refugees atop the train called The Beast coming up from Central America and Mexico, *not* the children of Detroit who had no clean water to drink, *not* the women giving birth in tents as they were protesting the Dakota Pipeline.

Those children were not even blips on our collective TV screen.

Instead, there was this blustery man, his head hanging over the landscape, all puff and noise, like the Wizard of Oz before the curtain is opened. He pulls the levers. The show begins. Even if we see through the smoke, we are riveted.

A few minutes later, they wheeled my daughter in on her bed. Baby A, the smaller of the two, only four pounds, was lying on her chest, the blanket tented over both of them. I was so relieved to see my daughter still alive, her hand stroking her baby's back.

That evening, as the shift changed, the nurses stood in the corner of the room, one briefing the other. I heard about the T cut, an inverted T—they'd had to make a second incision, up from the first, through the uterine wall to save Baby B. After Baby A came out, there had been a vacuum and the uterus had clamped down, trapping Baby B up under her ribs. Since they shared a placenta, once Baby A's cord had been cut, Baby B couldn't get any oxygen. I looked at my daughter. She was still so drugged. She turned her face to me and said, I could feel them pulling on him and pulling on him and pulling on him. I kept talking to Dad, asking him to help us.

Down in the NICU, Baby B was lying face down on a warm bed, tubes in and out of him, helping him breathe. He was so bruised, especially his legs and feet, where they had tried to pull him out. I wanted to touch him, I stroked his back, but he started crying. The alarms went off. The nurse ran in. His skin is too sensitive, she said. It's like someone feverish with the flu. If you want to touch him, just place your hand, like this, over the top of his head.

The next day, as the election results came in, my son-in-law kept turning the TV on and off. On, because we were in suspense; off, because, as he said, "We're not watching this." We took a picture of Baby A flipping the bird with his tiny hand. We visited Baby B in the NICU. My daughter was still vomiting from the medication.

By Thanksgiving, both babies were home and my son came to visit with his wife and their two sons. My grandsons were playing a video game in the other room and I kept hearing the older one say, "I'll sacrifice myself for you." I knew it was a game, but it made my heart hurt.

My son told me he was going to Standing Rock with other people from his church. This was when they were blasting the protestors with water canons, even though the temperatures were freezing and below and the water could endanger their lives. This was when Veterans and people of faith had vowed to go and put their bodies between the canons and the protestors, when others were shoring up the shelters for the winter, when the authorities ordered an evacuation out of a concern for "public health."

"This is not the first time we have survived winters here," one of the Sioux leaders said. But, of course, it would be the first time with the water canons, I thought. "I'll sacrifice myself for you," my son's son kept saying, but I did not want my son to stand in front of that wintery assault.

We had relatives who were Sioux and relatives who were Yaqui and, of course, over half of our family was Mexican, although they had been born here, for generations, even when the land was part of New Spain and Mexico. What does it take for us to be considered Americans, my husband used to ask—even though his grandfather had served in WWI and his uncles in WWII, Korea, Vietnam. My nieces and nephews kept posting on Facebook their fears of the Trump presidency and how it would affect their children. I kept imagining the way the force of the water would bruise my son's flesh, the ice crystals in his hair, the water in his lungs.

"Don't go," I wanted to say to him even though I knew he and his wife put themselves on the line for social justice all the time. They live their faith. Almost all faiths, all myths, even all fairytales, are about self-sacrifice for the greater good. "I will sacrifice myself for you," one grandson says to the other. He was the preemie and, even now, at age eleven, has arms like toothpicks. He has painted his fingernails red and wears a safety pin on his shirt even though, in the schoolyard, I've seen his sturdier seven-year-old brother have to stand between him and a bully.

As we sat around the Thanksgiving table, I thought of the irony of what was happening in North Dakota, and I realized that only two of us were not Mexican, not Jewish, not gay. In other words, only two of us were white, Anglo Saxon, Protestant, and straight. Only two of us were not marginalized in some way, not vulnerable to persecution. Discrimination, after all, is the political made personal.

Later, maybe the next day, my daughter and I were holding the babies, their soft bodies yielding against our chests. Snow had been falling for days. I remembered this feeling. It was like praying. "What shall I put on their Social Security forms?" she asked me. "Hispanic? Latino? White?"

When I was a young mother, my imagination was apocalyptic. I feared every-thing. I was afraid there might come a day when someone would try to take my children away from me because I was white and they and their father were brown. I would pray that something like that, which had happened in history, could never happen again. Not here. But I didn't know if that was why she was asking—if she wanted to record that her children were white, even though she wasn't, to keep them safe. Or if she wanted to record that they were brown, like her, so they couldn't be taken away.

Have faith? Oh, dear, dear America. Don't tell me to have faith. Faith might help us bear our burdens, it might help us devote ourselves to others, but it can't change what will happen when flesh meets steel or a wall of freezing water.

We have this thing where we tell ourselves: it is nothing. One election. That's all. It can't change the course of history. But, of course, it can. The arc of history is not inevitable: some of us have hoped and believed that we will keep evolving until the promise of liberty and justice for all is fulfilled. But now we see. That kind of faith is blind.

Doug Anderson

Inauguration, 2017

Under leaf-rot and rock-slime it stirs, faceless
but looking for faces, looking for form in the fear-
fog. It has fists talons fangs and toxins bred
of long coal-to-diamond crush under the rockpile
of wealth. One tube-foot at a time it reaches out
and snags a torn heart here, there, and then
a phalanx of them carrying heads on pikes and
singing for the death of all who would love
the world as one large thing, human and vulnerable.
Now comes the spike-footed centipede jack-booting
the inner thigh of tenderness: they will kill us for
questioning the juggernaut. Swastika and starlight
and a choir of shout-me-downs have come to call.
Let us in, they cry. Let us drink from this punchbowl
of your blood. Let us wear a necklace of your eyes,
let us burn your books, extirpate the mind-zone
that might offer a heaven on earth.
The apocalypse is too much fun, lynch mob sexy.
Let us revel, they sing, in our God-promised apoplexy.

Tara Ballard

A Post-Election Aubade from Saudi Arabia

With a line from Robert Hass

I squeak open
the window's security shutters
to reveal the world outside:

gray-white sky, sun huddled
behind the city's box-like buildings:
brown dust covers walls and rooftops
where even pigeons still sleep.

Blanket in hand, I settle now
into the L of our couch, shiver
in what-is-Red-Sea-coast-cold,
push the television remote
out of reach. I sit, curled up,
noiseless, and try not to worry
about what happened. I pull
the blanket close, hear my husband
turn over in our nearby bedroom.

And in all this
               slow waking,
the tea kettle begins its whistle.
I find myself thinking:
Maybe, *maybe[,] you need to write
a poem about grace.*

Tara Ballard

Unfinished Letters to Officer [Insert Name]

I.

May you read Joseph Conrad's *Heart of Darkness.*
May you fear yourself young, and black, and there.
May your stomach churn.
May you reside in a neighborhood with fifty-percent unemployment for your skin.
May you question location, direction, and life.
May you see yourself Lady Macbeth. *Out, out, damned spot!*
    (You will have to scrub harder.)
      May you witness the beauty of a village in northern Ethiopia.
      May you find time to view Al Jazeera's "Fault Lines."
      (There are a few episodes you might find interesting.)
May you lie down on a city street to feel the press of gravel into your chest and cheek.
May you take a break from reading comics.
May your lover avert her eyes.
May you experience hospitality in Ghana.
May you wake at midnight and tremble.
May you memorize Langston Hughes' "The Negro Speaks of Rivers."
May you dream oak trees.

II.

My husband is African American.

He is from St. Louis.
He is educated, reads Wordsworth and Yeats,
studies Biblical history.

His brother is a policeman.

If you saw my husband
walking toward you today,
would you cross the street?

25

III.

Say your name aloud. The world knows it.

A merchant selling cork outside
the city of Lisbon knows it.

A grandfather sipping mint tea
in Gaza knows it.

A college student protesting
in India knows it.

IV.

What are your thoughts on education?
Did you ever imagine yourself famous?
How do you feel about Edward Snowden?
Have you studied Maslow's Hierarchy of Needs?
Are you comfortable?

What are you thinking right now?
Have you read *Othello* or *The Invisible Man*?
Where do you see yourself in ten years? Twenty?
Who is your brother, Officer?

What brings you fear?

V.

[Insert Name],
remember those adolescent years.

May I call you
[Insert Name]?

VI.

Yes—I have smoked weed, rolled blunts.
I have listened to rap music, watched
Belly and *Boyz n the Hood*.

I have said bad words and taken photos
with my middle finger to the sky.

When I was fourteen,
I braided my hair, Officer.

How many times
would you fire that gun at me?

VII.

Forgive me for I have sinned.
My hands are lifted.

VIII.

Officer [Insert Name],
what is your crime?

Aliki Barnstone

So That They Shall Not Say, This Is Jezebel

1
The one who tells the story has power to erase
a story, a nation, a faith, "so that they shall not say, This is Jezebel,"
Phoenician princess who became Queen of Israel.
So that a woman shall not speak, a woman shall not
have power to tell the story.

2
Emily Dickinson wrote "The Bible is an antique Volume
Written by faded men." Skilled at the artful smear
such men make a Queen faithful to her own
a harlot, a fleshpot, a despot.

3
He looms behind her as she speaks,
taunts her for daring to lead.

4
The King of Greed rants she is pushy,
brags he grabs pussy, rapes a child, lies
every 196 seconds, fact-checkers reckon.

5
The teachings say she was a dominating wife,
with "force of intellect and will," and none
of the "nobler feminine qualities" of selflessness.

6
Faded men with faded skin, evolved from migrating North,
away from sunlight and warmth, away from the Mother God
brown-skinned Isis, whose name they disgrace, make a terror curse—
Isis, friend of slaves and artisans,
icon of the icon of Mother and Child.

7

After her son was murdered, knowing she, too, would be killed,
Queen Jezebel dressed, arranged her hair, and lined her eyes with kohl,
prepared herself for the grave where she would never be lain.
Her last question: "Does he have peace, who slays his Lord?"

8

His answer: "Throw her down!" Pushed out the high window,
adorned in a gold embroidered and tasseled hyacinth gown,
her blood splashed on her palace wall and on her assassins' horses.
"He trode her under foot" till he was king
and he left his Queen's corpse to be eaten by dogs,
except the skull, feet, and palms.

9

"And her carcass shall be as dung on the field…
so that they shall not say, This is Jezebel," write the faded men
who deem their story the Word of the Lord.

Appeared in *Spark and Echo*

Aliki Barnstone

Late January Thaw, Refugees, Fragments

The Christmas cactus opens like white gulls
diving toward the sea, their red beaks leading.

The late January thaw gives my muscles peace
and I put off deadlines.

If I could join
my breath with others
across oceans, if we
could share the air,
atmosphere be
love's common lungs.

The student recently released from solitary in Iran says his cell was six by seven,
and he's over six feet tall. There was no bed but he took comfort to know others
in the building, also in solitary, were journalists, professors, artists, thinkers, poets.

Five geese walk in unison over ice.
Others drift in the oval where ice has melted.
Near the lake's far shady bank still others rest,
heads tucked into their bodies.

My feet are cold when his radio words enter me.
My toes curl beneath my chair.
My socks and sweater are navy blue and soft.
My black cat in the seat beside me purrs,
mewing a bit, and bumping the top of her head
against my elbow.

A fragment.
A boat sinking
off the coast
of Samos.

All at once the whole flock rises,
their wide wings flickering
shadows on ice.

Gusting wind.
Rusty oak leaves wobble wildly
but do not fall.
Oppressed on Lesvos, Sappho wrote her daughter,
I have no embroidered headband
for you, Kleis …

Fragments of clothing, plastic, or wood
on the water's surface.
24 dead. 9 of them children.
Yesterday
alone.

The tea kettle wails to my soul,
Aflame, aflame.
A video shows ambulances racing from the quay.

A fragment
of understanding.
Words in Arabic,
Greek, English.
Fake life preservers
piled on the beach.

Tamman Azzam (musical name) photoshopped
Gustav Klimt's *The Kiss* over a bombed out
Syrian building.

Ancient walls
or new.
Fabric of craters.
The Kiss
on ghosts
of living-
quarters.

Even so, the parents tie a bright ribbon around their little daughter's head
before they board the unsafe boat.

Today the sun makes gray ice and clouds
luminous silver, though some would call it white.

Today an African violet bloomed and looks out
from a corner of windowpane at bird feeders swinging in a breeze,
geese huddled on the ice.

Tonight another freeze.
The hours of sun become
glowing fragments
in wintertime.

A crowded raft.
Another raft behind it.
Rescuers with red cross vests wade out.
A bottle of water.
A snack.
Some dry shoes and clothes offered
from bins lining the beach
where once were chaise lounges
and generous umbrellas.

Samos, Rhodos, Kos, Leros, Lesvos.

In the State Historical Society of Missouri hangs the painting, Order Number 11.
The guides explains the self-emancipated slaves, who are fleeing toward us, out
of the picture plane, are refugees.

A boy and a man.
A man who hides his face
in his hands.
A wide-eyed boy
in rags.

The candles burning on my dining room table are for memory,
Oh, transporting scents.

No. The little flames
focus attention
inside where
there are no
            borders.

House sparrows fight over birdseed.
They came from Europe.
They kill off the native bluebirds.

Somewhere in Syria, Yazidi women are slaves.

The enterprising refugees
gather discarded pool toys,
life preservers, so-called,
fashion them into purses
and messenger bags.

The sewing machines—
gifts from the people of Lesvos
where Sappho wrote poems
not intended to be fragments:

>   *The bright*
> *ribbon reminds me of those days*
> *when our enemies were in exile.*

On the high hill above the beach and ruined rafts and wooden boats
and full graveyards, people from all over the world gather
life jackets and water wings and form an enormous peace sign.

A sign made
of wrecked
life preservers.
Preserve life.
A sign to be
seen by people
from the air,
breathing air.

Appeared in *Rattle's* "Poets Respond"
January 31, 2016

Rick Bass

Open Letter To What Comes Next

Nobody saw it coming. For the second time in as many decades, a Democratic presidential candidate received a significant majority of the popular vote but lost the election.

What happened? What many saw as repugnant and undignified, others gawked at and then, seeing there were no repercussions for bad behavior, that indeed those antics garnered attention, they cast their lot with Donald Trump: decided to look past racism and misogyny. I can guess why some economically-marginalized middle-aged white men, watching the last of their 1950s world-of-power slip away years ago, and never dreaming it would return, rallied. But I don't understand how even one person of non-white color, or one woman, voted for Trump: a prisoner, voting for the warden. Millions did, though.

For the other millions who voted for Clinton, or against Trump, or both, we miss already the grace, dignity, and poise of our old leader. As we prepare to descend into darkness and gird ourselves for a cultural and ecological war, there are spots of lamplight to which our eyes are fixed in the dimming: last gestures a man of courage and hope, earned hope, can deliver to us, before the darkness. Things we elected President Obama to do, and which he can still, while his term, his job, yet exists: the grand and the minute.

The current demographics of the Supreme Court are such that it is not beyond possibility that we could go from a 4-to-4 balance of justice to an 8-1 archconservative majority during a Trump presidency. It is not inconceivable that in a few more years, all the pieces are in place for us to turn into a country as religiously and socially austere and abusive as, say, the Taliban, with codification of men telling women what they can or cannot do with their bodies, and that one must pay to vote. That a handful of paying corporations will continue to receive unaccounted and uncountable subsidies, while the poor get poorer.

Trump's nomination of Exxon's Rex Tillerson as Secretary of State, at a time when the world is burning, gagging on carbon, and pipelines are rupturing and spraying all over the West and Midwest—does anyone still even remember the Exxon Valdez?—and Scott Pruitt as head of EPA is a gargantuan leap back in time, one that threatens to change not just the physical health of the country, but the world. It is more than an embarrassment, it is a clear and present danger. The Arctic is melting. International oil companies are seeking to drill within the boundaries of the Arctic National Wildlife Refuge. The Refuge should be declared a National Monument and protected forever. Leonard Peltier, a political prisoner, awaits freedom every four to eight years; another need. So much good is yet undone, here in late December of 2016, and so much terrible is rising to the top of the aggressors' agenda.

Fifty tribes have signed a letter to Obama requesting there not be a trophy hunt on Yellowstone's grizzly bears, though he has not yet responded. (The nation's leading scientists have also written a letter, detailing evidence of how global warming places the grizzlies in peril, and of the government's extremely flawed methodology—counting whitebark pine trees rather than crop yields, for instance, and missing 60% of the dying trees in their survey, even at that. Science is in freefall, as if in a return to the Dark Ages.)

In the diminutive Yaak Valley, where neighbors once fought for generations over land issues, collaborative agreements have been hammered out that create jobs removing fuel from overstocked forests around communities while protecting the farthest, most special places on the public lands. Such forward-thinking experiments in peacemaking should be given authority and support to succeed. (A previous midnight rider on a Congressional bill by a single Representative has authorized a human high-recreation highway of over 4000 users annually to be directed through designated core grizzly habitat, over the wishes of the collaborative, and over the findings of a Congressionally-authorized study).

The grand and the small. All of this unfinished business has in common the dignity of long years of hard work on behalf of the public and the future and a responsibility toward those who come after us. For a little while longer yet, his and our time is still now, and these things, good work still undone, endure yet.

I remember watching Al Gore—another popular vote winner—leaving D.C. by helicopter, as if departing the fall of Saigon. I am preparing myself for the close of eight years of things we did not get done. How fast time flies. How much harder we could all have worked. I still have hope, but hope without works is empty. Or as Ed Abbey said, Sentiment without action is the ruination of the soul.

We're in a tight spot. The way forward is narrow, rocky, unclear. Four or five states hold the key to the world. My beloved West—my beloved Montana—holds the majority of the country's coal "reserves." (And the Carlisle Group holds the majority of those leases on federal land; they've been waiting, patiently). We are looking for a new leader, an opposition leader, around whom we can rally, and surge, in democratic counter-response to the ugliness that just happened. But in the meantime, there is always work to be done at home—a kind of decentralization of democracy, and greater involvement, I suspect, in local issues.

This is why democracy takes so very long to change, but then changes suddenly, when it does.

We are casting for a larger narrative, amid the rubble. Yes, misogyny is a terrible thing—is plain and simple hatred without-a-cause—as is racism. Yes, the destruction of the earth, clawing and gouging and dozing all that can be reached on the public lands—greed—is a bad thing. The would-be oppressors are braiding and branching out like floodrivers; we will be called upon to defend our values locally, but are searching, again, for a clean line of narrative to reject the would-be oppressors.

I don't want to think of this as speaking truth to power. I want to think of it as speaking truth to greed. I think all bullies operate from a place of fear, terrible fear. As they should. There are weaknesses—in this instance, a monstrous greed—and we will find them.

There are no new tricks in politics. Cutting off the money supply is vital. Other than that, the old fundamentals, old verities, still apply: all politics is local, and success will come from endless pressure, ceaselessly applied.

We all let up, last time. It won't happen again.

Kate Bell

Hair On Fire

Thick knit knowledge does no good-
a pale flame, a dark cell,
hot coffee, cold vodka,
white-out silver ice, honey locust
blind light, no light - - steering, no steering
collapsed lung
collapsed legs

and when the rocks can no longer hear
they gasp

Hair on fire
white clouds roll in
no escaping this slice of tight solid ice
blazing night white-out on the pass,
and a stranger arrives wielding a gun or a knife

and when the trees can no longer see
they moan

and if the snow never stops falling
people will forget the colors of flowers
Blue River rose and the marble moon,
grim over the mountains
rising.

Kate Bell

In March

The lion devours the lamb
as a pale blue malaise settles
and political powers provoke -
is there a collective concern
or are we numb?

Scrub jays scatter, squawk
blue upon black
into the grey sky.

The moon hangs heavy and wet
in the morning, the tips of the trees
are swollen, auburn colored twigs
cover the edge of meadow and
we are bruised by the media over and over again-
we wail, ache for a song –
a rising up, a revolution – and
a hemlock resting on a lonely ridge.

And finally one morning in May
(for April has dissolved in the hard
rocky soil like our thoughts
about dictators devouring lambs)
a flock of mountain bluebirds
appear with an undeniable sweetness-
and there is a streak of bold blue and wild orange flowers.

Kate Bell

December Twenty-Seventh, Droney Gulch – First Foot of Snow

The ridge white as cake, sky like a hero's song - brilliant blue
ahead of us a wall of white pinnacles
we stomp with pleasure as winter sun
lights our faces with fire
ancient junipers wide spiraling trunks, textures of time
wood given into the wind
chickadees grin
we follow the arroyo to where the
ponderosas appear
guarding the way

How like a Mondrian painting this small day journey,
we slip into the ease of our friendship here in the sage and snow

Push away the injustices and violence of the past year
the sprawling pain, a year of Pollock's incoherent internal rhythms-
hungry mouths, guns taking down Black American Men, and the
disappearance of children
poison our dreams
as a sharp-shinned hawk takes to the air above us
the old dog bounds into deep drifts
we laugh, calculate how many more miles
to reach the trailhead

We walk with the mystics to the mountains
not just for joy but to recall all the people of our tribe-
and like the juniper to stand against the wind and
the suffering

Marvin Bell

The Book of the Dead Man (The Election)

Live as if you were already dead.
Zen admonition

1. About the Dead Man and the Election

The dead man ate and went to bed.
The morning after the election, he was once again uneasy.
He worried about who now had the ear of the president-elect.
He had qualms about the cocksure ex-professor back in vogue.
He swam in a flood of late reports from the cults, cliques and cabals.
He felt the bewilderment of those who thought much of the country an
       undifferentiated flyover.
He thought back to the calamities of "the best and the brightest."
He had watched the humanities wither on the ivy.
He saw again an aggregate of interests shattered by single-issue voters.

2. More About the Dead Man and the Election

He, too, heard the plans of the high-flyers, the salt of the earthbound, the
       prideful *summa cum laud-ies* and dishonest Abes, the impetuous
       fresh-faced and the grumps against change.
He has felt the heat of the self-righteous and the bully-pulpit bullies.
He has seen the best of Congress sapped in the hunt for cash.
The dead man is not surprised, he is never surprised, those who know they
       live in the preposthumous will never be surprised.
He does not forget that minorities everywhere have had to know what's up
       and where to stand.
The question recurs, whether to stay or go.
There will be no absolution for the ideologues, the for-hire celebrities, the
       vain talking heads, the provincial dailies of the cities, the rich who
       stiff workers.
The dead man does not want to say that he is better than anyone, and
       Mercutio had it right, but *this*?
A nation ruled by the wickedly rich.

Wendell Berry

1993

1

No, no, there is no going back.
Less and less you are
That possibility you were.
More and more you have become
those lives and deaths
that have belonged to you.
You have become a sort of grave
containing much that was
and is no more in time, beloved
then, now, and always.
And you have become a sort of tree
standing over a grave.
Now more than ever you can be
generous toward each day
that comes, young, to disappear
forever, and yet remain
unaging in the mind.
Every day you have less reason
not to give yourself away.

(THIS DAY: Sabbath Poems Collected and New,
1979-2013 and LEAVINGS, Counterpoint Press, 2013.)

Wendell Berry

2005

XII

If we have become a people incapable
of thought, then the brute-thought
of mere power and mere greed
will think for us.

If we have become incapable
of denying ourselves anything,
then all that we have
will be taken from us.

If we have no compassion
we will suffer alone, we will suffer
alone the destruction of ourselves.

These are merely the laws of this world
as known to Shakespeare, as known to Milton:

When we cease from human thought,
a low and effective cunning
stirs in the most inhuman minds.

(THIS DAY: Sabbath Poems Collected and New,
1979-2013 and LEAVINGS, Counterpoint Press, 2013.)

Wendell Berry

2007

II
The nation is a boat,
as some have said, ourselves
its passengers. How troubling
now to ride it drifting
down the flow from the old
high vision of dignity, freedom,
holy writ of habeas corpus,
and the land's abundance—down
to waste, want, fear, tyranny,
torture, caricature
of vision in a characterless time,
while the abyss whirls below.

*

To save yourselves heartwhole
in life, in death, go back
upstream, if you have to swim
ashore and walk. Walk
upsteam along the bank
of the Kentucky River, the bank
of Cane Run, and step from
stone to stone up Camp Branch
through the cutdown, longtime
returning woods. Go back
through the narrowing valleys
to the waters of origin, the dry
leaves, the bare wintering trees,
the dead, the unreturning.
Go from the corrupted nation
To the running country. With the land
Again make common cause.
In loving it, be free.

Diminished as it is,
grant it your grief and care,
whole in heart, in mind
free, though you die or live.
So late, begin again.

*

The abyss of no-meaning—what
can prevail against it? Love
for the water in its standing
fall through the hill's wrist
from the town down to the river.
There is no love but this,
and it extends from Heaven
to the land destroyed,
to the hurt man in his cage,
to the dead man in his grave.

*

Shall we do without hope? Some days
There will be none. But now
to the dead and dry woods floor
they come again, the first
flowers of the year, the assembly
of the faithful, the beautiful,
wholly given to being.
And in this long season
Of machines and mechanical will
there have been small human acts
of compassion, acts of care, work
flowerlike in selfless loveliness.
Leaving hope to the dark
and to a better day,
receive these beauties freely
given, and give thanks.

(THIS DAY: Sabbath Poems Collected and New,
1979-2013, Counterpoint Press, 2013.)

Sherwin Bitsui

Empire

They announced you *captive*.

They *nouned* you on the television screen.

They strung cut ears around their necks
and winked from the parade when their horses
stood on hind legs
          absorbing the morning light
                    with blood on their hooves.

They picked scabs of dark from cigarette-lit streets
siphoned gasoline from walls lathered over babies beginning to teethe,
and slapped the fox from the lamb's soggy neck.

In the soup line,
          your army held their leggings above the wet floor,
and kept smoke from slithering out,
          when the announcer announced your language captive also,
          caged outside
                    where it mattered only when it barked,
                    where they named you thief
                              as you jumped
                                        to bite the bone.

First published in *Red Ink Magazine* Vol. 11 Number 1.

Roger Bonair-Agard

Allegory of Fire – 38 of 365

I'm back home and it's Winter. Immediately the dark
sheen of my skin in the sun that was once my home
is gone. I have to think again about different ways
to be Black. In Georgetown Grand Cayman I set off
the alarm in my aunt's home, and my first thought
was to peel away at high speed from the house
before the police came to see me standing there
and made of me something extraordinary to sing.
Then I remembered I was not in America. I called
got the code, re-entered the house, took off the alarm.

Meanwhile back home, Trump promises to privatize
well… everything. I'm struggling with how to use
the word – home. My daughter, I remind myself,
is American. For that matter, so am I, but all I can think
of right now is that a boy I knew from my childhood
a fellow we called Panther, died last week.
He was in his fifties. He was dark as I remember.
That family had several sons. The last one
closer to my age, we called Sunshine. He was light
skinned, what we called at home, a red man.
Panther and Sunshine, brothers in the Moses family.
I'm amazed I can remember their real names. The village
is adept at naming what it sees, regardless of what it's called
before that moment. This is the way of villages
and bush people.

Meanwhile, we're busy in America not naming
what it is we see. We knew what Trump was
all the way until he won, now the most official
owners of the rights of naming things, call things
by shadow, name things by proxy. Alt-right
they say. White working class angst, they crow.
He felt the pulse of the people, they prevaricate.

Meanwhile men attack Islamic women on trains,
burn men wearing turbans on freeways. It has begun –
the burning that is. It always seems to be the way
of another kind of not-naming – the cleanse.
Books, witches, Blacks, Mexicans – we know
the burn. Octavia Butler dystopifies the role
of fire in Parable of the Sower. A drug makes
watching fires feel even better than sex, and so fires
are set. I made up a word to name what Octavia did.
I could see no other way. Perhaps this is what education
does – distorts the ways we see. From the Latin
e-ducere, to draw out. Perhaps it is not what is drawn out
of us, but how we are drawn out of ourselves. Perhaps
that's how we come to see fire, as cleanse, as a way
to make ourselves new again.

My grandfather set fires to get rid of our garbage
when I was a boy. I loved to watch those. At home,
the LaBasse is where all the country's garbage goes.
The poor salvage what they can from its massive
mountains. They set fires all the time. Fires
set themselves in those giant dung heaps.
The smell is enormous and nothing comes clean.
In Grand Cayman it is illegal to set fires. Still,
some do. We stood for a moment to watch one
smolder. We looked into the charred wreckage
trying to figure out what was there before. Frames,
shadows, husks of what had been, but enough
to put a bare bone story together. That's the trouble,
and the beauty of fire. It removes, but it can't make it
come completely clean.

Heil Trump, say his supporters – an ecstasy of remembering
amongst them not there to know what burning does,
what it did, what it continues to do, how the fire
seldom only takes what is set, ablaze. At least
they're naming what they see, their love
for smoldering notwithstanding. Everyone
in love with fires feels they can be proud
now. See them theorizing on the television. See them
doing and not naming. See them lie, which is the same
as staring into the mouth of a lion
and calling it a cave.

My skin is peeling. It does not hurt. My body
is immediately making me ready for Winter,
sparing me the agony of remembrance. Forget
the warmth and the black people who work
and the store owners who address you
as one would, a man. The Sun too, knows
something about burning, about scrubbing the skin
clean. The Universe knows how to protect its host
organisms even when they're bent
on annihilating themselves.

Right before we harvest the sugar cane, we set fire
to it – the leaves, the straw, the tops, all burned.
The burning kills microorganisms and the trash.
We leave those in the fields to keep the soil
rich. At home, in Trinidad, the burning of the canes
meant intense work for the slaves – cannes brulées
we called it. And after slavery, Canboulay
as celebration of slave uprising, of emancipation
as African re-purposing of carnival to speak
a new truth, a truth that wasn't previously being told.
We re-named the burning, and the celebration and the cane
and being Black and being Trinidadian. The colonizers
banned Canboulay in 1884. They banned percussion.
Imagine that. They thought they found
a way to stop the burning. Pan was yet to come.
Tubal Uriah Butler was about to be born.
The Midnight Robber was going to tell truths
anyway. Look them up. I'm riffing
on how we're going to survive. Of course
we started something else. We covered ourselves,
in mud, in oil, in color, in sound. Something else
was beginning. We called on the darkness
to sing the Sun up. We called it J'ouvert.

Christopher Boucher

Lo and Behold

That winter I took my daughter out to the blank pages of my hometown – Appleseed, Massachusetts – to see the place and plant some stories. My wife was against the trip – "It'll just depress her even more," she said – and she was right that the town was just an old, sad version of its former self. But that's exactly why I wanted to go. I still believed that stories had value – that they could change things over time.

So much of Appleseed had died under the Fathers' rule, though – these days it was just worryfields, empty pages, as far as the eye could see. We parked my truck on the margin near a worry where I used to run around as a kid, and my daughter and I trudged through the deadweeds and out into the center of the page. My daughter, who was four at the time, already looked bored. "Where *is* everybody?" she said.

"No one lives out here anymore," I said. "They have their own worrypages, somewhere else in the story."

My daughter scrunched up her face.

I put the shovel to the page and started digging. I thought the fibers might be frozen, but I was able to dig deep enough to bury the words. My daughter sat down on the page with her backpack and pulled her stuffed moose next to her. "You cold, honey?" I asked her.

She shook her head and whispered something to her moose. Then she said, "Moose wants to know if this was a good place to grow up."

I shrugged. "I didn't think so at the time? But it was OK. I used to ride my bike everywhere – that was cool," I said.

"You rode your bike in the grass?"

"There used to be a street right here. And my house," I pointed, "was right there."

"Where is the street now?" she said.

"It died," I said.

"Why did it die?"

"Everything dies unless you take care of it," I said.

She thought about that.

"Let's see those stories," I said.

My daughter opened the backpack and started pulling out the clumps of words I'd packed. One was a backstory about my aunt, who'd died the previous fall. Another story was about us – me, my wife, my daughter and my son – making it through these difficult Father years intact as a family. I put those two stories in the ground and started sifting some page over them. "See?" said my daughter to her moose, showing him the freshly-turned white space. Then she looked up at me and said, "What happens now?"

"We'll see if they take root – some do and some don't." Then I said, "There should be one more story in there."

My daughter reached into the bag and retrieved a tangle of rusted words. "These?" she said.

I nodded and she gave me the words. "They're cobwebby," she said. "What are they about?"

I shook my head and laughed. "You wouldn't believe me if I told you."

My daughter's face darkened.

I leaned down. "This story?" I whispered. "Is about the Mothers."

"Who are the Mothers?"

"They're are a secret team of protectors," I said. "They live in these buildings
called 'Nests,' way high up in the sky. When I was a kid, the Mothers used to fly overhead – "

"They can fly?"

"– looking for ways to help people. People who were hurt or mistreated. They've always done that, all through history. Did you know your grandmother was a Mother?"

My daughter's eyes widened. "Where are the Mothers now?"

I shook my head. "No one knows," I said. "They were exiled – that means kicked out – by the Fathers."

"Are they still alive?"

"That story says so," I said. "It says they're in hiding. But it also says that, eventually? More and more people – men and women – will abandon the Fathers and join the Mothers. That the Mothers come back someday stronger than ever, and make a town where people take care of each other."

My daughter's face was a holiday. "Can I plant this story?" she said.

"Oh. Sure," I said. I stood up and stepped aside, and my daughter scurried to the row of new stories and pressed the rusty words into the soil. "You can do it, little story," she whispered to the words. Then she stood up and wiped the page off her hands.

Right at that moment, something shifted; we heard a great crack, and the thunderous sound of earth moving and roots snapping. Then the page itself began to shake. "Move!" I shouted, but my daughter was frozen in place. I picked her up and carried her off the page and back to the car. We turned just in time to see the field crease and fold.

"What's happening?" my daughter hollered.

"The page is turning!" I shouted.

The white field raised high on one side and eased over, coughing page-dust on us. But the flipside – the next page – was ripe with stories. There was my street – Converse Street – and there was my old house and my neighbor Loam with his skateboard. I heard a whoosh overhead and looked up to see the shadow of flapping skirts in the sun. "Look," I said to my daughter, and pointed at them.

"Mothers," she said.

Without even thinking about, I stepped forward onto the new story. Then I motioned for my daughter to follow me.

"Is it safe?" she said.

I said it was and she took a careful step onto the sidewalk. Then she smiled up at me and skipped off across the new page.

Karen Brennan

Imminence

Red shouldered hawk sits on a wire waiting for the doves which he will kill. We sit in the car watching the hawk await its prey. Red shouldered hawk, very stationary, very beautiful, very noble, with a bold slice of orangey red on each shoulder. We light cigarettes and observe. We observe the spaces in the sky which are empty.   We observe the smoke filling the car's interior like an image (such as the hawk) fills the caverns of our imaginations. With our usual composure, we observe the ruthlessness of nature: one creature about to swoop upon another. Red-shouldered hawk snaps his head to the left. In the distance, the tender clamor of doves about to descend.   Is all life so misguided? we wonder. We light fresh cigarettes. The real show is about to begin.

From *Monsters*, Four Way Books, 2016.

Karen Brennan

2016 post-election walk in the desert upon fearing we had lost everything…

This narrow desert path
   Like life I think

The habit of metaphor crops up annoyingly
   But I can't transform the light

     Into anything other than it is
Sharpening the tips of things

A consolation to count
     Holes pocking the ground

   To creep into
Certain times of year (like now)

& rocks everywhere (to hurl)
    Composing mountains

   The Catalinas and Rincons
Still there

    The sky's true blueness
Still there

    A pile of desiccated brush, all
Silver webs and branches, hides a pale

  Thumb-sized barrel cactus
That managed to find shade enough to flourish in--

    Correction: that tries to flourish
  In the shade.

Nickole Brown

Trump's Tic Tacs

—"I've got to use some Tic Tacs, just in case . . . I just start kissing
them. . . . I don't even wait."

The night after my country loaded you
into its chamber and cocked
that long gun aimed straight for my
home, my wife and I were stuck
in a nearly dystopian line of unmoving
traffic. And because sugar comforts her
she popped those half-calorie candies
into her mouth and was bound to eat
the whole box herself until she shook out
from that hard plastic case the oranges ones,
just for me.

You see, Donald, this good woman,
she loves me. And she knows how the taste
of artificial orange makes me feel—
safe—makes me remember fevers broken
by the chalk tangerine of baby aspirin,
cool rags upon me, and a soft knock
on my door saying, Baby, don't get up;
mama's just checking on you again.
That was back when another man
not so unlike you was insecure enough
to also think it best to freshen himself before
grabbing at me, and to this day
I don't remember much except: Don't worry.
I took a shower; it's clean.

Donald, the news coming through the radio
made me sick. We had to turn it off.
We drove in stand-still, bumper-to-bumper
silence, unable to speak, especially not
of you. Yet there you still were,
a rattling under my tongue—those three orange
candies now tiny bullets, pills with a powdery zest
that never really were tasty but just mindless, addictive
in that high chemical way, not doing a damn thing
to sweeten anyone's breath. I could not spit
and could not swallow and helpless
let it dissolve in my mouth.

Sarah Browning

In Guantanamo

A man composes a poem
pressing his thumbnail
into the white permanence

of his Styrofoam cup –
Arabic script of praise song,
of lament, circling the cup,

cup of our disdain. Hail the
cup, singing its squeaky dirge
in the land of our castoffs.

Hail the poet's nail, thumb,
muscle and hail his nerve.

Sarah Browning

Drinking as a Political Act

The way my Virginia daddy made them,
mint juleps were a sacrament:

He folded ice cubes inside a clean
tea towel then pulverized them
with a wooden mallet that wasn't used
for any other purpose,

picked mint he'd grown and tended
in a strip of rich black earth that
hugged the south side of our house
on the south side of Chicago.

My Virginia daddy'd been with
Dr. King on the bridge in Selma, so
I didn't know 'til I was a middle-aged
white woman that some Black folks did not

share my view of the julep as a rare
and noble drink, but, rather, knew it
for what it was, plantation-born: ice
crushed by the strong arms of their

ancestors, sweetened with the blood
of others sold south to cut the cane.

I don't mean we forget my Virginia forebears
who sat out on their wide porches and sipped
the minty coolness of the labors of people
they took to be their property. I don't mean

forgiveness, even. I mean, let me make you
a sweet, ass-kicking julep. Let's raise a glass
to those who unmade that hideous life,

who, with their hard, truth-telling love,
keep unmaking it each day.

Christopher Buckley

Oil, Nostalgia, Immigration Reform, & The Decline of the West

All right, geniuses, what do you expect? The Texaco filling station atten-dants who snapped-to in their white uniforms, caps, and bow ties on Milton Ber-le's Texaco Star Theater are long gone—no one's going to wash your windshield, smiling as they check your tire pressure and oil. No trickle-down economics will bring back that '50s quartet harmonizing "We are the Men of Texaco, We work from Maine to Mexico" as they pump Fire Chief into the tank of your Hummer. You've been carrying home MTBE on your hands for years now and paying ten times as much as you used to for the privilege. Checked the rising rate of autism lately? Your portfolio manager tells you the answer is to buy more Exxon/Mobile stock. 76 Union had to scrape away half the town of Avila Bay and dump the oil-leached earth into someone else's back yard.

News Flash: Orange County chapters of The Young Republicans are not lining up for work in kitchens San Diego to L.A., or for five bucks an hour under the table shoveling out the stables at Santa Anita, Del Mar, and Hollywood Park. Congress men & women drink year round at the public trough—health care, franking privileges, airline tickets, all on the house. Over half of them on the Hill still like Ike, and can remember most of what Reagan forgot.

They're not turning away troops of Boy Scouts from the strawberry fields around Santa Maria. Some poor SOBs spend 60 hours a week with their backs bent in ditches so we can go to Vons and buy something for an attractive des-ert. Where did they hide the ballots in Florida? Enron ricocheted 40 billion from California in an energy scheme, Schwartzenegger poaches two billion from kids in classrooms, Karl Rove scripts the White House leaks, the earth is at its hottest in 400 years, and you have this problem with The Law!? With undocumented people mowing lawns, cleaning out your restrooms?

We're not in Brooklyn anymore—this is no '40s Bing Crosby film where the worst thing anyone can say is, "Hey, Mac, what's the big idea?" or "Sorry Bud, no dice" just before the millionaire donates his new building to the nuns. Back in the day Cisco & Pancho actually put the *bandidos* in jail, took no kick-backs or percentage off the top. The Mexicans were here before us and Standard Oil.

And who made a bundle off Jimmy Durante on the Colgate Comedy Hour, the "great schnozzola," who sang "Smile," "Make Someone Happy," and "Inka Dinka Doo," who was not a language poet, who told the truth in his baggy suit, who never got credit—or cash—for his song writing?   Each week he stepped back in black & white into the diminishing spotlights saying good night to Mrs. Calabash, doffing a forlorn fedora to honest inspiration. Who was it who said, "You've Gotta Have Heart" . . . "Wide as the ocean, deep as the sea"? Not the shareholders, not the board members of the executive committee, not the CFO of the Catholic Church. Every *saludo* and ticket stub of good will expired, unredeemable as Avila Bay dirt.

Instead of a six-shooter, they're using Supply & Demand when you fill up, and, if you buy that explanation, I do have a bridge in Brooklyn . . . .   No one's left who'll say, Howdy, partner, sit and rest a spell. Make yourself at home, Have a cigar, How are you fixed for dough, or, Step right up Sonny Boy, Have one on me. Whatever happened to So Long? Stay tuned? and Yours Truly?

Politicians, administrators, CEOs, I'll trust them as far as I can throw a house, when cows can fly. Never in a million years—that'll be the day. Fold it five ways and put it where the sun don't shine . . . twice on Sunday. Whatever spin they put on it, I'll bet you dollars to donuts there's not a snowball's chance in hell any of them will put the planet in front of profits.

If there is a God, a God of vengeance that all the red states thump the dust from their Bibles for, leave your number on his pager because He's not picking up. Thanks for nothing, sucker. And, Same to you!

Christopher Buckley

Social Contracts, Neocons, & Clichés

Each morning the Under Secretary and
Procurement Appropriations Mngr.s
arrive at their Defense Department jobs
lamenting the Welfare State,
creeping Norwegian Socialism. . . .
In the commissary, over their
Salades Niçoise, they wonder
where all the tax money goes—
complaining with the tea baggers about
food stamps for the dispossessed,
school lunches for inner-city kids.

Keep your eye on the ball,
your mind in the game—drift a bit
off base, and it's Goodnight Irene
for your prescription benefits.
Age as a pre-existing condition.
Ten in gets you five out—
sure as shootin'—you paid into
Social Security for 50 years
and it's now an "entitlement."
Your turn again in the unemployment
barrel. You might as well try
to throw liverwurst past the wolves
as bank on their lip-service
to community values . . .
sure as Mary had a lamb.

Their next socially responsible idea
will be their first, right after
one more five year plan
to cut the rich another break.
As majority leader, LBJ
saw 1 filibuster in 6 years;

Harry Reid faced 248 in 4,
most of them phoned-in;
I say make them stand there
and read the damned phone book
until they drop, every last one!

Throw the lobbyists out
with the sea water from
the nuclear reactors. Easy as pie,
piece of cake, which, despite the old
admonishment, they've never had
any intention of letting anyone eat.
If all the trains ran on time,
we'd form a more perfect Union,
and if my aunt had wheels she'd be a wagon—
we'd all wear black shirts
and ostrich plumes in our silly hats
as we click our heels
and try to take over Africa.
Dick Cheney and a select committee
are working on a scheme to privatize light—
double rates for Iceland.

The top hats are gone, but there's
no question who's riding in the coaches
and who's cleaning up after the horses.
I've got the heart of a poet and
the wallet to match. They still don't
do business with people they don't
do business with—the motto of CEOs
and drug cartels everywhere.
No dice Buster—that don't cut no ice
with us, say the underwriters
and actuaries.
            Haven't they always
wanted more than they wanted?
Trickle-down economics and tax loop holes
for squires, that's a lot of tom cats
and sour cream, and your bowl's
still empty isn't it? But everyone
with a pressed shirt and a sport coat
believes they see the bigger picture,
believes there's a metaphysical
coefficient for accumulation
which will appreciate and secure

their minimal spiritual investment.
Plenary Indulgences still on offer,
insider trading, golden handshakes,
a wink and a nod to the boys
in the back room is all it takes—
it's all good—and they're sure
that one day they will hear
all the angels sing.

But the older you get
the easier it is to see the diminishing
returns. So, just in case you lose
your way, here's a map to the nearest galaxy
should you really think you're going
anywhere when the job's over here,
should you believe there's no final
markdown, no accounting in the stars.

Excerpted from THE COLLECTED TWEETS OF CHUCK CALABREZE

Chuck Calabreze @ChuckCalabreze Feb 26
New poem from Donald Trump!

THE WALL
By Donald Trump

We're going to have our borders nice and strong.
We're going to build the wall, you know that.
We're going to build a wall.
Mexico is going to pay for the wall, right?
It's going to happen. It's going to happen.
They know it. I know it. We all know it.
They'll pay for the wall.
They'll be very happy about it.
Believe me. I'll talk to them.
They're going to be very, very thrilled.
They're going to be thrilled to be paying for the wall.

Chuck Calabreze @ChuckCalabreze Mar 5
Breaking news: Immigrants propose building wall around Donald Trump.

Chuck Calabreze @ChuckCalabreze Mar 15
Backbones are overrated. The vertebrates will be the first to go.

Chuck Calabreze @ChuckCalabreze Mar 20
Making America Grate Again.

Chuck Calabreze @ChuckCalabreze Jul 19
RNC on Melania Trump's speech: That wasn't plagiarism; that was sampling.

Chuck Calabreze @ChuckCalabreze Jul 19
Never mind his tax return. I want to see Trump's genome. Need to get to the bottom of this.

Chuck Calabreze @ChuckCalabreze Sep 1
Because you can't have an apocalypse without measurable outcomes.

Carmen Calatayud

Summer Storm Dance

*After Alton Sterling's murder by
two white Baton Rouge police officers
in a convenience store parking lot
on July 5, 2016*

1.
Pray to the crack in the sky,
night of a thousand clouds

where deer dance through steam
under July's Thunder Moon.

Skilled legs react as they race
from the spray of pale men

who believe in dominion by
machine gun rounds.

2.
Pray to the crack in the sky,
night of a thousand clouds.

Another shooting on a Baton Rouge street
where testosterone feeds on dark skin.

Summer wind begins to fill its lungs &
all moments pause inside this one.

Listen: Time barely exhales
& the satellite of hate chokes cable news.

3.
Pray to the crack in the sky,
night of a thousand clouds.

Muffled dread rises like steam,
creates leaky valves as blood

overflows from the four chambers
of our collective heart.

Fear overtakes the humid air while
the breeze has lost its common sense.

4.
Pray to the crack in the sky,
night of a thousand clouds.

How to stop sorrow of hot gator air
from tranquilizing the mind:

Move in grace.
Paint the night with a purple sky.

Stand Cypress-tree tall in the gut of darkness.
Dance like lightning when it's time to run.

Rosemary Catecalos

Catastrophe, Likenesses of

after Sontag

Here, take this image, make it *like* the world, no.
This image is not like the world, made or unmade.
No, neither does it *like* the world.

Here, take this image of the world, no.
This image is not *of* the world, not *like* the world, no.
No, not *as* the world. Either.

Here, take this picture of the world which *is.*
The world in the image of what has been made.
Here is an image of it. One of many you've made.

Here is an image you've made. No. It is History.
Take a picture of children mining diamonds.
Slave children. Thin. Diamonds are forever.

Here, *take* a picture as the world has it. Has them.
No. Or if not the world, then who? Or what?
Is it time? No. Is there time?

Here, take this image to *show.* Time. No.
Space. No. An image of the made world. Yes.
Also unmade. Greenbelt abutting desert. No.

Here, an image of an Indian reservation abutting
country club sprinklers. Yes. Of lush Golan condos
abutting dust, graffiti, shrinking land. No. Yes.

Here, take a picture of what we make.
No. Take a picture to stop. Time. Yes. No.
Take the time. To still. Believe. Resist.

Teresa Mei Chuc

Quan Âm on a Dragon

Mother shows me a lacquered painting on a plaque
of Quan Âm, bodhisattva of compassion, riding a dragon.

It is misty around the bodhisattva and the dragon.
The picture looks so real, almost like a photo.

A sacred vase in one hand and a willow branch
in the other to bless devotees with the divine nectar of life.

Mother says that she and other boat refugees saw Quan Âm as we were
fleeing Vietnam after the war in a freight boat with 2,450 refugees.

When she looked up towards Heaven, in the clouds, she saw
the bodhisattva in her white, flowing robe riding a dragon.

Mother says that the goddess was there to guide and save us
from the strong waves of the South China Sea. I should know

better than to believe her though she swears it's true.
I ask again and she nods, says really, I saw Quan Âm in the clouds

as we were escaping. I should know better than to believe her.
But, a part of me wants to believe in a bodhisattva, in compassion

riding on a mythical creature, to believe that somehow something
more than just our mere human selves wanted us to live.

(first appeared in *Whitefish Review*)

Teresa Mei Chuc

Love After Fukushima

I want the
courage of
the elderly who
volunteered
in the clean-up
at the
Daiichi plant

To be filled
with a desire
to live
and know that death
is a reality of
isotopes rearranging
in the body

Five years later
cesium-137
cesium-134
are still leaking
into the Pacific

Bluefin tuna
a neon green

I think I am
growing two
hearts
They beat one
after the other
in a constant
drumming with
no silence in
between.

(first appeared in *San Gabriel Valley Poetry Quarterly*)

Teresa Mei Chuc

Depleted Uranium

The water runs
a neon color
in the village.

All the villagers
know why
the babies

are born dead
and deformed.

Others say
there is no
proof it was
the war.

Sometimes
truth can
only be
understood:

the father carries
the little body
wrapped in a
blanket.
She will be buried
with a wooden
grave marker,
her name
inscribed
with a knife.

There are coffins
that are only
six inches long.

If you place
your hand
inside,
it will fit.

(First appeared in *Hypothetical Review*)

Alfred Corn

Global Chiaroscuro

Depression. The sort
subbasement midnight brings.
Then the mania of light
and heat at equatorial
noonday. Note too
that Arctic and Antarctic
play an electromagnetic role
in the bipolar planet's psyche.

Gone untreated,
its temperature too high,
Earth in its gloom
at last creeps toward
dawn, quaking with
a fracturing illness
experts diagnose
as human in origin.

Which can be addressed
only if humans can—
can we?—be cured.

Glover Davis

The Neoteric Poets

When power-drunk generals decided things
they massed their cohorts in a city square.
Anyone trying to stop them could be "proscribed."
You'd see his head impaled on an iron spike,
and this is how they murdered Cicero.
The republic died forever on that day.

The unnamed Emperor might take his seat
with other senators but they all knew
wherever he might sit would be a throne.
Because of this the Neoteric Poets
retreated to their gardens; there would be
few patriotic poems, no epics till
Virgil composed the Aeneid despite
himself but instructed his heirs to burn
it when he died.
                    Virgil, Propertius,
Horace and Catullus all believed they should
concentrate on details: "keep your sheep fat
and your lines thin."
                         We are so much like them,
carding our lives for things we'd weave like wool
Into the lines we station on a page.
Disgusted by our governments, puerile and corrupt,
we will concern ourselves with little things
surrounding us in the green shadows, moist
from watering like the blossoms just beyond us
in patches of light swaying on their stems.

Alison Deming

Dear America

The heat is just beginning to wane here in Arizona in the November ending the hottest five years on record. I've had to adjust my inner thermostat too, living here in terrain associated in many of the world's religions with spiritual testing. The election results threaten to undermine every cause that I as an educator, poet, and essayist have worked for in the past 50 years: women's rights, civil rights, environmental justice, science literacy, civil discourse, and empathy—and underlying all, the informed and reflective thinking required for democracy to thrive.

Only 25 percent of the American electorate voted for Donald Trump. That means 75 percent of Americans did not vote for deportation of Mexicans, banning of Muslims, denigrating and denying science, wasting this glorious planet for the sake of personal and corporate gain, hate speech, racist and misogynist words and deeds, or autocratic decision-making. The reasons that only 25 percent of Americans voted for Hillary Clinton will become more clear with analysis, though some elements of this outcome I suspect will remain opaque.

The reasons that the remaining 50 percent of Americans did not vote for any candidate include despair, cynicism, principle, and challenges to the right to vote. I will not castigate non-voters. I will praise them for not voting for a dangerous, ill-informed, disrespectful, undignified, greedy, and hate-filled bully. The fact that 75 percent of Americans did not vote for this candidate makes clear that Trump values are not American values. This vote says that whatever the reasons might have been for not voting, we need you now to avow your majority position in being publicly vigilant, articulate, respectful of difference, and caring toward the most vulnerable among our people and creatures with whom we share the planet.

We have seen language used to manipulate people, distort reality, deny facts, and betray our American ideals of liberty and justice. We need now to believe in the power of language to help us connect across our differences, express empathy, form new alliances, fuel our better natures, and live more fully the values we espouse. Surely surprising acts of resistance will rise from the spirit of resilience and solidarity energized by this dangerous turn in American leadership. Maybe all the women who attend the Million Women March in Washington should wear the hijab in solidarity with those who feel the very real vulnerability arising from the threatening rhetoric of the campaign.

I think of this remembering the symbolic power of an action taken just days after the terrorist attacks in Paris in November 2015 when public protests were banned. Ten thousand pairs of shoes were lined up in the Place de la Republique—shoes from Pope Francis, shoes from the Dalai Lama, shoes of the living, and shoes of the dead. They stood in for the 200,000 people anticipated to gather on Paris streets ahead of the Paris climate summit.

Sure, take to streets, sign petitions, move to a red state and run for the school board, donate to organizations that work on the local level or promote human rights. Think of the great spirit of inventiveness the Earth calls forth after each major disturbance it suffers. Be artful, inventive, and just, my friends, but do not be silent.

Reprinted with the author's permission from <u>terrain.org</u>, 2016

Chard deNiord

Prophecy Against Those

They will grow ass's ears and stand
and stand like guards at the funerals of their own mothers.

They will forget history as if it were
a bad memory they can live without.

They will become victims of their own crimes.

They will confuse art with propaganda and advertisements.

They will be devoid of human leaps and other lives.

They will become famous for their towers.

They will pass eye exams year after year.

They will grow blind to others.

They will cease from studying tragedy
and find humor in violence.

They will dress sharply and abuse women.

They will deny their loneliness on the street
and hone their wit.

They will get ahead.

They will have no literature.

They will turn into boards with infinite splinters.

They will misprize and misprize.

They will see no connection between themselves
and a hazelnut.

They will destroy the Earth with luxuries.

They will recoil with disdain at poetry.

They will take pride in their faithlessness
and win at the table.

They will do what they want
and laugh at Orpheus.

They will sew lids to their lids
and carry knives to school.

They will lose the mouth to their soul's great hunger.

They will dream unceasingly of cocks crowing.

Natalie Diaz

Reservation Grass

I keep no account with lamentation
Walt Whitman

We smoke more grass than we ever promise to plant.
Our front yards are green and brown, triangles of glass— *What is the*
      grass?—emeralds and garnets sewed like seeds in the dirt.
The shards of glass grow men bunched together— *multitudes*—men larger
      than weeds and Whitman, leaning against the sides of houses—
      dance with the dancers and drink with the drinkers—upon dirt not
      lawn.

Corned beef comes on the first of every month— *this the meat of hunger*—
      in white cans with bold black writing.
We— *myself and mine*—toss it in a pot and wonder how it will ever feed
      us all— *witness and wait*—but never worry, never fret, never give a
      damn, over mowing the grass.

What have we— *the red aborigines—out of hopeful green stuff woven*?

Reprinted with the author's permission from *My Brother Was An Aztec*,
Copper Canyon, 2012

Natalie Diaz

Cloud Watching

Betsy Ross needled hot stars to Mr. Washington's bedspread—
        they weren't hers to give. So, when the cavalry came,
                we ate their horses. Then, unfortunately, our bellies were filled
                        with bullet holes.

Pack the suitcases with white cans of corned beef—
        when we leave, our hunger will go with us,
                following behind, a dog with ribs like a harp.

Blue gourds glow and rattle like a two-man band:
        Hotchkiss on backup vocals and Gatling on drums.
                The rhythm is set by our boys dancing the warpath—
                        the meth 3-step. Grandmothers dance their legs off—
                                who now will teach us to stand?

We carry dimming lamps like god cages—
        they help us see that it is dark. In the dark our hands
                pretend to pray but really make love.
                        Soon we'll give birth to fists—they'll open up
                                black eyes and split grins—we'll all cry out.

History has chapped lips, unkissable lips—
        he gave me a coral necklace that shines bright as a chokehold.
                He gives and gives—census names given to Mojaves:
                        George and Martha Washington, Abraham Lincoln,
                                Robin Hood, Rip Van Winkle.

Loot bag ghosts float fatly in dark museum corners—
        I see my grandfather's flutes and rabbit sticks in their guts.
                About the beautiful dresses emptied of breasts…
                        they were nothing compared to the emptied bodies.

Splintering cradleboards sing bone lullabies—
       they hush the mention of half-breed babies buried or left on riverbanks.
          When you ask about officers who chased our screaming women
             into the arrowweeds, they only hum.

A tongue will wrestle its mouth to death and lose—
       language is a cemetery.
          Tribal dentists light lab-coat pyres in memoriam of lost molars—
            our cavities are larger than HUD houses.
               Some Indians' wisdom teeth never stop growing back in—
             we were made to bite back—
                 until we learn to bite first.

Reprinted with the author's permission from *My Brother Was An Aztec*,
Copper Canyon, 2012

Natalie Diaz

Orange Alert

There are certain words
you can't say in airports—
words that mean bomb, blow up, jihad,
hijack, terrorist, terrorism, terrorize,
terrific fucking terror.
     And words like *orange*—
small citrus grenades,
laced with steel seeds, rinds lined
with anthrax.
     Security cameras scan and scrutinize
Californians. Floridians
are profiled, picked for full-body
fondlings—everyone knows Florida
is the Axis of Oranges.
     Loudspeakers announce:
All passengers' navels
must be covered or checked in baggage.
Congress is considering mandatory
navelectomies.
Orange Alert paranoia eats away
at the nation like a very hungry caterpillar.
     The Mexicans, known agents of oranges,
are scared—taking to the streets, picketing,
fighting for *naranjas* as if they were their own
corazones. They don't understand—
We don't fly, they say. *If we want to travel*
we borrow Tia Silvi's mini van.
     Pamphlets flutter from the sky
telling how to tell
if someone's a terrorist: They tell jokes
with punch lines like:
Orange you glad I didn't say banana?
     Women with B cups, men with certain-
sized crotches, even those with

man-boobs, are squeezed, bobbled in search
of forbidden fruits—questioned
about stowed-away pomelos, tangelos,
sun-kissed improvised explosive devices,
quarters of tart dynamite.
      Orchards are napalmed.
Homeland Security says, *Convert them all*
      to parking lots. Go, men! Go!
We're out for blood oranges.
      Orange Aide to Third World fruit stands
was canceled.
The U.S. expunged
the Oranges for Oil campaign.
It doesn't stop there—
      patriot posses mow down highway cones,
the DOT revolted and wrecked their fleets
of clementine-colored trucks,
school crossing guards are mauled in their tangy vests—
beaten with Walk signs
by packs of anti-mandarin kindergarteners.
O.J. Simpson's in jail.
      Tropicana sold out to V8.
Orange County is a mere smudge
in the West Coast sky.
      Halloween was banned—
Jehovah's Witnesses shake their heads
saying, *We told you so.*
In the haze of this early winter,
blue flames engulf the cities.
Wait—what's that you say?
We've been bumped to red alert?
But that's like apples and oranges.

Reprinted with the author's permission from *My Brother Was An Aztec,* Copper
Canyon, 2012

Sean Thomas Dougherty

At Least Not Here

in my mouth in the small silences in the asphalt
or the gut or what is left behind is leaving
or not or even there in the joints or the bell ringing
at the retirement center where Mr. Marconi
is being fed the place where your grandfather
died the place where the grandmothers play cards
and when they slip the old tongues
come the red dirt Georgia singing
the Baptist Churches with their roofs
burning places the pogroms and the secret police
the old century sliding into the last head stones
and us here in this new one this new unknowing
language they are forming we are trying out
for the first time and who can claim
where what will be lost and when we will drop
anchor when we will drop our vowels
and the ashes and the urns and the unbearable
lightness and the winter when the cops arrested
nobody at least not here not here where they say the poor
are draining the country where they can put you away
where they can deem you an enemy and you cannot ask
for a lawyer where the food is spliced where the rain
is acid where they've bottled and sold the lakes at least
not here in our bodies in this basement in the space
between our breath and the grainy black and white images
of our ancestors being taken away when we are done
covered in sweat we will open the book
the one that is always burning and we will step inside it
till we are reborn till we are more than a caption
the same as Muhammad Bouazizi
who the police in Tunisia confiscated the fruit
he was selling on the street so he had nothing
he doused his body in gasoline and transformed
his grief into a burning not here they said at least

not here a hundred then a thousand then a million
carrying that stench saying at least not here we will
his burning body when I touch you when touch becomes
more than touch when hands are linked like the opposite
of handcuffs like the gleaming bodies of strangers
joined singing in the downpour outside of the palace
outside of Parliament the gated places unlocked with your voice
is all voices and the burning is ours we will finally refuse to kneel

Rita Dove

Black on a Saturday Night

This is no place for lilac
or somebody on a trip
to themselves. Hips
are an asset here, and color
calculated to flash
lemon bronze cerise
in the course of a dip and turn.
Beauty's been caught lying
and the truth's rubbed raw:
Here, you get your remorse
as a constitutional right.

It's always what we don't
fear that happens, always
not now and why are
you people acting this way
(meaning we put in petunias
instead of hydrangeas and reject
ecru as a fashion statement).

But we can't do it — naw, because
the wages of living are sin
and the wages of sin are love
and the wages of love are pain
and the wages of pain are philosophy
and that leads definitely to an attitude
and an attitude will get you
nowhere fast so you might as well
keep dancing dancing till
tomorrow gives up with a shout,

'cause there is only
Saturday night, and we are in it −
black as black can,
black as black does,
not a concept
nor a percentage
but a natural law.

Reprinted with the author's permission from *Collected Poems 1974-2004* by
Rita Dove. W.W. Norton & Co., Inc. ©1999, 2016.

Rita Dove

"The situation is intolerable"

Intolerable: that civilized word.
Aren't we civilized, too? Shoes shined,
each starched cuff unyielding,
each dove-gray pleated trouser leg
a righteous sword advancing
onto the field of battle
in the name of the Lord . . .

Hush, now. Assay
the terrain: all around us dark
and the perimeter in flames,
but the stars —
tiny, missionary stars —
on high, serene, studding
the inky brow of heaven.

So what if we were born up a creek
and knocked flat with the paddle,
if we ain't got a pot to piss in
and nowhere to put it if we did?
Our situation is intolerable, but what's worse
is to sit here and do nothing.
O yes. O mercy on our souls.

Reprinted with the author's permission from *Collected Poems 1974-2004* by Rita
Dove. W.W. Norton & Co., Inc. ©1999, 2016.

Rita Dove

Freedom Ride

As if, after High Street
and the left turn onto Exchange,
the view would veer onto
someplace fresh: Curacao,
or a mosque adrift on a milk-fed pond.
But there's just more cloud cover,
and germy air
condensing on the tinted glass,
and the little houses with
their fearful patches of yard
rushing into the flames.

Pull the cord a stop too soon, and
you'll find yourself walking
a gauntlet of stares.
Daydream, and you'll wake up
in the stale dark of a cinema,
Dallas playing its mistake over and over
until even that sad reel won't stay
stuck – there's still
Bobby and Malcolm and Memphis,
at every corner the same
scorched brick, darkened windows.

Make no mistake: There's fire
back where you came from, too.
Pick any stop: You can ride
into the afternoon singing with strangers,
or rush home to the scotch
you've been pouring all day –
but where you sit is where you'll be
when the fire hits.

Reprinted with the author's permission from *Collected Poems 1974-2004* by Rita Dove. W.W. Norton & Co., Inc. ©1999, 2016.

Rita Dove

Aubade East

Harlem, a.m.

Today's the day, I can taste it.
Got my gray sweats pouting in a breeze
so soft, I feel like I'm still wrapped for sleeping
as I head uptown in my undercover power-suit,
bitch sunlight fingering the spaced-out tenements.

This morning there ain't nothing I *can't* do.
This is my territory, I know all of it –
ten long blocks flanked by mighty water.
Walking any Avenue is like riding
a cosmic surfboard on the biggest wave

of the goddam century, the East River
twerking her bedazzled behind
while sky spills coin like a luck-crazed
Vegas granny flush at the slots. Today

I'm gonna make out like a bandit myself:
hook up with my buds to drop
a few shots on the courts, ogle the ladies,
then play the rest of the day

as it comes   see where it goes
feeling good
feeling good
somewhere over the Hudson
the sun   heading home

First published in *The Georgia Review,* Vol. LXX, No. 1, Spring 2016.

Rita Dove

Aubade West

Ferguson, Missouri

Everywhere absence mocks me:
Jimmy, jettisoned like rotten fruit.
Franklin blown away.
Heat aplenty of all kinds,
especially when August blows its horn—
cops and summer and no ventilation
make piss-poor running buddies.
A day just like all the others,
me out here on the streets
skittery as a bug crossing a skillet,
no lungs big enough to strain
this scalded broth into brain and tissues,
plump my arteries, my soul . . .

Voice in my ear hissing *Go ahead, leave.*
Look around. No gates, no barbed wire.
As if I could walk on water.
As if water ever told one good truth,
lisping her lullabies as she rocks
another cracked cradle of Somalis
until it splits and she can pour
her final solution right through.
Me watching from the other side of the world,
high and dry on this street
running straight as a line of smack,
sun shouting down its glory:

No one's stopping you.
What are you waiting for?

First published in *The Georgia Review*, Vol. LXX, No. 1, Spring 2016.

Rita Dove

Ghettoland: Exeunt

follow the morning star

Tell yourself it's only a sliver of sun
burning into your chest, a cap of gold
or radiant halo justly worn by
the righteous at heart –

then take it off, stomp it, rip out the seams.

Wherever a wall goes up, it smolders.
Gate or street corner, buried canal—
you'll catch yourself before crossing,
stumble over perfectly flat stones,
skirt the worn curb to avoid a cart
rumbling past three centuries ago.

You stop to gaze up at the softening sky
because there is nowhere else to look
without remembering pity and contempt,
without harboring rage.

First published in *The Georgia Review*, Vol. LXX, No. 1, Spring 2016.

Alex Drummond

Calling Ed Abbey

Listen, Ed, gotta shake you
outta your desert slumber
the unthinkable is here
presidency trumped
both houses of congress
most state legislatures
hamfisted to the right
supreme court going going soon gone
beyond reach of reason,
hey Ed, plans already on paper,
gilded plank in the coming congress
to give away, sell, America's
public lands and resources--
Republican elephant, tusks and necktie
sitting at a billboard booth
sign says "supplies limited
get 'em while they last"--
national parks, monuments, forests
wildlife preserves and wetlands
wilderness, wild and scenic rivers
grazing lands and watersheds
gonna be up for grabs.

Ed, come help us fight
tell us how we can get
the coyotes to howl with us,
teach us the serpent stare,
the warning rattle
of we the people, not backing down,
when we face rifle squads and bulldozers
tell us if a sandstone arch
will hold the weight of all
the people needed to save it,
show us how to take back
each two barrels of water
before they're used
to pump one barrel of oil.
Ed we need you right now
dead or alive
back on stage.

Heid E. Erdrich

The Pacifist Grows Mean

Courage   when it speaks
might be a small peaceful man
Gray-haired   of no color   Unrighteous
                              But right

You would be as kind but no
Inside every handshake is a fist
Your deep-born peace also knows this

Your peace grows gravel-voiced   erodes
Grains of sand in wind   two centuries
of scouring abrasion   day to day to day

At first it hurts   like a voice leaving
or the opposite   a stillness taken over
Hundreds of years of whispers in one roar

Your peace defeats itself
Called to defend   your peace finds a line
then finds any line takes sides

One day your blood jumps up
One day your warrior blood jeers
You speak your piece

You boo   and hiss and rant
You spend years drowning out
that sound without sound   your peace

You damp it down   cache it deep
that largeness of humanity—
that quiet that once held you

Before you were claimed by your chorus
before your peace worked for others
before you grew to know   what it might mean
                              to be so mean

Martín Espada

Sleeping on the Bus

How we drift in the twilight of bus stations,
how we shrink in overcoats as we sit,
how we wait for the loudspeaker
to tell us when the bus is leaving,
how we bang on soda machines
for lost silver, how bewildered we are
at the vision of our own faces
in white-lit bathroom mirrors.

How we forget the bus stations of Alabama,
Birmingham to Montgomery,
how the Freedom Riders were abandoned
to the beckoning mob, how afterwards
their faces were tender and lopsided as spoiled fruit,
fingers searching the mouth for lost teeth,
and how the riders, descendants
of Africa and Europe both, kept riding
even as the mob with pleading hands wept fiercely
for the ancient laws of segregation.

How we forget Biloxi, Mississippi, a decade before,
where no witnesses spoke to cameras,
how a brown man in military uniform
was pulled from the bus by police
when he sneered at the custom of the back seat,
how the magistrate proclaimed a week in jail
and went back to bed with a shot of whiskey,
how the brownskinned soldier could not sleep
as he listened for the prowling of his jailers,
the muttering and cardplaying of the hangmen
they might become.
His name is not in the index;
he did not tell his family for years.
How he told me, and still I forget.

How we doze upright on buses,
how the night overtakes us
in the babble of headphones,
how the singing and clapping
of another generation
fade like distant radio
as we ride, forehead
heavy on the window,
how we sleep, how we sleep.

Reprinted with the author's permission from *Imagine The Angels of Bread*, W.W. Norton, 1996

Martín Espada

Heal the Cracks in the Bell of the World

*For the community of Newtown, Connecticut, where twenty students and six educators
lost their lives to a gunman at Sandy Hook Elementary School, December 14, 2012*

Now the bells speak with their tongues of bronze.
Now the bells open their mouths of bronze to say:
Listen to the bells a world away. Listen to the bell in the ruins
of a city where children gathered copper shells like beach glass,
and the copper boiled in the foundry, and the bell born
in the foundry says: *I was born of bullets, but now I sing
of a world where bullets melt into bells.* Listen to the bell
in a city where cannons from the armies of the Great War
sank into molten metal bubbling like a vat of chocolate,
and the many mouths that once spoke the tongue of smoke
form the one mouth of a bell that says: *I was born of cannons,
but now I sing of a world where cannons melt into bells.*

Listen to the bells in a town with a flagpole on Main Street,
a rooster weathervane keeping watch atop the Meeting House,
the congregation gathering to sing in times of great silence.
Here the bells rock their heads of bronze as if to say:
Melt the bullets into bells, melt the bullets into bells.
Here the bells raise their heavy heads as if to say:
Melt the cannons into bells, melt the cannons into bells.
Here the bells sing of a world where weapons crumble deep
in the earth, and no one remembers where they were buried.
Now the bells pass the word at midnight in the ancient language
of bronze, from bell to bell, like ships smuggling news of liberation
from island to island, the song rippling through the clouds.

Now the bells chime like the muscle beating in every chest,
heal the cracks in the bell of every face listening to the bells.
The chimes heal the cracks in the bell of the moon.
The chimes heal the cracks in the bell of the world.

Reprinted with the author's permission from *Vivas to Those Who Have Failed*,
W.W. Norton, 2016

Martín Espada

Imagine the Angels of Bread

This is the year that squatters evict landlords,
gazing like admirals from the rail
of the roofdeck
or levitating hands in praise
of steam in the shower;
this is the year
that shawled refugees deport judges,
who stare at the floor
and their swollen feet
as files are stamped
with their destination;
this is the year that police revolvers,
stove-hot, blister the fingers
of raging cops,
and nightsticks splinter
in their palms;
this is the year
that darkskinned men
lynched a century ago
return to sip coffee quietly
with the apologizing descendants
of their executioners.

This is the year that those
who swim the border's undertow
and shiver in boxcars
are greeted with trumpets and drums
at the first railroad crossing
on the other side;
this is the year that the hands
pulling tomatoes from the vine
uproot the deed to the earth that sprouts the vine,
the hands canning tomatoes
are named in the will

that owns the bedlam of the cannery;
this is the year that the eyes
stinging from the poison that purifies toilets
awaken at last to the sight
of a rooster-loud hillside,
pilgrimage of immigrant birth;
this is the year that cockroaches
become extinct, that no doctor
finds a roach embedded
in the ear of an infant;
this is the year that the food stamps
of adolescent mothers
are auctioned like gold doubloons,
and no coin is given to buy machetes
for the next bouquet of severed heads
in coffee plantation country.

If the abolition of slave-manacles
began as a vision of hands without manacles,
then this is the year;
if the shutdown of extermination camps
began as imagination of a land
without barbed wire or the crematorium,
then this is the year;
if every rebellion begins with the idea
that conquerors on horseback
are not many-legged gods, that they too drown
if plunged in the river,
then this is the year.

So may every humiliated mouth,
teeth like desecrated headstones,
fill with the angels of bread.

Reprinted with the author's permission from *Imagine the Angels of Bread*, W.W.
Norton, 1996

Martín Espada

Jorge the Church Janitor Finally Quits

Cambridge, Massachusetts, 1989

No one asks
where I am from,
I must be
from the country of janitors,
I have always mopped this floor.
Honduras, you are a squatter's camp
outside the city
of their understanding.

No one can speak
my name,
I host the fiesta
of the bathroom,
stirring the toilet
like a punchbowl.
The Spanish music of my name
is lost
when the guests complain
about toilet paper.

What they say
must be true:
I am smart,
but I have a bad attitude.

No one knows
that I quit tonight,
maybe the mop
will push on without me,
sniffing along the floor
like a crazy squid
with stringy gray tentacles.
They will call it Jorge.

Reprinted with the author's permission from *Rebellion is the Circle of a Lover's Hands*, Curbstone, 1990

Martín Espada

Alabanza: In Praise of Local 100

*for the 43 members of Hotel Employees and Restaurant Employees
Local 100, working at the Windows on the World restaurant,
who lost their lives in the attack on the World Trade Center*

Alabanza. Praise the cook with a shaven head
and a tattoo on his shoulder that said *Oye,*
a blue-eyed Puerto Rican with people from Fajardo,
the harbor of pirates centuries ago.
Praise the lighthouse in Fajardo, candle
glimmering white to worship the dark saint of the sea.
Alabanza. Praise the cook's yellow Pirates cap
worn in the name of Roberto Clemente, his plane
that flamed into the ocean loaded with cans for Nicaragua,
for all the mouths chewing the ash of earthquakes.
Alabanza. Praise the kitchen radio, dial clicked
even before the dial on the oven, so that music and Spanish
rose before bread. Praise the bread. *Alabanza.*

Praise Manhattan from a hundred and seven flights up,
like Atlantis glimpsed through the windows of an ancient aquarium.
Praise the great windows where immigrants from the kitchen
could squint and almost see their world, hear the chant of nations:
*Ecuador, México, República Dominicana,
Haiti, Yemen, Ghana, Bangladesh.*
Alabanza. Praise the kitchen in the morning,
where the gas burned blue on every stove
and exhaust fans fired their diminutive propellers,
hands cracked eggs with quick thumbs
or sliced open cartons to build an altar of cans.
Alabanza. Praise the busboy's music, the *chime-chime*
of his dishes and silverware in the tub.

Alabanza. Praise the dish-dog, the dishwasher
who worked that morning because another dishwasher
could not stop coughing, or because he needed overtime
to pile the sacks of rice and beans for a family
floating away on some Caribbean island plagued by frogs.

Alabanza. Praise the waitress who heard the radio in the kitchen
and sang to herself about a man gone. *Alabanza.*

After the thunder wilder than thunder,
after the shudder deep in the glass of the great windows,
after the radio stopped singing like a tree full of terrified frogs,
after night burst the dam of day and flooded the kitchen,
for a time the stoves glowed in darkness like the lighthouse in Fajardo,
like a cook's soul. Soul I say, even if the dead cannot tell us
about the bristles of God's beard because God has no face,
soul I say, to name the smoke-beings flung in constellations
across the night sky of this city and cities to come.
Alabanza I say, even if God has no face.

Alabanza. When the war began, from Manhattan and Kabul
two constellations of smoke rose and drifted to each other,
mingling in icy air, and one said with an Afghan tongue:
Teach me to dance. We have no music here.
And the other said with a Spanish tongue:
I will teach you. Music is all we have.

Reprinted with the author's permission from *Alabanza: New and Selected Poems*, W.W. Norton, 2003

Howie Faerstein

Hung Jury

Always the wide plank of fear,
whirling lights blinding,
sirens at the highest
pitch of human sound.

We all watched the man running.
You can watch him running even now.
Walter Scott forever fleeing.
Walter Scott dying endlessly.
Officer Slager twice discharges his Taser,
then shoots at the fleeing man,
fires eight times into his back.
You can isolate, then listen
to each pistol shot,
watch the video in slo-mo.

When pulled over
because of a traffic violation
Walter Scott decided to run,
Slager chose to fire,
broken brake light,
eight rounds in a half a minute,
a distance of fifteen feet.
Broken brake light.
The dead unarmed man
on the ground even now.

You don't need to visualize.
This is the United States after all.

You can see Walter Scott was running for his life.
You can see Michael Slager approach the fallen man,
handcuff him, plant his Taser next to Walter's body,
the man he executed, a traffic violation.
Slager said later he *feared for his life.*

The trial ended with no verdict reached,
a hung jury.

They all saw Walter Scott running.

Blas Falconer

Revolution

Plantain trees gather at the edge
of the orchard, clamor for light

in the foreground. They seem to grow
as one, as if they'd fill the field

and the mountains behind them,
leaves large and frayed. We stood

there, once, or someplace like it, so
here we are again, it seems,

years later, branches leaning over
the road, you in your long skirt,

looking out as if to recall something
you meant to do. *My country,* I hear

you say still. But if that's dusk
in the hills, you know what's

coming to the field. You'll stand
among them till there's nothing left

to see. I'll wait beside you, though
I don't know what we're waiting for.[1]

---

1   When considering Myrna Baez's painting "Platanal," E. Carmen Ramos explains, "When Puerto Rico was a Spanish colony, artists like Francisco Oller depicted the plantain as both a key accoutrement to the jibaro (rural peasant) and a metaphor for the island's independent cultural identity."

Annie Finch

Allegiance

November 9, 2016

We knew we needed sisters.
We hoped to make them count
The way we thought our brothers did.
We craved. We yearned. We spent

Our closest words in silence,
Heard matriarchy scorned,
Sucked hard the food of insult,
Forgot how we were born.

Today is for moss and quietness,
A path for salty hurt
From intimate directions:
Beside, behind, in front.

Walk this brilliant forest,
Hugging and bleeding. Spell
Wisdom how our wombs do.
The love we birth is real.

Remember the ways we govern,
sorting the truths of things
Out through our tangible kinships—
Exultant spiralings.

We have never been islands.
The whole planet hangs in our balance.
Yes, they have weapons that mean
It's time. Pledge allegiance

Ann Fisher-Wirth

Day After

We drive out through the Delta to Parchman, the Mississippi State Penitentiary, aka the notorious Farm, where we team-teach every week, Patrick and I—he, African American literature, I, poetry—to thirteen men in the Prison to College Pipeline Program that Patrick and our colleague Otis are creating. Our students are men in the pre-release program, which means they will be out within two years. Unless not. Two of the men, apparently not. Not ever.

Finally it's not 97 degrees with 97 per cent humidity, as it was through September and most of October. Today we see this land, this scarred battered overfarmed impoverished and chemically poisoned land, at its most golden. The fields stretch away on either side of the road. The cotton has been picked now, but some bolls still linger on the stalks. Twice, we drive through groves of pecan trees, and once, past a swampy pond with cattle egrets like slender angels. Nature smiles, the way nature always seems to smile here after a catastrophe.

Seems cruel, how beautiful the day is.

Lucky pecan trees, I'm thinking. Lucky cattle egrets. Lucky clouds, lucky fields, lucky swampy little pond. You don't have to know. You don't have to know, like our students who've come up through Mississippi, that a man was just elected who despises you. Who will only hurt you more.

.   .   .

A week ago in class I was explaining the concept of environmental justice, that, though in the modern world all environments are degraded, certain human communities bear a disproportionate environmental burden; damage to the environment is inflicted disproportionately on people of color and the poor. To put it simply, for example, toxic waste sites are not built in Beverly Hills. Though the Mississippi Delta epitomizes environmental injustice, our students had not heard of this before. One, a 65-year-old blues musician named Pinkie who has toured the world and played to audiences of 20,000, said, "Does this idea also apply to us convicts?" "What do you mean?" I asked. "Nobody care about *us*," he replied.

I'm certain," Patrick told me later, as we were driving back to Oxford, "there's a lot of struggle bound up in his question. I've *never* heard the men openly refer to themselves as convicts.

.   .   .

And of course they're struggling.

I can't even begin to imagine how they're struggling.

I write on the board these words from Bertoldt Brecht: "Will there be singing in the dark times? Yes, there will be singing. About the dark times."

We spend my part of our team-taught hours together, this day after the election, talking about poetry in the dark times. About Ross Gay's fig tree in *Catalog of Unabashed Gratitude* that gathers a spontaneous community to itself one day in Philadelphia with its copious gift of fruit. We workshop our student Brendell's beautiful and grave poem with its evocation of "the moon, my love, who knows me best." They ask me to discuss my poem "Dream Cabinet" that's excerpted in *The Ecopoetry Anthology*," so I tell how in that poem—which is about a week my husband and I once spent on a tiny island in Sweden—I am trying to juxtapose the knowledge and fear of global warming with the natural beauty of the Stockholm archipelago.

I have taught for more than forty years, but I've never taught a class I care about more. Whatever these men have done, whatever Patrick or I have done—for as Patrick says to me often, if justice were equal we'd all be cooked—all this becomes immaterial. These are hours that combat the "soul death" of incarceration with the soul depth of beauty and truth and imagination. I love these students and learn from these students, so many things I don't know how to say.

.   .   .

What we face now in our country isn't new. We know that. No matter how we cut it, it's been a long time coming. But maybe now we can see it clearly.

Keith Flynn

Democracy

It's coming through a crack in the wall,
on a visionary flood of alcohol,
from the staggering account
of the Sermon on the Mount,
which I don't pretend to understand at all.

"Democracy"
---Leonard Cohen

The President is so still the people can hear the planets
scraping through space like a fork on a plate.
In their little closets, draped in black flags, the voting hands
grip the iron ball of the one-armed bandit,
listening to the jingle jangle gamble of the capitalist machinery.

Like mercury unable to be trapped beneath your thumb,
the numb citizen, facing that horrible mirror of election,
sees every constituency's refracted self-interest reflected but their own.
When the people stop to consider their choices
they are like clews of worms beneath the ground so busy
that the Senators can feel the earth moving the walls of their Coliseum.

We assign a day and the soul's lead filaments scatter to its magnet.
More women commit suicide on Mother's Day, for instance,
and Black History Month loosens the racist tongues.
The prostitute is a book of knowledge, says the cop
and wakes every morning with a yes on her mind,
drawing to her the nefarious elements.

In the late nineteenth century you could see the hats holding men
by their heads against the ground. Great Lakes Indians

knew their enemies would be coming soon
when the honeybees preceded them. European flies, the Natives
called when they pointed at the bold black clouds as Columbus
restored Pangaea and viruses stormed out of the ship's hold.

The founding fathers, in their powdered wigs, could not
have conceived of satellites or cyberspace, and politely believed
that the citizens would become as one, so thankful for their freedom
from tyranny, that if given a choice, they would always commiserate
and that the deathly grave and greedy glance would give way

to the love of country, and though comprised of a thousand
darkened guesses, the Patriot would rush from shadow to shadow
until he embraced and held the one that housed Salvation,
and patiently wait until the ocean was frozen in place, and time
had mended its savage mandate, which lo and behold, all along
had been focused on a bandage, on the far side of the moon,

a true Super Bowl, where the people in a wave are brushing
and braiding the frayed rope ends of their broken and scattered
commitments, guessing at what new form awaits them
on the opposite humming shore, while below in the Coliseum
playground, the Senators have formed a single block
and cannot be moved, entangled like dogs in heat.

Their interns take turns throwing water on the heap of suits,
but they have come to resemble in their spectacle, a giant log
approaching a waterfall, fixed in its course upon a raging river
and covered in swarming teams of black and silent ants,
all of them calmly refusing to communicate, ignoring the roar
beyond their barge, each convinced they are the one in charge.

Carolyn Forché

Mourning

A peacock on an olive branch looks beyond
the grove to the road, beyond the road to the sea,
blank-lit, where a sailboat anchors to a cove.
As it is morning, below deck a man is pouring water into a cup,
listening to the radio-talk of the ships: barges dead
in the calms awaiting port call, pleasure boats whose lights
hours ago went out, fishermen setting their nets for mullet,
as summer tavernas hang octopus to dry on their lines,
whisper smoke into wood ovens, sweep the terraces
clear of night, putting the music out with morning
light, and for the breath of an hour it is possible
to consider the waters of this sea *wine-dark*, to remember
that there was no word for blue among the ancients,
but there was the whirring sound before the oars
of the great triremes sang out of the seam of world,
through pine-sieved winds silvered by salt flats until
they were light enough to pass for breath from the heavens,
troubled enough to fell ships and darken thought—
then as now the clouds pass, roosters sleep in their huts,
the sea flattens under glass air, but there is nothing to hold us there:
not the quiet of marble nor the luff of sail, fields of thyme,
a vineyard at harvest, and the sea filled with the bones of those
in flight from wars east and south, our wars, their remains
scavenged on the sea floor and in its caves, belongings now
a flotsam washed to the rocks. Stand here and look
into the distant haze, there where the holy mountain
with its thousand monks wraps itself in shawls of rain,
then look to the west, where the rubber boats tipped
into the tough waves. Rest your eyes there, remembering the words
of Anacreon, himself a refugee of war, who appears
in the writings of Herodotus:
I love and do not love, I am mad and I am not mad.
For if the earth is a camp and the sea an ossuary of souls,
light your signal fires wherever you find yourselves.
Come the morning, launch your boats.

First appeared in *Poetry Magazine.*

Yahya Frederickson

Holiday Lights

Fargo, North Dakota

The neighbor's house down the street throbs like a jackpot:
blue lights pacing along gutters, candy canes and stockings
high-kicking from the windows, Santa and reindeer
flashing red on the peak. In the yard, the snow so fluffy and clean

it challenges belief, a life-size crêche glows like a display
of giant lava lamps. My seven-year-old son Abdu,
born in Arabia, asks, "Daddy, why do they have Muslims
in their yard?" And sure enough, there is the Virgin

Maryam, her whole body, even her hair, draped in blue *chador,*
while bearded men in turbans and long gowns gaze with her
at the baby 'Eisa wrapped in an immaculate rag,
everyone so aglow with bulbs inside that I have to wonder

what is being proclaimed: the more lit, the more free?
In Afghanistan, bombs the size of Volkswagens
cut into mountains. How lovely a million lights
must look from above. In a Quranic parable, olive oil

glows amber within a lamp whose flame glows within a glass flue,
the flue glowing within a niche, the niche lighting a dark corner.
This exponential glow is what Allah is. O bungalow in snow,
your lights are gaudy and cold, your television bodes death

for seven million foreigners this winter. So I send a check.
My son sacrifices two dollars from his commemorative quarter collection.
This year, he has learned to pledge his allegiance and sing "Jingle Bells."
With his American grandparents he eats turkey at Thanksgiving.

He is thankful for candy. Swimming pools. Batteries. Forgive me,
Allah, if I sound cynical. I must remember that it is Ramadan and I am fasting,
that this month words should be kind and tempered, words should be
peaceful unless, of course, they are necessary for one's defense.

CMarie Fuhrman

Squaw

I let the word clear my throat
Squaw
I hold the s a little longer
than I should, let the *q* push
against my back teeth and land
flat against my tongue and back
of my closed throat. The final sound
does not move my lips

I say *Squaw*
again and I feel it
on my thighs
climbing back inside of me
finding safety in my ovaries, searching
for its home in my blood, in the gentle
lining of my scarred cervix where a decade
of knives sterilized, tried clear up this Indian
problem.   *Squaw*

and I hear it from the lips
of white men. I hear john wayne
run it over his big cowboy teeth
like the hungry tongue of a weasel
and my stomach tightens
and I want to steal the word back
from his swaggering mouth
put it inside my big woman bones
hide it in my marrow, feed it back
to the mouths and the bodies
it was stolen from.

and I trace it on a map. I find it
a valley, a mountain, maybe this body
is where it belongs. in the obscurities of

places named Nigger Dick, Bitch
Creek, Jewtown. The land of pejoratives
where the locals hunt deer, ride
motorbikes, pull fish from clear lakes
and say *Squaw*, like they are saying
Woman, like they are saying, Tuesday
like they are saying nothing at all.

Christian Anton Gerard

On Down the Line

…Here is action untied from strings necessarily blind to particulars and details…
–Whitman

Joplin's Crush Collision March
Jesus. Ma played it non-stop.
That old player-piano worked its ass off
bringing them two trains toward oblivion.
It really happened, you know?
Baroque died with Bach.
Classical died with Mozart.
Ragtime died with Joplin.
Missouri's got a town called Joplin.
I looked at a map last week.
What's in a name? A rose
by any other name. A kiss.
I used to watch the keys move and
imagine the piano knew something
I didn't. It did of course. Ma said.
She'd leave the sheet music there
so the ghost of her first kiss could
sit and feel at home. I guess
his great-grand-daddy was there,
when The Spectacle was staged and
them two engines hit sixty and didn't stop,
couldn't. The railroad needed something.
Twenty thousand came to see it go down.
Three of'em died. Thirty in the hospital.
Spectacle shrapnel. Twentieth century impatience.
Ma's first kiss still lives in this town.
She don't ever say his name.
I don't know what to call you.
What's in a name? The Spectacle.
Don't it feel like that when we kiss?
How many'd end up wounded
if we kissed in front of the White House now?

I looked at a map last week.
There's a way to get anywhere.
I don't need a crowd but I want something
and it ain't a ghost. What
do I call you? What are you on my lips?
What happens if I turn to cough and
we're metal against metal in the night?
You know how long it takes a train to stop?
I stand in front of 'em sometimes
just to see the fireworks show
when you're somewhere else not kissing me.
In the right moment bitter tastes good
and necessary. Grapefruit, maybe.
Its own sweet in kind. A kiss's ghost, spectre.
The past don't have to be a haunt.
In front of a train I'm living.
In front of you I'm living.
Being alive's no sequence of events.
The moon tonight. Look. A heart full.
There is what happened and
what's happening and it's all
happening at the same time.
We ain't in it. We are it.
I have tried to sleep through tyranny.
Sleep is no verb anymore. It is a noun,
proper. Like love. Not like.
Love is not like anything.
Tell me about love without making metaphor.
Spectacle. Try to say you love your country,
try to say it and sleep as if sleep was a verb
now, as if it could be. Two engines runnin' sixty.
Sleep will not come if you try.
Baroque died with Bach.
Classical died with Mozart.
Ragtime died with Joplin.
How a man can kill what don't know
it's staring down a gun's barrel.
Ma loved her country. Didn't know
a man or woman or child couldn't sing
one march or another, a man who hadn't gone to war
with pride in one hand, a march in his heart.
She'd begged her love, that old ghost, to

take her to D.C. where all them folks
were Mr. Smith and all roads led to
something worth dying for, some dream.
All those people. All those people
watching them iron horses carrying
so much freight, so much conscience.
That old piano knew something I didn't
'bout signs and times and things bigger'n itself.
When a horse can't work there ain't no choice.

Greg Glazner

And Yet Believe

The kid, sixteen or seventeen, freckled, his new haircut left about as long on his ears and collar as he can get away with, is standing between his friend Lee, who's singing tenor, and Jim Bob, the preacher's son, who's singing bass. He's trying to keep his voice in the eight-part harmonies of "Blessed Are Those Who Have Not Seen" focused on the Lord. But across the half-parenthesis their octet makes on the church stage, one of the altos, Janet, glances up from her microphone, smiling to him in a way that can only means she likes him. She's out of his league, partly because she's the most beautiful girl in high school, mostly because she's been with Jackie Paul, the town's one dangerous drug dealer, for two years now and doesn't see a way for that to change. The kid knows how safe she would feel with him. She's wearing the same beige chiffon dress the others wear. He's wearing a powder blue leisure suit and white patent leather slip-ons like the other guys. And yet maybe he doesn't belong with them at all. He's beaming and afraid. His footing on the precipice, at the infinite drop, is perilous.

Sin is not what puts him in so much danger. Letting the adoration in his singing slip over to her is readily forgivable, if he asks, and he asks in his mind already. Nor does he have the sin of ingratitude. He's thankful for growing up right, thankful to have a decent singing voice and to be using it for the highest good, in church. His problem is worse than sin. The saving power comes to you through the Bible, he knows this, and also through the sanctuary air, into your heart. It has to really happen, so powerful you can feel it, when you open yourself to belief. Almost everyone he knows is in the sanctuary, listening. They believe; they've felt the saving power. He's not so confident he ever has, standing there on the precipice of hell in his white slip-on shoes.

I want to help him, reach back more than forty years to put my arm around his shoulders, shore him up for the shocks to come. In a couple of years, in college, contradictions and impossibilities and divinely-sanctioned massacres show up in his inerrant Bible. In his dorm room with the Led Zeppelin poster and the Sears stereo, he fights the sense that he's one breath's length away from hell as he tries to think this through. And often he's back behind the eyes of the singing kid. Lightheaded, he can't look for long at the believers watching him. He knows them all, and yet aren't they strangers now? "Blessed are those who have not seen," the song goes, "and yet believe." His own voice in his ears sounds not so much earnest, after all, as it does compliant, anything to believe, any vowel or tone that might steady a young man struggling to keep his footing, when the cost of slipping is so high. The auditorium has been drained of all standing, the regulars and deacons and Sunday school teachers transformed. They look on, not so much truthful, or wise, or solid, but credulous. He has a strong queasy feeling, as if the nave had always been rolling like a great ship. It's hard to keep standing as it keels. Some are smiling, a few with their hands waving in the air, and he knows, nineteen years old, that he will have no way to ever quite be home again.

I want to go back there, let him lean on me a while, tell him I've got this so he can rest. But who am I kidding? I wake up in the mornings trying to get my breath, the pulse in my ears. A friend has been shoved up against her car, cold coffee thrown in her face, told to get used to it, because that's how it's going to be for women now. A friend's been shouted down, told to go back to the country he came from, a friend's rainbow flag has been set on fire. Spray-painted swastikas and slurs are blossoming on the pavements and facades, the beatings are ongoing, and the forces aren't even gathered fully into power, save the racist propagandist, the spokesman for paranoia, and the registrar of the first-to-be-accused. What generosity do I have left to spare for some kid lost ages ago?

And yet I've slipped back there, just singing, not helping at all. The listeners, alarmingly regressed after all these years, are credulous as children, and the stays in me keep giving way, the who to trust, the right from wrong, the what is sane. I keep falling in and in. Thinking is the only antidote, and always the little flash of hell that first accompanies thought, and then the thinking that must follow, cooling the fear steadily, until the burn is gone. This is not a game. Saving your mind never is, nor is history.

When the Baptist Church barred slaveholders from missionary work in 1844, The Southern Baptist Church was formed in response, to support slavers. Divine scriptures fortified the sermons. Ephesians was a cornerstone, "Slaves obey your earthly masters." Inerrant verses later fortified the sermons against women's suffrage and equality, later fortified sermons in favor of Jim Crow segregation. When the church publicly repented of its racist history at the end of the 20th century, inerrant verses, in support of repentance from the racism that inerrant verses had originally inspired, fortified some sermons for a while. From the end of the 20th century on, in light of inerrant scripture, pastors and seminary professors have been required to affirm that women should submit to men.

How do you ever think, how do you ever break away? The kid's maybe seventeen, standing at the precipice, most of what his life's built on no more than a terrifying string of thoughts away from vanishing. He's singing and shifting his weight, his plastic shoe soles slick on the carpet. His heart is swelling when she glances up, and he repents of that, though he's almost floating on it too. Soon enough, though, somehow, he will apply his mind, with his entire will, and the only world he's known will fall away.

My townswomen and townsmen, I've read about the political sermons you've heard, you to whom the truest measure of things is made manifest in the heart. I know how, as the hum of cool air poured down on you in the auditoriums, you could feel the threats arrayed against you—permissive, dangerous, other-than-you, unbiblical—and you knew what was true, since conviction in the heart is how truth works. I've seen you in news photos, praying for political results, with hands out, eyes shut like sleepwalkers. We needed you desperately, but it was almost impossible, I realize. It would have taken risking your families, your friends, stepping where you've always feared hell is, to think. You won't be listening, but I'm talking anyway. Whatever it was you believed you said yes to, you didn't say no to torture, to racial hate and religious registries, to killing the families of terrorists. Did you imagine shooting the baby, the elementary age schoolgirl, the young mother? You said yes to a man whose predatory sexual boastings, had your sons uttered them, would have driven you to beat them until they couldn't walk. You said yes, go ahead, put the world at his feet, the nuclear codes in his hands.

Shouldn't you be down on your knees for forgiveness, by the tens of millions? But I look around, and where are you? There's only me, forming words, contending with that sick feeling I can't seem to shake anymore. I'm guess I'm talking to myself. So I can never let myself hate you, because self-loathing is the most dangerous thing of all, a thing that can't be reasoned with, a mortal danger, a wild beast. I admit, trying to unfist the weapon in my chest, that it's myself I'm admonishing daily, that I may need to do this until I stop breathing, it's myself I'm forcing over the precipice and into thought, and so I must take some care, must never abandon myself to hate, since I'm talking to myself.

But you, also, whom I can never hate, you who paid me in ones when I'd mowed your lawns and who set iced tea in front of me in your kitchens, who brought flowers and foil-wrapped meals and prayers to my mother's hospital room, came to my high school graduation in your navy suits and floral dresses, taught me Bible verses, fishing knots, the way to throw a big looping two-finger curveball—

you, and your children, and theirs, who, when fascism came to America as promised, "wrapped in a flag and carrying a cross," you broke in favor of it by four to one, you with old blood and new on your songbooks and your pale hands—

I am also, by God, and so help me, talking to you.

Richard Grossman MD

Recall The Past History of Abortion—3-20-2016

I returned to our room in the cheap hotel in Paris to find a bloody mess. My roommate, John, left a note that he had gone to the hospital with his girlfriend.

We were in college and were spending the summer studying the French language. John had met Ruth in London, our first stop. She was already pregnant and had decided, although it wasn't legal, to abort the pregnancy. She arrived in Paris several days later and thought that everything had gone well. Immediately after she got to our room she started to hemorrhage. John called an ambulance, she was hospitalized, transfused and had a D&C. She recovered eventually.

That was my first introduction, as an innocent 20 year-old, to the subject of abortion, and my first brush with gynecology. It made a lasting impression.

Two years later my fiancée (and later, wife) was in graduate school and I in medical school in a different city. One of Gail's roommates had been out of town, then spent a night in the hospital. After she returned to the apartment the police came for an official and frightening visit. The hospital reported that Jane had had an abortion and the visit was to find the identity of the doctor who had performed it. The officials interrogated her at length but left without that information.

Fast forward to when I was in general practice in New Mexico. The records of a new patient showed that she had had a hysterectomy—not unusual for a middle-aged woman. But what was surprising was the pathology report. In addition to the expected uterus, it showed a 6-inch long splinter of wood! I asked the woman how the splinter got there. She replied that she didn't know, that she was as mystified as me. We both knew what the real story was.

During my residency I was called to the emergency room one evening to see a woman who was pregnant and bleeding. This was her 4th pregnancy; she had 3 young children at home. I thought she could be having a miscarriage. Spotting could also be an indication that the woman was trying to cause an abortion by introducing something into her uterus. Abortion was already legal in all states in the USA, although the Supreme Court decision was less than a year old.

Back then I used to warn all women with a threatened miscarriage that it was important to tell me if they had done anything to abort the pregnancy. This was because nonmedical abortions were still common, and because of the risk of a serious infection. This woman responded "no", she would never do that—she was a member of a religion that didn't believe in abortion.

I was surprised a few hours later when the same woman returned to the ER. She told me that she returned because what I had told her worried her. She couldn't be sick because her children needed her. She admitted that she had, indeed, tried to cause an abortion with a knitting needle.

These are cases that I can remember well of women who faced unwanted pregnancies. All of these cases are long past history, thank goodness, because now safe abortion services are available. Regrettably some people are trying to take away access to safe, empathetic and legal abortion. Worldwide over 20 million women have unsafe abortions, resulting in 50,000 maternal deaths and many more serious injuries. "Not Yet Rain" is a video made in Ethiopia about the difficulty young women have in getting safe abortions after rape. Studies show that abortion is actually more common where it is illegal.

An unplanned, unwanted pregnancy is a difficult situation for a woman to face. Sometimes things work out well and the child is adopted. Sometimes the child is raised by the mother and loved despite an inauspicious beginning. But often things don't work out well. Currently women in the USA occasionally resort to unsafe abortions because of increased difficulty in accessing safe abortion services.

Some politicians are trying to overthrow the Supreme Court's Roe v. Wade ruling. They put hurdles in the way of women to decrease access to abortions. They also decrease access to contraception, the best way to decrease the need for abortion, by defunding Planned Parenthood. They advocate needless requirements for clinics that have provided safe abortion services for years without them. For women's sake and for the sake of our already overcrowded planet we must maintain access to safe, legal abortion services.

Hedy Habra

Even the Sun has its Dark Side

but does it really matter,
        unless
we could enter that hidden space,
        the way grains of sand
                would suddenly rise
in an hourglass,
        reshape themselves,
        regain their initial place.
I wonder what is lost behind a picture,
        rippled in its negative
as I often try to read between the lines,
        sense clenched teeth,
            or grasp an unspoken word.

When I set to bridge these gaps,
my blood warms up in tides,
        revealing a tightness inside the chest
            as if memories,
        pressed in a tin can
        kept near one's heart,
could sweep away the grayness outside.

We lost everything when we fled,
except for an album
        full of my childhood pictures in Egypt
        and my children born in Beirut.
"You're so lucky," everyone said,
        our family unharmed,
            not one of their fingers
            was worth the whole world
left behind.
        Our beds were made in places
        where the sun teased us, hiding
        most of the time, forcing us to master

the local motto
        ...make sunshine inside...
Christmases followed one another
        offering versions of our lives,
                each fragmented image
evoking a new face,
        a recipe ...an absence...

Whenever I sort them out,
        I see myself floating in a fluid
                lining edges
in search of a referent that has vanished,
                leaving only an empty shell, crumpled,
        discolored like fallen leaves.

I felt constantly renewed,
        peeled off like an onion,
                shedding layer after layer
                until what was left
        was so tender,
                une primeur à déguster,
                        yet so vulnerable.

First published by *Inclined to Speak: An Anthology of Contemporary Arab American Poetry* (2008)
From *Tea in Heliopolis* (Press 53 2013)

Teri Hairston

Invisible...but not today!

It was the day after the elections. I was still numb. I moved throughout the day as if I had just awakened from a deep fretful sleep. I wore disappointment like a heavy secondhand coat bought from the Goodwill Store. Complete with the overwhelming smell of mothballs and too many years stored unworn in the back of somebody's closet.

I couldn't eat. I had been convinced that day, I would be, along with everyone else, celebrating the election of our nation's first female president. As easy as it was to think that the outcome was unbelievable, I told myself that I had to believe it. This is, after all, America. And this feeling that I was feeling, of helplessness, was no new thing.

I have felt it before. I have never had any real power. My father began molesting me when I was three years old and I was powerless to stop him. I was raised in poverty in a family of ten siblings, I was number eight of ten so I was pretty low on the totem pole in the hierarchy of brothers and sisters. I married and divorced two abusive men. I worked low paying unskilled jobs where I was the subordinate and often devalued as a human being. My life as a poor black woman has generally sucked.

I know what it felt like to be invisible. For the "others" in society to not notice me, or only notice me in negative stereotypical ways. Like when I've gone into a store only to have a guard follow me or stop me as I walk out to check my bag and receipt. Or not notice that I was often the first person at work after having had to ride two buses to get there while some of my white boss historically arrived fifteen minutes late having driven to work. Few ever noticed that.

For a long time I didn't know that this feeling of powerlessness or invisibility had a name. Then one day I heard it on the news and looked it up. Marginalized: to put or keep (someone) in a powerless or unimportant position within a society or group. I learned it went even deeper than my personal feeling of disenfranchisement or alienation. The social exclusion and discriminatory practices that were my normal affected people of color, people with disabilities, LGBT people, old and young people, and people addicted to drugs. And the result of this marginalization is that those of us affected by it are prevented from fully participating in every aspect of life like the "others."

Donald Trump is the "other." His campaign brought the face and feelings of the "other" out in full force. The "others" have all the power and privilege that go with it. Some of the "others" don't see me. To them I am invisible.

Today, I stood second in line at the gas station. I was the only black person in the store. The lady in front of me was Hispanic. An elderly white woman walked in the store and walked past me to stand directly in front of the white man who was the cashier. She neither looked at me, or the Hispanic woman, and immediately engaged the white man in pleasant casual conversation. He diverted his attention to her and after completing the transaction with the Hispanic woman he began to transact a sale with the elderly white woman.

I have felt this before. But today after having heard months of Donald Trump advocating the building of walls, using divisive campaigning that was causing race relations to further deteriorate and emboldening racist and hate groups to show themselves publicly, learning of how he demeans women and hearing his voice repeatedly saying, "grab them by the pussy," as he described what power and privilege afforded him. I made myself visible. I spoke up. Loudly. I told the cashier that I was next in line. I startled him and the elderly white woman who didn't see me standing there in plain view waiting my turn in line.

As the Hispanic woman and I walked out the door she said, "Donald Trump is President." I cried all the way to my car.

Teri Hairston

Illiterate

From the gut
of the potbellied
stove
he used to
burn my books
in

I gathered myself
ash by ash
singeing my fingers
to write
words
he cannot read

Sam Hamill

Approaching Winter Solstice

A bitter wind out of the north,
gulls frozen to their icy perches,
and a lone tug inching its way
across the bay. On the eastern horizon,
the great mountain in a robe
of new snow, the sky turquoise blue.

I have come far enough to know
the snows that bury dreams and wishes,
the blizzard in the soul that cries
for the warm embrace of love
in the harshest season. But the world
remains silent, but for moaning winds
and the faint drone of mindless traffic
in the distance. Who am I now,
old and weathered, almost worn out,
but still that hunger, that faint light burning?

I am a seeker, a wanderer in a world
I never imagined. A soul seeks itself
in a kindred soul, the need for a touch,
a knowing glance that makes the fire roar.
Smoke and ash and an old man's
merciless hunger. May the gods
chew my gnarled bones when that time comes,
but in this soul there still is a story
waiting to be told, still a mystery
to unfold, still a spark in the tinder
of unknowing.

first appeared in *Vox Populi* 12/16

Joy Harjo

For Calling the Spirit Back from Wandering the Earth in Its Human Feet

Put down that bag of potato chips, that white bread, that bottle of pop.

Turn off that cellphone, computer, and remote control.

Open the door, then close it behind you.

Take a breath offered by friendly winds. They travel the earth gathering essences of plants to clean.

Give it back with gratitude.

If you sing it will give your spirit lift to fly to the stars' ears and back

Acknowledge this earth who has cared for you since you were a dream planting itself precisely within your parents' desire.

Let your moccasin feet take you to the encampment of the guardians who have known you before time, who will be there after time. They sit before the fire that has been there without time.

Let the earth stabilize your postcolonial insecure jitters.

Be respectful of the small insects, birds and animal people
who accompany you.
Ask their forgiveness for the harm we humans have brought
down upon them.

Don't worry.
The heart knows the way though there may be high-rises,
interstates, checkpoints, armed soldiers, massacres, wars, and
those who will despise you because they despise themselves.

The journey might take you a few hours, a day, a year, a few
years, a hundred, a thousand or even more.

Watch you mind. Without training it might run away and
leave your heart for the immense human feast set by the
thieves of time.

Do not hold regrets.

When you find your way to the circle, to the fire kept burning
by the keepers of your soul, you will be welcomed.

You must clean yourself with cedar, sage, or other healing plant.

Cut the ties you have to failure and shame.

Let go the pain you are holding in your mind, your shoulders,
your heart, all the way to your feet. Let go the pain of your

ancestors to make way for those who are heading in our
direction.

Ask for forgiveness.

Call upon the help of those who love you. These helpers take

many forms: animal, element, bird, angel, saint, or
ancestor.

Call your spirit back. It may be caught in corners and
creases of shame, judgment, and human abuse.
You must call in a way that your spirit will want to return.
Speak to it as you would to a beloved child.

Welcome your spirit back from its wandering. It may return
in pieces, in tatters. Gather them together. They will be
happy to be found after being lost for so long.

Your spirit will need to sleep awhile after it is bathed and
given clean shoes.

Now you have a party. Invite everyone you know who
loves and supports you. Keep room for those who have no
place else to go.

Make a giveaway, and remember, keep the speeches short.

Then, you must do this: help the next person find their way
through the dark.

*For any spark to make a song it must be transformed
by pressure. There must be unspeakable need, muscle of
belief, and wild, unknowable elements. I am singing a
song that can only be born after losing a country.*

Reprinted with the author's permission from *Conflict Resolution For Holy Beings*,
W.W. Norton, 2015.

Joy Harjo

Rabbit Is Up to Tricks

In a world long before this one, there was enough for
    everyone,
Until somebody got out of line.
We heard it was Rabbit, fooling around with clay and the
    wind.
Everybody was tired of his tricks and no one would play
    with him;
He was lonely in this world.
So Rabbit thought to make a person.
And when he blew into the mouth of that crude figure to see
What would happen,
The clay man stood up.
Rabbit showed the clay man how to steal a chicken.
The clay man obeyed.
Then he showed him how to steal someone else's wife.
The clay man obeyed.
Rabbit felt important and powerful.
The clay man felt important and powerful.
And once that clay man started he could not stop.
Once he took that chicken he wanted all the chickens.
And once he took that corn he wanted all the corn.
And once he took that wife, he wanted all the wives.
He was insatiable.
Then he had a taste of gold and he wanted all the gold.
Then it was land and anything else he saw.
His wanting only made him want more.
Soon it was countries, and then it was trade.
The wanting infected the earth.
We lost track of the purpose and reason for life.
We began to forgot songs. We forgot our stories.
We could no longer see or hear our ancestors,
Or talk with each other across the kitchen table.

Forests were being mowed down all over the world.
And Rabbit had no place to play.
Rabbit's trick had backfired.
Rabbit tried to call the clay man back,
But when the clay man wouldn't listen
Rabbit realized he'd made a clay man with no ears.

Reprinted with the author's permission from *Conflict Resolution For Holy Beings*,
W.W. Norton, 2015.

Linda Hogan

Singing For Water

We are singing for water and for the protectors of earth's waters. We sing for water; it is the element all life on earth needs water to exist and to thrive. Long-legged birds stand at the edges of lakes and rivers to watch for fish, their nests hidden in the rushes. A doe crosses the land and stands guard as her little one drinks. All our brother and sister animals follow their paths worn to needed waters. Trees and plants subsist with the rain, snow, and groundwater in a place where this watershed and living earth supported the large herds of bison for thousands of years.

As for us, we were water beings from the very beginning. We rained from the broken waters of our mothers to enter this world. We drank from our mothers to thrive. Water is our life-blood and like all creations on this blue planet, we were born to its currents and passages. So we sing for those who pray for the wide, long Missouri River on its elemental journey.

Near the Cannonball River, a place of chokecherries and other plants, thousands of people are camped. They know that by legal treaty rights the Missouri River and land of this region belongs to the Standing Rock Sioux. Waters flow beneath the skin of this earth body and vast clear oceans called aquifers lie deeper in the near ground, with rivers and tributaries beneath and on the earth surface. The "Plains" may be the wrong word to use for places existing in the midst of all the ground water and watersheds that support life here; animals, birds, food and medicine plants, with expanses of wildflowers in the spring and harsh, cold seasons of winter. The tall grasses live because of waters from beneath and above, from snow and rain.

My own nation, the *Chicaza* lived with the Mississippi River throughout much of our long history. We called that wide rush of water, *The Long Person*. She was our Grandmother and supplied everything we needed to survive. With great sorrow, we were removed from our homeland in 1837, and we left largely to avoid future genocide. The U.S. government planned to place all tribes into Indian Territory and build a wall around it, opening the rest of the country to settlers. Large numbers of Native peoples were chased toward "Indian Territory," now Oklahoma, but many of the plains nations managed to remain, avoid capture, or to return to their beloved homelands, although the people continued to suffer constant warfare from the military.

While many Northern Plains nations escaped life in Oklahoma, every action of the federal government resulted in a shrinking land base for the Dakota and Lakota, including the Dawes Act of 1889. However, the Ft. Laramie Treaty is the only treaty that remains not broken by the United States. Now it is a corporation breaking the heart of the people and the water guaranteed to the Sioux by the 1868 treaty.

Throughout the entire continent and other countries, most people are hoping the Standing Rock Nation will hold steady all their treaty rights to the Missouri River, and that the land and water will remain healthy and intact, that the Dakota Access Pipeline will never pass dangerously beneath the river or cross the land in any way.

Thousands of water protectors have arrived to show their solidarity. The chiefs and leaders of over three hundred tribal nations have been there to speak and to show their own concern for the water and land. Tribal leaders from other locations have sent water, money, and supplies.

Along these waterways the land has a long history, with many negotiations.... but each time, the land here grew smaller. But the river system grew even more important, as trail, trade, and especially as survival and sustenance for people who refused to give up this land for any amount of money offered by the United States.

Other states are affected by work on the Bakken Pipeline of crude oil. Numerous citizens in Iowa have already had their homes condemned by the Texas Company that began fracking the Bakken fields with plans to run a fragile pipeline all the way to the Gulf of Mexico where it will be processed and exported to another country. Fracking makes the land more vulnerable and more likely to shift and move. It affects the tectonic plates. Water is removed and injected back into earth with unknown toxic chemicals protected by copyright. This makes for a vulnerable earth. At least the lawsuits in Iowa have slowed operations.

Bakken crude comes from one of the most dangerous work sites now in operation. Working men have been charred to death by explosions and fires, electrocuted, and injured, all without financial compensation. The company makes no promises. Also, Native women who have been in these "man camps" are subject to abuse, rape, and sometimes have disappeared, often into the sex trafficking business, but some have been killed.

Standing Rock and this part of the plains is the world of well-known leader and holy man Sitting Bull. It is land crossed during the time of the Ft. Laramie Treaty signed in what is now Wyoming. In my mind's eye as I've studied the history, I see many nations of the past crossing the land to negotiate with the American government. Wearing beautifully made regalia, most traveled on horseback or wagons, the chiefs and the women ambassadors of nations who thought the Ft. Laramie Treaty would be a resolution to their problems. Those who had earlier disputes with one another came together in kinship, camping near one another, sharing, and creating new relationships.

Now, in 2016, the chiefs of many tribal nations and other representatives arrived once again, this time to join in protection for the water of this earth and to show solidarity with the Standing Rock and Lakota people who have been victimized by the Texas company.

It is still the land of the Standing Rock Sioux and other Lakota Nations who refused to give up their treaty for millions of dollars. It is still held together by the words and memory of Sitting Bull who loved and protected his people.

No one has the right to take a thin, dirty business through it, a pipe already certain to break, endangering water and contaminating the future. Yet the oil corporation has decided to invade this land because those in better locations didn't want to risk their own water.

It is as if, now in 2016, the corporation with their private, aggressive militia, has declared war on the people. With the amount of harassment, the people would certainly be in danger. It is a tough situation. If one person reacts, the nation loses. If no one does, they will be harassed for as long as the corporation wants to continue. If the Indian and other people leave the campsite, the pipeline with be built even without their agreement. The aggression is painful. After being told where the burial sites and sacred lands were, the bulldozers went to those areas and tore through the earth. That was the opposite of what was expected to happen. What drives such hostility is hard to imagine.

The plane and helicopters have been flying over, spraying unknown substances on elders and infants, the vulnerable, the past and future of the land. What looks like SWAT teams and men with assault rifles are set loose to aim the weapons of their anger at the people who are only protecting and watching over the water, or cooking for the others until the armed men arrived. As I said, what drives this hatred is hard to grasp.

I think of the pilots and these men and wonder, do they go home at night to happiness, to their own? Do they carefully tend gardens or gently touch their loved ones? Do those with such fury on their faces think that the others are human beings like themselves? Do they realize that flying over the lands of the first people causes fear? I think of one picture, quickly removed, showing a man point an assault rifle close to a crying girl who was maybe eight years old.

I am a Chickasaw woman no longer on the waters of the Mississippi, but my daughters and grandchildren are Oglala Lakota. We know how many tribes in the South became extinct centuries before fur trappers and gold-seekers journeyed to the Northern Plains. Those of us living all survived massacres and hunger from the loss of our food sources, or from freezing winters, even before the time of the Custer wars in this region.

Photographs from space reveal that earth is a water planet. No living thing survives without water. It is for that reason, space explorers search for planets that may contain this element; it is a sure sign of life.

Most people have chants or songs about the sacred nature of water. Water is even used in Christianity for baptisms. Even the waters have their distinct songs as they journey toward the oceans.

We live on a single globe of water, all of it only one water. It is alive, this elemental force, this yearning sacred creation longing to reach an ocean in all health. This element carries and sustains us. It is our body and perhaps we are part of its soul. It is always moving away, traveling and returning in its glorious circle, and we know that when we sing for the water, we sing for ourselves.

***

[Note: At this time, we need to pray and sing for water in other locations as well. To name only a few, the Animas River and San Juan is still too polluted for use by the Navajo after the great wall of pollution from the Gold King Mine spill. The Menomenee are fighting a mining site at their water's source. California tribes have had water taken by bottling companies and their sacred springs have dried. The Amazon and other rivers in South America are under duress from mining, oil, deforestation, and mega-dam builders.]

first appeared in *YES MAGAZINE*, 2016

Cynthia Hogue

After the War There Was Another War

The man's cousin, 6 years older when drafted
to Algeria, *saw things*, they said,
the war being fought by then *with gloves off.*
                                    How history's
trace resides in a country's language.
50 years later, the cousin gasping for breath,

the man understood that all the white
wine, harsh and constant cigarettes
were also a language,
                            that his cousin's other-
worldly laughter welled from an ancient memory
of having once *belly* laughed.

Like riding a bike, they said. Time heals
nothing. Defeated, the colonizers created
for their children a doctored history.
When conscripted, the man whiled his time
cleaning the rifle he still keeps in the upper closet,
oiled and ready.

Cynthia Hogue

The Pacifist

War
was
wasteland,
was a way
of putting it.

Loud boombadaboom of the bombs.
Sometimes distant sometimes close.
Each moment a splinter a spark a birth.
Each person a singular globe until
out, out—

No pigs left we did not eat pork.
No cows we did not drink milk.
No chickens we did not boil eggs.
What did we eat I do not remember
eating. Or not eating.

I remember washing maybe once a month maybe once a year.
I wasn't happy or sad neither clean nor unclean.
Mother washing sheets in the stream out back.
Mother selling the rabbit weren't there more we could eat?
Rabbit's dear.

War's a way of living not living.
Question it doesn't matter it's just war always called the
just war. I saw through words used to just-
ify war as if glass sharpening sunlight into fire.
I was forever on fire.

Garrett Hongo

96 Tears

In high school, I was in a special group,
the "AP" classes, advanced placement,
segregated from the rest of the student body.
In them were mostly Japanese kids,
a few whites, and a black or two-
there were never any Chicanos- and
that was when the idea of hierarchies,
categories, and "rank" was finally made clear
to me. It's certain I'd noticed, thought
about it before - in Hawaii, when I was a child,
there were always those of us who could speak,
write, a proper kind of English (we were
always favored) and those who had only
the pidgin. I remember a boy I was trying
to help write a composition. The teacher,
Mrs. Yamamoto, had assigned me to him
as a kind of tutor (I would have been
humiliated had it happened to me), and I
was reading over his work, dismayed that it
was written in pencil rather than ink,
huddling over his shoulder, my hand on his back
like an umpire's on a catcher's, following along
as he read it aloud to me. "Spelling first,"
I said. "We check dah spelling," my own propriety
sensing this occasion as a scene for pidgin,
a discretionary moment of logocentrism
amidst this scene of discipline and *ecriture.*
". . . and went the bird *ladat,*" he read,
flatly, without the risk of emphasis.
"What?" I said, suddenly puzzled.
"And den the bird *ladat* went?"
he asked, tentatively, feeling corrected,
changing his story as a suspect does
when leaned on by cop or D.A. *Interrogated.*

"What's *ladat*?" I asked again. "You know,"
he answered, suddenly confident, relieved
that I had probably only misheard him,
that it wasn't grammar or the esoteric
subtleties of idiomatic, Mainland syntax
I was questioning. "*ladat*! I went hit
dah bird *ladat*! *Ladat* I hit dah ball
wit dah bat *ladat*!" he said, popping
his fists together, chopping down, rolling
his wrists in sweet imitation of a crisp,
Aaronish swing. "Ladat," I said. "Yeah."

So, by high school, on the Mainland,
I'd already internalized
the principles of difference between the dim
and the quick, counted myself pridefully
among the sullen elite, and, jive as I was,
carried armfuls of books wherever I went
in order to show it. It was my identity,
and added sign that, I felt, cast me
tropologically free from the anonymity of other,
drifting signifiers as they swaggered
by the lockers, making time with chicks,
jingling lunch money, scuffling their feet
in a cruiser's walk so the steel taps
on their shoes would click and scrape,
rhythmically, on the pavement.
They wore their shirts open,
dark wool Pendletons in winter,
loud satins, loose and pajamalike
in the hot weather, lustrous as fishbelly,
exposing a thin jersey undershirt,
sexual, strangely cummerbundish
in its subculture formality, the rules of its wear,
and Christophers, gaudy crucifixes, or later,
and black and red leather *mo-jo* pouches
dangling like *mamori* from their necks,
signifying, testifying, and talking trash.
They were a lateral dance of signifieds,
transcendental, Temptations-like
free and unoppressed as they walked.

"Free, white, and twenty-one" is the formulaic.
Cynical and exclusive, it doesn't mean
"Emancipation," that freedman's word,

signifying unlimited potential, and open road
like Whitman saw, a view from the prospect
of *Democratic Vistas*, a sense of magnificence
and of election.

               I had two friends in school,
one Jewish, one Japanese, both very bright,
who became presidents of our student body.
They wanted the recognition
and the experience of it, I suppose,
the status and familiarity with leadership,
both as a role for themselves and as an access
to power, its rules and disdainful possessors.
We all wanted to get out.

               Our school was
three thousand, urban, poor and middle class
intermingled, bordered by two freeways,
a drainage channel and corridor for power lines
with their monstrous platoons of buzzing towers
approaching campus through yellow smog.
Their lines emerged through the inland distance,
across marshlands thick with cricket pumps
and the junkyards along Figueroa.
They receded west down Artesia
over the derelict rails and crossties of the Santa Fe
down to Redondo steamplant and the invisible sea.
I won't forget the drive-in on the east side.
Singular then, it's now a multiple,
four screens mounted like newly risen moons
over the zebraed asphalt and speaker trees
of four separate lots. Adventure movies,
Disney features, and screwball comedies,
puerile sixties Day and Hudson sex romps then,
now they show soft-core porn sometimes,
white and ethnic ladies in polyester negligees
cuddling with some biker or shoe salesman
on the large rectangles stuttering with images
just visible through the stands of the football field.
On Fridays, when the spectators cheer,
sometimes it's for a good play or touchdown,
others it could be for an on-screen, comedic feel.

Not to say in my time things were nobler,
more dignified. They were not. We went

a long way for a bad joke: Steve Hamada
carved out a compartment for his portable radio
in the dense pages of the ham-sized,
Dictionary of Philosophy I think it was,
so he could tune in on KGFJ, "The Soul of L.A.,"
letting the organ-preachy strains of *96 Tears*
or some other Top 40s hit of the day
filter through the chem lab as we titrated,
90lb. girls giggling under decorously curved hands,
we boys feigning cool, staring into the wretched paisley
of an Erlenmeyer flask full of dark precipitate,
while our short, pastry-haired teacher
(he used Wildroot, a lanoline saturate)
in his sharkskin suit bellowed threats
down the lab aisles, policing his way past
burbling tubes and long glass stir-sticks
tinkering like feeble tongues
in the pale froth of the beakers;

or the time Higashi brought in the deck
of Tijuana playing cards to sophomore gym.
I remember one card in particular,
of rose-colored and cloud- purple genitals,
a blank look of humiliation or boredom
on the aging woman's face
(the Queen of Hearts or of Spades, unmitred),
rills of fat deliquescent along her belly,
her legs parted, knees up, the dark beard
undisguised and fibrous, frank as malice
or the desires of industry, her eyes unglazed,
looking straight into the camera lens
minus the obliged and sham ecstasy
on the faces of others in the deck.
I remember my own face then, hot with puzzlement,
abashed at my own craving, exchanging
that deep glance with the nameless woman's eyes.

There are none of us elect. Jap of Sheenie
hawking rags in New York streets,
nothing matters under corrosive skies,
the burdened light that bears down on us
with the tremulous weight of guilt and outrage.

Garrett Hongo

O-Bon: Dance for the Dead

I have no memories or photograph of my father
coming home from war, thin as a caneworker,
a splinter of flesh in his olive greens
and khakis and spit-shined G.I. shoes;

Or of my grandfather in his flower-print shirt,
humming his bar-tunes, tying the bandana
to his head to hold the sweat back form his face
as he bent to weed and hoe the garden that Sunday
while swarms of planes maneuvered overhead.

I have no memories of the radio that day
or the clatter of machetes in the Filipino camp,
the long wail of news from over the mountains,
or the glimmerings and sheaths of fear in the village.

I have no story to tell about lacquer shrines
or filial ashes, about a small brass bell,
and incense smoldering in jade bowls, about the silvered,
black face of Miroku gleaming with detachment,
anthurium crowns in the stoneware vase
the hearts and wheels of fire behind her.

And though I've mapped and studied the strike march
from the North Shore to town in 1921, though I've
sung psalms at festival and dipped the bamboo cup
in the stone bowl on the Day of the Dead,
though I've pitched coins and took my turn
at the *taiko* drum, and folded paper fortunes
and strung them on the graveyard's *hala* tree;

Though I've made a life and raised my house
oceans east of my birth, though I've craned
my neck and cocked my ear for the sound of flute

and *shamisen* jangling its tune of woe -

The music nonetheless echoes in its slotted box,
the cold sea chafes the land and swirls over gravestones,
and wind sighs its passionless song through ironwood trees.

More than memory or the image of the slant of grey rain
pounding the thatch coats and peaked hats
of townsmen racing across the blond arch of a bridge,
more than the past and its aches and brocade
of tales and ritual, its dry mouth of repetition,

I want the cold stone in my hand to pound the earth,
I want the splash of cool or steaming water to wash my feet,
I want the dead beside me when I dance, to help me
flesh the notes of my song, to tell me it's all right.

Pam Houston

My father was a sour man

My father was a sour man. He took pleasure in only a very few things: tennis, vodka, watching sports on television, and breaking anyone he perceived had done him wrong. I did my father wrong by being born, by having needs that required some of my mother's attention, and--even worse—some portion of his paycheck. My father made no secret of his deep resentment——he would explain it to our family friends repeatedly, believing that if he could find the exact words to describe all the ways he'd been cheated by my arrival, his friends would stop pointing out that I was just a baby/toddler/child, and finally take his side.

My father broke my femur when I was four. Because I was in a 3/4 body cast for nearly four months, there is plentiful documentation of this particular episode of breakage. But it was not the first or the last time he hurt me with the intent to do permanent harm. My mother and I tiptoed around my father, determined to keep from doing anything that would insult or defy him, determined not to invoke his wrath. But he was so thin-skinned, so eager for rage and revenge that acceptable behavior was always a moving target, one that was impossible, with any consistency, to hit.

All hatred is self-hatred, said the great James Baldwin, and every thinking person knows this to be true. My father believed—above all else—that only money could make him happy, and so he dedicated his entire life to gathering as much as possible at the expense of every other good thing he might have had: a lively intellectual life, the love of his wife and daughter, the deep pleasure of cultivating a faithful and compassionate heart. He made a decent living, and we lived more comfortably some years than others. But one thing my father was not, for even one day, was happy.

He used to say, *Pam, one of these days you are going to wake up and realize you spend your whole life lying in the gutter with somebody else's foot on your neck.* But when I went to college at seventeen, I found out the only foot that had ever been on my neck was his. All I needed was five foot-free minutes to explode out of the oppression of my father's house and into a life where, whatever else happened, I would never have anyone else's foot on my neck again.

I'd been lucky enough to get a scholarship to Denison University, a small liberal arts college in Ohio, where my professors wore ceramic peace signs around their necks and IUD's as earrings, and said things that were in direct opposition to my father's mantra. One example: *You can be anything you want to be, as long as you commit to it with all your heart and always keep in mind the greater good.* Going from my father's house to the English Department at Denison University was like being hauled up out of a car stuck in a continuous spin on black ice in the middle of the night in a Pennsylvania blizzard, and then dropped down into a hammock on Hanalei Bay where somebody has already put an organic pineapple smoothie into my hand. By some happy accident of grades, SAT scores, and an admissions officer's good will, the entire world had been remade around me, and all I had to do was say yes, please, I prefer this one…how might I be permitted to stay?

But years before I escaped to Denison I had come to the understanding that the only way my father could truly beat me, is if I lost my ability to imagine an alternative world, the one I wished to inhabit. Had I at any time in those first seventeen years, stopped being able to see the alternative, I wouldn't have made it through. There is part of me that still suspects that Denison University was created, not by the Ohio Baptist Education Society in 1831 but by the power of my imagination, and the sheer force of my will to survive.

Since I left my father's house, I've had forty wonderful years of living with no foot on my neck, but a no less acute memory of the seventeen when it was there. One of my legs came out of that 3/4 body cast a little crooked, and the pain in my back and hip works on me like Chekov's hammer. *You got out alive*, it says, *now do something with yourself.*

I don't waste time imagining who I would be if I had had a different father because so much of who I am, for better and worse originates with him. And I know well that it was in the moments when I most vulnerable to my father's abuses—when he was hurling me across the room into a piece of furniture, for example, or dragging me into the shower with him by my hair—that all his incapacities were so starkly revealed. If he killed me, I saw in those moments, he would be killing me out of weakness, but if I survived, I would have almost infinite power to make my own life.

So it follows, then, that on a cold December night in 2016, I have gotten busy imagining a world I wish to inhabit. In the world I envision, the ACLU raises 15 million dollars in two weeks from 241,480 donors, and organizations as various as Planned Parenthood, the Sierra Club, the Trevor Project and the Council on American-Islamic Relations see their donations skyrocket beyond their wildest dreams. Here, hundreds of non-Muslim students form a circle of protection around their Muslim counterparts to protect them during their five daily prayers, two thousand veterans travel to Standing Rock to form a human shield around the Water Protectors, and the Army Corps of Engineers denies the permit for the Dakota pipeline to be built. In the world I am imagining, thousands of writers come together at hundreds of simultaneous readings all over the country to raise money for organizations that protect women, the natural world, and the civil rights of all Americans, and the day after the inauguration, millions of women march on the Mall in Washington DC. Here, Americans step in and speak out whenever they see hate crimes and bullying, and principled members of congress from both sides of the aisle work together to protect the US Constitution. In this world, we vow never to sell each other out, nor go back to sleep, nor to the mall, nor to the bar, nor to any other anesthetization. We vow never to forget that the power of love is exponentially greater than the power of hatred. Above all else, we vow to believe in each other, and our collective power to make a world.

LeAnne Howe

Lesson 11,131,719

And then I meet the Woman On All Fours
Her back is up
But she says nothing.

Waiting for a reply,
I lie down across her panther-mound, weeping,
Salting ticks and crickets

The view from her mound near the river pains
Of ancient vessels and seal's wax, eons of
Cruel lessons from trespassers trumpeting change

Another old king comes ashore, his throne an office chair.
Killing she-panthers, opossums, airplanes, yellow sunflowers,
The Woman On All Fours he rapes; then strangles water and air

No one knows how many die, how many more mounds destroyed,
Strangers, peculiar bedfellows, his awkward friends vanish; he's
Bent on claiming everything, even privacy

A 24-7 king, he tweets, "I alone can fix it."
Meanwhile fluids and semen flow, stock markets fluctuate and finally sputter-stop
Like an old heart in blunt trauma. Alas, the deplorable is dead.

I am told the world has ended 11,131,719 times,
Who keeps account of such things?
Fear not, says the Woman On All Fours, rising from her mound.

We must rise together
We must rise together
We will rise together

Arise

LeAnne Howe

Reburial

Dig up his bones, his trumpets,
Rebury them.
Finding again, sensing they're still too lively,
Rebury them.
Dig up his bones, his hair, his trumpets,
Sniff any lasting traces,
Rebury them.
Dig up his bones, his hair, his ties, his trumpets
One last time
Before the odors of bone and blood fade,
Turning into something else,
Something useful like mulch or detritus, or
Fecal material, something other parasites recognize.
Rebury in a place where even the dogs can't find them.

Richard Jackson

Litany of the Self's Broken Horizon

The finite has no genuine being.
There soon creeps in the misconception of already knowing before you know.
                    -GWF Hegel

When our dreams drive off into bottomless ditches.
When the moon refuses to shine on the tombstones.
When the presumptuous clocks abandon memory.
When the sky fades out before dawn has a chance.
When the shadows break camp and march on us.
When a mine sprouts through the earth at someone's step.
It doesn't matter if we hang our words from steeple
to steeple. If love breaks the rung on the ladder below it.
If the curtain of the sky slips from its window.
There's a carload of futures circling the block.
There's a wrinkled emphysemiac at the emergency
room blowing smoke into a plastic liter bottler so he can
breathe again. There's another in his underwear calling to
to the angels who don't listen. Down the street there's a rusted
metal sign, its words worn out, clanging its message
to an improbable future. It was Hegel who knew that everything
we know is contradicted by something else we know.
I have never revealed my dream of the charred waves.
I have no idea where the mastless sails took me.
The only horizons are the ones we have passed.
The world is everything it is about to be.
There is no sense in becoming the grave robbers of our failures.
At every moment we have reached the middle of our lives.
You turn your head but it wasn't you who was being called.
The wearer of a bomb vest invests in every compass point.
Every slogan has its own hive of lies that roam about freely.
Our windows fog with theory. Mallarme knew the mind is
a spider web whose ideas are trapped by chance. As when
our words are known by the bomb craters they leave.
When our futures begin to betray the pasts we cherished.
When every stone contains countless colliding asteroids.
When we fight the border wars between desire and memory.

When we find ourselves strangers in our own minds.
That's when our hearts hang from the sweetest fruit trees.
When each word becomes an orchestra with no conductor.
When the flocks of our ideas fly off in all directions.
When truth is the scandal the nightingale sings about.
When the tree frogs know more than we will ever know.
When the old truths no longer open the soul's locks.
When one lovely war replaces another. When the stars begin
to flatter one another for favors. When one god promises
its candle wax will not flow like tears, when one skeleton
spies on another skeleton, when their gossip becomes law.
How many bodies must be splattered on how many
café walls to arrive at a truth that will soon fail everyone.
Someone has been knocking at the door of my dream.
Every word becomes eventually its own prison.
Therefore, the galaxy turns cartwheels without end.
Therefore, the trees bow down to the wind they never see.
Therefore, I disguise myself as myself while I am
waiting to see whatever the stars might hatch into.

Richard Jackson

How to Live, What to Do

There was the man playing his invisible violin on the street corner this morning, the roofers racing against the coming storm, the geese concerned with the right formation, the boy sling-shotting pigeons in the park, the man tasting his vintage cabernet, all in the midst of dreams that float like feathers from a bird the cats have caught, sayings that leak meanings they never intended, numbers too large to reveal what they hide like the Syrian homeless hiding beneath the shattered shells of their homes, and there is this box turtle eating the grapes I've left for him, circling the house like a planet or moon, though every moment contains all time for him as he follows star maps he's traced on the inside of his shell, whole constellations that lead him from one story to another, stories that say, yes, you can notice also this, the way the grass rises again after your step, how the rose petal leaves its sheen between your fingers, how the wind brings tickets for journeys hidden in words you have not yet discovered, stories that teach you it is all right to love the world again.

Patricia Spears Jones

Good bourbon helps

And old songs sung well
By well hung song makers
Ah Leonard Cohen, you must have been
As smooth as the bourbon on my tongue tonight
Before the moon grew larger
And sirens blasted Brooklyn's avenues
Wave after wave

On the streets of Portland, Denver, Chicago, New York
Detroit,—it feels like a Heat wave!
Combustion and courage—the ardent media watchers
Are loving the chaos they raised for ratings.

But lives are on the line. The "billionaire" and his bride
have entered the White House
But the cameras are off
So, what will the man with the very small hands do?

Martha Reeves full throttle voice could not make any of this
Better. Not the bourbon. Or the street marching. My students
Want him gone from their vision. Funny to think that a hip grandmother
Was more preferable to the young. They know that reality tv is hard work

For seconds of edited tape. This is reel time in real time and the star
Is not equipped to deal with the real world in whatever time is real.

So best to read about a red dwarf that has haunted Detroit since 1701.
American history is full of strange ghosts that linger at corners, near
Minefields, where a bridge meets the street.

Tonight I listen to "everybody knows" and "I'm your man"
And remembered why I wanted to run away to join a rock & roll band

Youthful dreams are often conventional and silly, but the man's sepulchral

Voice-bourbon, whiskey the smoke of tobacco's sweet lore.
Bards are handsome
Are they not?

Ah, two days and we hold ourselves up against the mindful anger
Of the privileged claiming victimhood. It is vengeance they seek, not justice.
It is vengeance they shall reap—their own kind slow dancing an opioid ballet.
Each day a misery held by that spoon and needle routine. Dreamless.

We hear those blasting sirens vibrate the moon.

Patricia Spears Jones

The Room Behind The Room

Lethal police force was used
To insure the funeral of the fetus left behind
In a room behind the other room where the doctors
Met and talked about football

Or that is the story told
By the good elders of the Forever Praising His Name
Church, even if his name is not actually called.

They wanted to hang her or burn her.
The woman in the room behind the room
Where the doctors talked about football.

But burning women remains taboo. Hanging women
Seemed redundant.   And so
Shooting her seemed more acceptable.

The lethal police force did what lethal police force
Is told to do and once done, another funeral
Another grave
Another wave of disgust rises in the Texas
Streets, like heat in July. It shimmers.

And shivers the doors and windows
Of offices where the doctors talk
About football and sorrow and the indecent
Moaning of state lawmakers—their cries
Recall the voice of vultures after feasting.

Marilyn Kallet

Warrior Song, After Brexit

June 25th, 2016

Trump's gloating over torn Europe like a fat orange guppy
        with hair. "My children can't stop crying,"
a London poet wrote. Long ago Heather called
        from her room, "I can't sleep, Mommy!
        The trees are crying." Hacked for starter castles,
the oaks slammed down. Judas redbuds
        with heart-shaped leaves shuttled
broken-off in trash bags.
"You can't leave the poem there," a young poet says. I taught
        his class a Dakota song:
        "You cannot harm me.
        You cannot harm one
        who has dreamed a dream like mine."
Now I wrap myself
in dream songs, chant through the halls of our ivory tower.
Europe is crumbling like a biscuit,
the tyrant blusters,
eating it up. Fear's his favorite breakfast.
"You cannot harm me," the warrior sang.
Young poet asks, "How did that work out?"
Pretty ending would be
the new lie.
                        (November 9, 2016)
        Now, breaks-it is on us.
U.S.
        We don't want to leave the house.
bed,
        bottle.

Outside the library
        our students
raise signs: "No Rapist for Prez!"
        Two p.m., a Trump thug punched
Jazmin's friend in the face.

153

"They called us 'niggers!'"
Mona said. She called in sick
        yesterday.

Normal now to be sick-afraid, but we
need to circle the hurt,
be cells that speak to each other
in one new body.
        We"ll find each other, easy
with "Not My President!" signs.
We'll rebuild. Speak out.
        We know fear won't protect us.
Silence can't cure. *So it is better to*
        speak, our friend Audre said.
Jazmin, take my hand.
One by one and by twos,
        together we'll clear the air.
        Our children will laugh
at the myth of an orange gob who
        bullied his way to
power. They'll howl
at an orange buffoon.
        Even in the future, he will hate the sound
of their laughter.

Wiccans, we beg you: bind him
to his own voice, deafen
and defeat him.
By his own will, he is bound
to a white sheet
and orange toupee.

Bind him in
the hell of his own making,
Bedtime for Bonzo,
part two.
Unbind we-the-people,
from this wild
boar who is tearing up
the graves of our ancesters
and the future of green earth.

Willie James King

You Go Back, If You Want

From a nursing home bed
Aunt Eva looked up at me
and said: Leave me here!
You go back, if you want,
those old ways, old haunts.
I won't go back to Alabama.
I saw how they lynched men
then returned to sit over a hot
meal, servant-made, lowered
their heads, whispered, then
lifted them up in "Amen." I
won't go back there again.

I kept poisons hidden in hats,
hems, between the mattress,
in case they'd hurt my boy.
It was torment to take it out
hold it up above what I later
ladled, and I'd set it back, in
the end. I should have emptied
it, the whole box, fed them all
their last supper. I almost did
when they killed Emmett Till.

I almost had Christ castrated
out me. And then, when they
shot King, I made a big meal.
Lord knows, they would lynch
me for sure, at my age, if they
knew I served a pinch of poi-
son to them every day, in water
bread, and, in every other way.
I won't go back to those ghosts.
I sense it, somehow, those old
Confederates don't stay dead.

Willie James King

To Console Them

I wasn't asleep last night
when the wind quickened
its pace, and the long lull
of rain fell steady as slow
piss falling down upon us
from another planet. I got
up and paced the frigid tile
of my kitchen floor, bare-
foot, while my overfed black
cat cantered up and down the
hall like a horse tired of the
same, pitiful clumps of sage

in an undeveloped pasture
where even the weeds lack
the courage to try anymore.
A screech owl wept in the
steeple of a nearby church
and if it were not weeping

why did it make those
sobbing sounds I heard in
the voices of the victims of
Haiti, when the TV camera
panned on all of those people
who tried with all they had

to hold on to being human?
It is as if I were with them,
groping amidst the mental
and the physically harmed,
where a bottle of sleeping
pills couldn't consign me to

a pillow. Nothing can trick
me into ever believing that
there was just the wind, lilt
of rain, or owl in the steeple
of the church weeping, while
miles from me, no less than

seconds, minutes, it takes a
heart to measure, there are
too many in numbers untold
who've got nothing but this
cold winter night to console
them while the world sleeps.

Yahia Lababidi

Excerpts from Meditations on the Light

The right to free speech ends where hate speech begins.
When hate speech is tolerated, eventually, some murderous fool acts out on the latent violence in the air and people's hearts.

The bigot's crime is two-fold: not knowing others well enough to love them, and not knowing themselves enough even to recognize their own hatred.
Hate, too, is a species of love; perhaps our enemies are, after all, merely thwarted lovers.
We are responsible for our enemies. Compassion is to realize the role we play in their creation.
At the heart of every vice sits selfishness, yawning.
In our popular culture's commitment to amusing itself to death, you can catch a whiff of sheer fear.
Our morality is determined by the level of immorality that we can afford to live with.
It's a sign of spiritual maturity when lesser transgressions prick our conscience more than before.
Unheeded pricks of conscience might return as harpoons of circumstance.

We can lend ideas our breath, but Ideals require our entire lives.
To breathe easier, do what is harder.

As with all battles, how we fight determines who we become.

To win a battle, morally, seek to be as blameless as humanly possible.

The Deceiver only promises short-term release, while tightening our shackles.
The devil's siren song has always been the same: "Let it burn."

Every time we betray our conscience, we strangle an angel. Yet, it's not certain we are allotted an infinite supply of winged pardons.
Think of (the d)evil as scared and, all his counsel, issuing from

a place of desperation.
Where there are demons, there is something precious worth fighting for.
You can't bury pain, and not expect it to grow roots.
Gratitude is caring for what we've been given.
How attentive the forces of darkness are, how they rush to answer
our ill-conceived wishes.
As you progress to the light, notice how jealous shadows also redouble their
efforts.
In most cases, darkness is a choice; the light is worth fighting for, and hard.
How vast the future that
it can serve as bottomless
repository of all fears, hopes and dreams...
Strange, how one hate enables another; how they are like unconscious allies,
darkly united in blocking out the Light.

Buoyancy of the human spirit in the face of turbulence is the source of the miraculous.
In serving words, faithfully, we also serve one another.
Like incantations, certain words combinations can set a sentence or soul in motion.
To grow older is to grow tired... of pretending.
Philosopher as outsider: how else to evaluate the play - onstage, alongside other
actors?The artist, too, must cultivate a certain distance, so they might lend their
vision to others.
In the deep end, every stroke counts.

Our salvation lies on the other side of our gravest danger.
To sense we are always at a great turning point is a sign of spiritual vitality.
There is a point in unlearning, where we cannot proceed any further - without
Transformation.
The price of transformation is nothing less than our old life.
This is the symbolic life, the previous and the next are the real. What we love in
the next world, we begin by loving here, first.
Words, like us, must do their work here, first, on their way to somewhere else.
Heaven save us from tragic seriousness; teach us to play, divinely.
Perhaps, crisis is self-induced disaster—a last ditch effort we gift ourselves to,
finally, transform.
Best not flirt with disaster, lest it decide to commit.
We're here to pass around the ball of Light, while keeping our fingerprints off it.

Civilization is carefully stitched together, yet easily undone. Humans, too, are a
form of organized chaos, capable of unraveling for an instant or a lifetime.

The only failures are misanthropes.

Meditation is knowing when to stay awake and when to fall asleep.

Mistrust a person seeking power, without a sense of humor - it usually translates into a lack of mercy.

Politics: what makes smart people sound stupid and stupid people sound smart.

A lesson to bullies, big and small: Controlling others is a spiritual impossibility; those who try, must exist in a state of agitated insecurity.

Mercy is to cover the nakedness of others, and stand beside them - naked, yourself.

The problem with being full of yourself is that you cannot fill up with much else.

William Luvaas

One Week

11/8/16 p.m.:
We expect it to be over by now, given all the Republican women in Florida who are Supposed to be supporting Hillary, the Latino vote, the black vote in North Carolina? Which state is called first? Florida, Ohio (no big surprise), North Carolina? Michigan is a shocker, as is Pennsylvania. Wisconsin...impossible! We stare at the TV, our mouths open, watching the Midwestern train wreck The landslide we'd expected for Clinton has become a Trump tsunami. We finally eat dinner at 11, when we feel we can hold something down.

11/9/16 early a.m.:
Some states remain uncalled, but the outcome is certain. I watch a grinning, fist-pumping mob at Trump central in disbelief. After decades of disengagement, millions of angry white voters have crawled out from under the floorboards, summoned by the Pied Piper of bigotry, blue collar Dems among them. Unbelievable. What happened to the women's vote expected to usher Hillary into office? Did they stay home or hold their noses and vote for a foul-mouthed misogynist? She is amassing a victory in the popular vote nonetheless. Hurrah for the West Coast. Time to secede from the union. What a fine country we would make: Scandinavia West. Then an event that stuns us all, red and blue alike, Hillary concedes. What the hell!

11/9/16:
I didn't sleep much last night and must drag myself out of bed into Trumpland. Grief is physical: it weakens the body and numbs the mind. I sleepwalk, making coffee, brushing my teeth, letting Mimi out to pee. Cin turns on TV. Nothing has changed from last night's nightmare. "President-elect Trump." I gag on the words. A widening popular lead for Clinton. No matter.

Funny how a land that prides itself on being a democracy isn't one.

We take Mimi for a walk in Kenneth Hahn Park, needing nature's healing. A middle-aged black guy in a porkpie hat walks up to us as if we've known each other for years. "Awful thing," he says, "terrible. But we going to be all right. We going to make it." Maybe I'm projecting, but it seems like people in L.A. are being purposely kind to each other today. A statement of protest here in our multi-cultural haven. People nod and say hello as we stroll around the lake: all types, all ethnicities, all genders, all ages. This is not Trump's Amerika.

We live in the West Adam's District, Jefferson Park. Once a Japanese-American neighborhood, it became African-American, and now is mostly black and Latino with a smattering of Asians and whites. The friendliest place I've ever lived. We know our neighbors, know each other's dogs, stop to shoot the breeze with passersby on walks; people stop their cars to admire our big akita, Mimi; we have block parties; we look out for each other. No crime-stricken war zone but a vibrant multi-cultural neighborhood. Trump doesn't know such places exist. People take pride in their homes; lawns are green or gone drought tolerant or are colorful Mexican gardens planted with bougainvillea, roses and bird of paradise. I feel guilty that we have let our grass die. Allow whites into the neighborhood and the place goes to the dogs. Not Trumpland. No, not here.

11/10/16:

I post on social media: Not my president. Never. Don't normalize this election. But it's already being normalized by Obama, the media, pundits and pols. Sure, I know our republic depends on a peaceful transfer of power, but how can we normalize an abnormal, hateful, foul-mouthed, authoritarian president? We can't deny that he is president and can't accept it either. We must reject and accept him at the same time and don't know how. There's no script to follow for this dilemma.

We go out to dinner at the Twin Dragons on Pico. People are discussing the election all sides. A black couple at the table behind me talk about the vast expanses of white America that elected Trump (I, like many writers, am a shameless eavesdropper). "It's like when you go to Vegas," the guy is saying, "once you pass San Bernardino, all bets are off, baby." Absolutely. Riverside and San Bernardino Counties are Trump country. Armenian-Americans (possibly) at another table are talking about how Comey cost Hillary the election. I imagine people holding such discussions across America. There's a collective agitation; we all sense that the outcome will be hugely consequential. There's a mixture of dread and giddy excitement that feels pathological.

11/11/16:

A tumult of emotions: disbelief, alarm, grief, despair, fury...I can't sort them out. They gel together in a toxic brew and turn my stomach. We are in mourning, plodding through the stages of grief. Not so much for Hillary Clinton and the promise she offered, but for our polity, our constitutional republic. I've felt nothing like this since John Kennedy and Martin Luther King were murdered. But this is different. The assassinations stunned us, but once the shock had passed we slowly recovered and moved on. The same is true of 9/11: it brought us together rather than tore us apart. This grief will evolve to rage, as unpredictable as this fool's presidency will be. We are in unknown terrain. Though some would argue that we remain in a place we have never left behind: Jim Crow country, Civil War territory, Trumpland.

Polarization is more intractable than we care to admit. This election has proven it. We coexist in separate Americas largely hostile to and ignorant of each other. Look at all the red spilling across election night maps: rural/small town America dominates the heartland, with outposts of blue marking urban zones and coasts. Any outsider would chuckle and say, "No wonder you lost." Wall-to-wall trump signs in Kentucky and Ohio and along the I-5 corridor through California's Central Valley. We all know the standard caricatures: the God, guns, guts and glory heartland, mostly white and protestant (increasingly evangelical), versus the let-it-all-hang-out urban/suburban pluralist zones. Simplistic? Sure. Not very. At core, ours remains a conservative country, nativist, xenophobic, fearful of change—enough so to elect a bigoted, fear-mongering president. What is it his supporters want? To refight the Civil War, purge the nation of nonwhites, Jews and Muslims? The Mason/Dixon line has shifted, but it's still there; the Confederacy has expanded.

11/12/16:

How to live with this outrage? I can't think of Trump without clenching my teeth. I'm not getting much work done. Protests continue in the streets and will for a long time. I'll join them soon. We talk about going to a march in downtown L.A. this afternoon.

People search for reasons. Some blame Hillary, some Comey, some cable news for chasing ratings and giving Trump 24/7 coverage, some the long Republican witch-hunt against Clinton and their success in labeling her "dishonest," which Bernie reinforced with his Wall Street stooge rhetoric (sadly, it's true). Some credit voters' appetite for change, but when isn't there an appetite for change? How ridiculous to characterize billionaire playboy Donald Trump as a populist agent of change. This election wasn't about change. What greater change than to elect a woman president? A change that many fear in our not-so-liberated America. Few commentators mention misogyny as a factor, though it was front and center of Trump's rhetoric. How do we explain blue collar workers in Michigan and Wisconsin who supported Obama but not Clinton? People argue it wasn't sexism since their wives voted for Trump, too—as if women never buy into patriarchy. Fighting for Civil Rights in 1960s Alabama, I never met an admitted racist. Racism was the water they swam in; no one even noticed it—as they don't notice sexism in Trumpland.

This election wasn't about jobs. Hillary had her jobs program, too. Income inequality was surely on voters' minds. But to imagine rich boy narcissist Donald Trump was suddenly flooded with come-to-Jesus love for the working man and an urge to share the wealth is a laughable delusion.

This election was driven by whitelash and malelash. Hillary Clinton lost the presidency because she's a woman. Pure and simple. Voters know Trump is a foul-mouthed, unstable hate monger and sexist bully, but they prefer a warlock to a witch. They don't see him as a pathological liar but rather a straight talker. It wasn't just the emails that got her labeled "lying Hillary" but the decades-long hate campaign against a woman whose only crimes are ambition and steely resolve. A woman who aims to fly high must be devious, she must have evil intentions, she must use a broomstick, while a demonstrably devious man is only doing what men do: going for broke.

We go to see the Jim Crow era movie "Loving" about an interracial marriage in Virginia. Words play in my head: "We're not going back there....We're not going back there...."

11/13/16:

My thoughts and feelings are a jumble. I'm still not getting much work done. While I can rationally explain what has happened, I can't comprehend it. Can't accept that Americans would ignore their core values and promote a proto-fascist autocrat to the presidency. Impossible. Sad to say, people don't vote from the head or heart but the irrational, craving, swinish gut. I wonder if I still believe in democracy. It's a noble aspiration, but now it seems like a fool's errand.

Hillary is not perfect and wasn't a perfect candidate. But I believe she would have made a fine president: capable, pragmatic, smart, steady, experienced, fair-minded. Beyond that, she is nurturing, as women often are and men more rarely. Our fragile world needs a nurturing hand, and we've just blown the chance to have one. Shame on us. I am reading Elie Wiesel's NIGHT. We must refuse to enter this darkness. "Rage, rage against the dying of the light."

11/14/16:

A week later, I remain where I started: dejected. Some of our black and Jewish friends are honestly afraid that their lives and liberty are in peril after Trump's selection of Steve Bannon, an avowed anti-semite and white supremacist, as his Chief Strategist. This isn't possible in America. Goebbels in the White House!

Clarence Major

Sardines

Lower East Side, Mid-1960s

On weekends
Ray always came back drunk.
His key fumbling in the lock.
He would give up
and sink to the floor.
I'd open the door,
pick him up, and pull him inside.
Often beaten up and robbed
Ray came back crawling.
I walked the streets
to give him some privacy.
I was doing research
on the future of the human race.
I sat in Jimmy's
and made one beer last for hours.
The Lower East Side
was becoming the East Village.
The perfect place
to research the future
of the human race.
I lived on sardines
and Saltine crackers.
With sardine-breath,
I hung out in Tompkins Square Park
among acidheads and LDS-heads,
among hippies and Flower Children.
Hippies playing bongo drums
entertaining the Flower Children.
The smell of marijuana
filling the air and the trees.
Middle class kids from Long Island
shacked up in flophouses.
Where better to research
the future of the human race?

Walking 5th and 14th
and Houston and Broadway,
I was deep in my research
on the future of the human race.
I wandered down into Chinatown
and across the Brooklyn Bridge.
Looking for clues
to the future of the human race.
Everywhere I found evidence
of a future for the human race.
Searching, I walked
the whole seventy-nine square miles.
Saturday night music on the streets
and people dancing at The Cave.
I researched it all
for the future of the human race.
For twenty cents, I rode
the first air-conditioned subway.
Evidence of progress
for the human race.
I rode uptown
and walked the streets of Harlem
documenting
the future of the human race.
In midtown, I loved
the cool solitude of art museums.
Keeping in touch with creativity
for the future of the human race.
In Washington Square Park,
I sat on the fountain and took notes
for the future of the human race.

Winners of the

Joy Harjo Poetry Contest

~

Rick DeMarinis Short Story Contest

~

Barry Lopez Non Fiction Contest

~

Lorian Hemingway Short Story Contest

Shangyang Fang

If You Talk about Sadness, Fugue

1.
Paul Celan wasn't necessarily the saddest person
chronologically. Trakl could have been sadder though his sadness was personal.
The personal is unbearable.

2.
I returned to China in the summer and found
summer doesn't belong there.

3.
The loneliest music I've ever heard is Brahms's
First Piano Concerto. My friend said, *it's like drinking a bowl of Chinese herbs
in the dark.*

4.
Schubert is non-existence.

5.
Trakl wrote, *your body is a hyacinth.*
And Celan, who drank milk when the night came.

6.
This morning a boy in Syria, 5-yrs old, was rescued
from the dust. He wiped his head and saw the blood; he didn't cry.
In front of the television, people wiped their faces draining with tears.
They didn't bleed.

7.
In June, I bought a book
of Silver Age poets: Akhmatova was the moon of Russian poetry,
Pushkin, the sun.

8.
A girl, again, in Syria, cried and raised her hands to surrender
when a journalist took a photo of her. She thought the camera was a gun.

9.
I cried when I listened to Brahms. The dead became retongued.

10.
In August, my aunt drove two hours to my town
and ask me not to be a poet. She read the poetry under my pillow
and found out Akhmatova's son was arrested. Gumilyov killed. Tsvetaeva went mad.
Everyone else exiled.

11.
My aunt told me that we are still in a communist country.
I told her, *I am already exiled by my family.*

12.
The moon remembers; she witnesses in the dark.
I ask her to explain how *we have forgotten to start with forgiveness.*

13.
For that boy, the war never ends. He shall not be lonely.
He shall repeat that motion of wiping, of digging
his mother out of dust, out of war-memory, brushing
her hair stained with blood. He doesn't
remember his mother's name; he kisses her face.

14.
Schubert had the body of a hyacinth. He wilted so fast.
Trakl added, *the last gold of an expiring star.*

15.
Celan's mother died in the war; he wrote poems for her.
He remembered her name. He wrote, *It's falling, mother, snow falls in the Ukraine.*
Ukraine is the name of a place. His mother's name is *mother.*

16.
I stopped writing poems, as my aunt pleaded. I took the book back from her place.

17.
I close my eyes and touch the book as if blind,
to feel how cold each word is on the page, how sharp, like shattered glass;
I am afraid no one can hold it from falling apart.

18.
Remember, the personal is unbearable. Some day, the moon will fall apart
from her memories. All night, she stared at the fleeting water, then left,
nothing remained except
the calm stare of the ceaseless water.

2ND PLACE, 2016 JOY HARJO POETRY PRIZE

Timothy McBride

Indigenous Knowledge

—Falanke Kaina, Niger, USAID, 1992

When the funds dried up, we took our findings
and went home to publish scholarly reports
on yield potential in selected drought-resistant
millet seeds (which further studies could confirm)
and the efficiency of various machine-dug
catchment shapes in trapping an additional ounce
of precipitation (assuming the availability of machines)
for subsistence farmers in the West African Sahel.
Along the Hamdallaye watershed, outside of Niamey,
village life goes on unchanged. "Locusts sing,"
a Zarma elder says. "The rainbow drinks the rain."

Robert Davis Hoffman

Where's Grandmother?

The missionary tells us the mortuary poles
are not good for our dead,
we should put the bodies in the ground.

We should abandon these poles.
They will cause sickness.
He says he can save us,
that our shamans cannot.
What truths shall we live by now?
What laws shall we follow next?
Great-grandmother's bones
neatly arranged
in a case
behind glass
in the museum.
It's a sin.
A sacred reliquary
that held decorated chests
of human ashes
the pole tries to stand,
plank cover pried off
for display.
Detritus filters down
onto conservator's paper
at its base
waiting for analysis.

Just over a hundred years ago
this pole would have a natural life
and death.
It was salvaged

the catalog says.
I ask in my Peoples' tongue, so that it will be clear:
Goo su wa eh, ax daakanóox'u?

Where are you, Grandmother?

Ruth Knafo Setton

Sophie's Recipe for Love

1. Begin with a perfect girl...

The perfect girl was born in America.

She does not waste time daydreaming about living in the House on the Hill with blond parents who speak English without an accent and pack her lunches with sandwiches of Velveeta cheese in spongy white bread instead of weird-smelling foreign foods wrapped in foil paper that fall apart the instant you pick them up. The perfect girl doesn't daydream at all, especially not when she's working in the family restaurant, The Couscous Café. She does not dream of Tony Rivers' blue-eyed smile that time she bumped into him in the hall because she knows it's hopeless and he's one of the wild gang boys who spends every afternoon in detention.

She does not ask the Ouija Board if Tony will break up with slutty Steffi Rodriguez and love her instead, definitely does not sneak into her best friend's church and beg Jesus to make Tony like her, does not call herself Nancy when she has a perfectly good name of her own, does not bring home filthy unclean food stuffed in cans, does not skip downstairs three at a time and land with a thud in the restaurant dining room startling customers, does not fight baths because boys like girls who are clean, does not fight shampoos because broccoli and carrots will sprout in her dirty scalp, and does not spy on grown-ups or follow strangers just because she finds them suspicious.

The perfect girl knows the difference between right and wrong and she is a shining example of Jewish femininity, and she does not—she does—she always—she never—she is—she is not—well, the only thing we know for sure is that she is not Sophie "Nancy" Elmaleh.

Still. As Mom says, when you don't have the right ingredients, improvise. And, *ma fille*, never forget the importance of cinnamon.

2. Add a dreamy young man...

Tony Rivers, of course.

After daydreaming about him all day at school, I come home to find General Mom and her army preparing for my brother David's bar mitzvah party in two days (December 15th, 1964). Neighborhood men help Dad's bass player and guitarist move tables to the wall where they'll be crammed with food for the buffet, which will consist of every neighborhood woman's specialty, including Puerto Rican mofongo, Russian Apple Cake, Chicken Chettinad just like they make it in Madras, Syrian stuffed grape leaves with a hint of olives, and Georgia Sweet Potato Pudding, and of course, Mom's Moroccan specialties—couscous, *bstilla*, and spicy *cigares*. The floor will be crowded with rows of folding chairs so everyone can watch David recite his prayers on stage. And then Dad and the band will play on the small stage in back.

As soon as she sees me, Mom wraps a white apron around me, hands me a feather duster, and tells me to dust as if it's Passover and not leave a speck anywhere, and adds, "Carlos is moving out right after the bar mitzvah party."

I'm so stunned he didn't tell me himself that I can't move. Carlos, Dad's drummer. The only one who understands how my magical House on the Hill can exist at night but disappear in the day. Everyone else thinks I'm mental, but Carlos says, "*Claro,* it's real. The world is too crowded to see everything and everyone all at once."

I scan the room for him. My gorgeous grandmother, Josette—who will kill me if I call her Grandma—works on a wall display of baby pictures of David. My shy brother is busy poring over the tiny print of the Torah with Sam the owner of Sam's Pawnshop. Unlike my aunt, Tata Zizou, who has convinced herself she was in a concentration camp during the war and scrawls blue numbers on her arm, Sam's are real, so real they're fading with time while Zizou's remain bright with constant touch-ups.

As I watch my brother prepare his recitation and speech, it strikes me that boys are lucky: they know the exact instant they become a man. My brother will recite prayers in front of a crowd, and boom, he's a man.

Even though Josette says, "A woman can decide what age she is," and even though I'm only two months away from turning fourteen, Carlos still calls me, "Brat."

Josette also says, "Big breasts are a state of mind," but if that's true, then why do boys automatically like girls with enormous boobs, like Carlos's girlfriend Angela and my secret true love Tony Rivers' girlfriend, Steffi Rodriguez?

Majestically hooded in my pink blanket, Tata Zizou stands at the swinging doors that lead to the kitchen, between the life-size cardboard figures of James Dean and Gary Cooper (donated by the owner of the Electra Theatre). Her spikes of hennaed orange-gray hair always make her look like she just saw a ghost. Head tilted, she listens to Mom confer with her three best friends—one with gold turban askew, another in an orange dress with the sequined parrot leaping across her chest, and the third with a wreath of Christmas lights on her bleached blonde hair.

I spot Carlos standing on a table, stringing a clothesline of blue paper lanterns beneath the canvas tent roof—"like in Mexico," he told us. I move to the table and glare up his long legs in jeans to his muscular drummer's arms as he hammers in nails to hold up the lanterns. Usually he ties his dark hair back with a leather cord but today it hangs loose.

"Carlos!"

He doesn't hear me over the music (Ella Fitzgerald singing "The Nearness of You"), chanting (David), men yelling as they push the tables, and Mom shouting orders in French and English. I dust around his feet—long bare feet, toes clinging to the edge of the table—tickling his toes with the yellow feathers until his foot twitches, his knee jerks, he almost drops the hammer and lantern, and squints down at me, his head draped with the tent, like a desert chief. "Hey, brat!"

"Why didn't you tell me?"

His face immediately goes stoic, and he says cautiously, "I was going to."

I thrust out my jaw. "You're going to marry Angela."

A smile flickers across his face. "No."

"Then why?" It's a pure wail, and it scares me—how mad and lost I feel at that moment. "You can't go! You're my—"

His face tenses against what I'm going to say. *You're my* … My friend? My companion in the secret world? My secret deputy in the Water Street Mystery Club?

I clamp my lips together.

3. Stir in big breasts, a mountain laugh, and the secret of the Spy Shed...

After Mom's endless Thanksgiving feast two weeks ago, I wandered outside in soft-falling snow down the alley and as usual checked out the Spy Shed, a small rusted tin shed that sits mysteriously between the Mahendroo and Norton backyards. I have frequently mentioned the suspicious fact that neither family claims the shed. Each time I pass, I test the claw handle doorknob (locked, of course).

But that day I circled the shed, and to my shock, the door opened! The Russian spy himself emerged, a black knit cap pushed down low over his forehead. I glimpsed sophisticated spy equipment behind him, radios and transmitters, lights that glowed red.

He locked the door and turned. "Fuck off, kid."

Brave detective that I am, I ran home and dragged Carlos from the stage, and being Carlos (my secret deputy), he came without a word of protest, and we raced to the shed. He yanked the silver handle, probed the keyhole with his pocketknife, and with a flourish opened the door.

Inside the mysterious Spy Shed, at last! A garbage can crammed with butts and ashes. A small table, a single folding chair. Where did the radios disappear? Not even a light switch on the wall, but a large flashlight on the table. And piled high on the filthy floor, stacks of magazines.

"Spy manuals!" I cried. "Coded messages!"

While Carlos leafed through one, I peered over his arm. A naked woman cupped her breasts in both hands. Enormous breasts, way bigger than Angela's.

Outside the shed, wind slammed the tin walls. Choking on stale air, I leaned over to pick up a magazine. Women flicked past. Naked. Fleshy. Lying on their backs, legs spread. Crouched on all fours. Squeezing their own breasts and touching their breasts and between their legs.

I dropped the magazine as if it were burning my fingers.

Behind me, a sharp groan.

I wheeled around in terror.

Carlos. One palm pressed flat against the tin wall, he sank to a crouch. Laughing so hard tears squeezed from his eyes. The mountain laugh, like his mother and the old shamans from his village. He'd told me the laugh was rare, fierce, wild.

I leaned closer to understand the secret of this laugh and this stranger who was—yet was not—my family. He tried to speak but the laugh trembled behind his eyes and mouth, ready to erupt again. His eyes flickered wet like leaves in the rain. I was so close I saw the honey smudge in his eyes blur gold-black. He moaned, "Oh, Sophie," but I wasn't Sophie anymore, I was Nancy Drew, peering into a dark cave with a flashlight aimed at the heart of the mystery until with a breathless gasp I ran out of the shed and back up the alley.

Alone.

4. Throw in your secret true love, couscous, Madame Bensibal, the kingdom of bad Moroccan jokes, and stir with a feather duster until flames appear...

Since that day I haven't felt right. As Josette says, "You aren't good in your skin." At night I picture those enormous-breasted women with sultry smiles, and when I wake up, I'm sure my breasts have sprouted as large as Angela's, so huge they lift me in the air like balloons and I float to school. But when I hear Mom's siren wail, "Soph-eeeee!" in the morning and tumble out of bed, I realize it's not my breasts that have sprouted, but my feet. And my hands. And my nose. I bump into every piece of furniture, trip on the same loose nail on the steps twice a day, bang my head against the overhanging plaster in the second-floor bathroom.

"Listen, brat," Carlos says now, his eyes bright and troubled. "I need to ... go back to Mexico ... see my people."

"We are your people." I almost spit the words.

He gives me one of his brooding looks and hunkers down, one palm flat on the table, a wild animal about to pounce. "My name is not Elmaleh. It's Sandoval."

"Is this about getting a passport and license? Are you leaving because of papers? Don't be an idiot! We'll chip in and buy them for you."

"I don't want to buy papers. I don't want another name. It's like being a ghost, no reflection, no face. It's like I don't exist."

Around us people are moving, tables screeching, David chanting, Mom talking, Josette laughing. I lean forward, trembling down to my toes. Suddenly I'm back in the Spy Shed, aiming the flashlight at the dangerous criminal in the cave. "You exist for me," I tell him miserably.

He stares beyond me. "You were spying on Angela and me last night."

My cheeks flame. "I wasn't spying!"

"No? What do you call hiding behind the door and listening to every word we say?"

And watching you kiss her. I kneeled behind the kitchen screen door and peered through the tiny netted diamonds. An electrifying thrill shot through me. When Angela moaned, the thrill turned to an ache deep in my stomach. The wire screen burned my nose and cheeks, but I couldn't move until Carlos lifted his head.

"Well? Don't tell me you were doing research again." Not a muscle in his face moves but I know he's laughing at me.

"Stop it!"

"Stop what?"

"Stop laughing behind your eyes."

The smile slowly reaches his mouth. "You'll understand when you grow up."

He makes me furious. Talking to me as if he's an ancient, all-knowing guru when he's only twenty, exactly six years and two months older than me. Anyway, as Josette says, "It takes boys 7.5 years to catch up with girls," which means he'll never catch up with me.

"He's here, *ma belle*!" cries Josette. "Tony Rivers!"

I twist around.

Tony! In the doorway of the Café. Flanked by two fellow gang members: Billy and Pete Rodriguez, my enemy Steffi Rodriguez's brother. All three wear studded black leather jackets and slouch toward me.

I turn back to Carlos. He's standing again, his head draped by the tent roof. I can't see his eyes.

Josette nudges me. "What are you waiting for, *cherie*? Go to him!"

Before I take a single step toward Tony, Carlos is hammering again. With each step away from him, my breasts grow larger and heavier, tilting me forward. *Walk with grace and joy,* says Josette, *and sway your hips like the leaves of a palm tree. Remember the joy of being a woman.*

But I don't feel graceful or joyful. My breasts and feet are huge, and I don't want Carlos to leave us, and I'd rather curl up with a mystery than solve one. Of all days, why did Tony have to come today?

"Hey, Sophie."

I swallow hard. "Hey."

"Thought I'd try that couscous." Tony's dark eyes sweep over me, up and down, and stop at the feather duster. *Grace and joy and palm trees*, I remind myself.

Behind me, I hear Tata Zizou's raucous laugh followed by the two words that make my brother and me cringe to the depths of our souls: "Madame Bensibal."

No! My mind freezes in disbelief. It can't be. What on earth would possess Tata Zizou to bring up Madame Bensibal?

"Hey," says Pete Rodriguez, giving me the same up and down survey as Tony. "Looking good, Elmo-lay."

He and Billy snicker. I feel like waving the duster in their faces. "We're not really open," I begin.

"Yeah, getting ready for your Jew-party," says Pete. "Steffi told me you got the whole street involved."

I don't know if it's the dust floating around the air or Pete's presence or the mention of Steffi, but I sneeze. A loud, messy sneeze. Immediately followed by another one. Another sneeze threatens on the horizon. I have no tissue, nowhere to blow my nose. As I scrunch my face to try and hold it in, I hear Tata Zizou's voice again, "You don't know this story, Carlos."

Oh yes, he does, Zizou. Everyone in this family knows about the horrible Madame Bensibal. Tell her you know it, Carlos.

"One day in Mogador Madame Bensibal was walking in the crowded *souk,* the market square, when she farted. A loud, long one."

Of course she says this while the room is silent for an endless moment. *I hate Madame Bensibal.* Hate her hate her hate her. There's no one in the universe I hate more, except possibly Tata Zizou at this moment.

"What's this?" Mom approaches us, all concern. Is it possible someone has been in the Café for five minutes and not been offered food? "Are you boys hungry?"

"Couscous," mutters Tony, and Mom immediately takes charge. "Sophie, don't keep them standing." She turns to Tony. "So nice to see couscous fans among the young. As you can see, I'm busy getting ready for my son's bar mitzvah but I can prepare couscous with sweet potatoes in a few minutes."

Another snicker from Pete and Billy. The three guys sit at a table while I go to the kitchen to get Cokes and bread. Josette is on my heels, almost running after me into the kitchen. "Oh la la, the winds of love are blowing your way!"

She doesn't understand. Neither does Mom. While she boils water for the couscous, I ask her to call Tata Zizou to get her out of the dining room but Mom waves away my worries. "She's good today. She didn't draw numbers on her arm. Don't worry, *cherie.* All will be well."

I return to the dining room with my tray of sodas and bread with olive oil, and see a sight that chills me. Tata Zizou, seated at Tony's table. So God has answered my question: can things get worse? **Yes**, He says, **it can, and it will, and don't ask again, or I'll have her tell the story of Madame Bensibal to your friends.**

As I draw near, I hear Zizou considerately adapting the story for her American audience. Instead of the *souk,* explains Tata Zizou, the notorious Madame Bensibal stops at the A&P. Instead of living in Mogador, Madame Bensibal lives in Newark. As if these changes will make it more understandable. *Don't you see, Tata, some things just can't be translated?* She recaps the action to this point: "And so, poor Madame Bensibal was embarrassed when she let loose a large fart."

The ugliest word in the English language, the stupidest story in the world, and Madame Bensibal the most obnoxious creature in the universe. American families don't tell stories like this. I slam down the sodas, olive oil and bread.

"Tata Zizou, Mom needs you in the kitchen."

She gestures absently. "Later. So Madame Bensibal ran home and pulled her hair. What could she do to make up for this offense? She decided to bake cakes, many little cakes. Then she rushed back to the *souk,* ah *non*, the A&P, and handed them out. 'Excuse me everyone, I farted so here is a cake."

I allow myself a quick glance at Tony. He's staring at Zizou the way strangers do: as if she just walked out of their nightmares into the real world.

"But cakes are not enough. She packs and tells her husband, 'We must move because I farted in the *souk* of Newark.' They leave town in the night and run away, like tiptoe, to Newark. *Non*, I mean Trenton! They move to Trenton! Ten years pass."

The air in the dining room is even hotter than usual, red-tinted, as if a fire is burning. I can't leave her alone with them. Who knows what she'll say? I hover, tray in hand, and listen to the saga of Madame Bensibal unwind with the tragic inevitability of *Julius Caesar,* which we're studying in English class.

"Monsieur Bensibal is sure everyone forgot, but Madame Bensibal insists they return in disguise. Madame puts on dark glasses, Monsieur grew a mustache. They drive down their old street but their house is gone!"

Finally, finally, the end of the joke is in sight. I curse you, Madame Bensibal. May you and your husband turn into donkeys whose ears sprout cilantro. If my brother weren't lost in the Biblical world, he'd be shuddering with me. Just when we think stinky Madame Bensibal has been banished to the kingdom of bad Moroccan jokes, here she comes again. Just in time to ruin our lives.

"They see only white office buildings. They ask a man, 'Where are the houses that used to be here?' He is surprised. 'You must be new in town. They were torn down eight, no, seven years after Madame Bensibal's fart.'"

She gives a little cry of triumph, and with glowing eyes, looks around the table.

Pete hisses like the evil snake he is. Billy gives a weird bark that sounds like it could be a laugh. It almost makes me warm to him. Tony turns his head and looks at me. No trace of a smile. No trace of any emotion. Tony Rivers and Sophie Elmaleh are over, before we even had a chance to begin. Thank you, Tata Zizou.

5. The recipe is a disaster! What went wrong? Did you sneeze? Quickly, in a desperate attempt to salvage the mess, throw in cinnamon, almonds, raisins, sweet potatoes, ketchup… Improvise! Hurry!

With heavy steps I go to the kitchen. Mom has set out three large bowls of sweet potato couscous sprinkled with almonds and raisins. She sifts cinnamon over each serving. The couscous smells and looks as wonderful as ever, but it makes me feel sick to my stomach. Josette opens her mouth. I hold up my hand. "Don't ask. Don't say a word."

I push the swinging doors with my hip and advance with the tray. Tata Zizou is still there, of course, thrilled she told a story all the way to the end, and imagining the three gang members as her new friends. Silently, I hand them the steaming, fragrant couscous. To talk now, to say a single word, requires more strength than I've got.

Tony clears his throat. "So this is couscous."

Pete grumbles, "Looks like plain old rice to me."

"I don't like the smell," says Billy, and my momentary sympathy for him evaporates.

"Got any ketchup?" asks Pete.

Ketchup. For couscous. Zizou's eyes are bright and eager, following the guys' moves. Next she's going to scribble maps on napkins and invite them to the birthday party she's eternally planning, but that will never happen. I go to the kitchen and grab a bottle of ketchup, wishing I could squeeze it over Pete's oily head. With the same dragging steps I return to the dining room. Now what? The guys lean toward Zizou, all three of them, hair gleaming and noses pointed, rats narrowing in for the kill.

"Tat Zeez," says Pete in a voice that sounds like chalk scraping across a blackboard, "youse guys sell any couscous ice cream?"

"I'll take a strawberry couscous milkshake." Billy spears a sweet potato.

"Hot fudge couscous sundae," says Pete, talking as he chews. I see that all three of them, despite their sour faces, are managing to force Mom's cous-cous down their throats.

"Eh?" says Zizou.

Billy rubs his belly. "Got me a craving for couscous parmigian."

"Scrambled couscous and bacon." Pete holds up his hand. "Hold the couscous."

"Pardon?" asks Zizou.

"Bullwinkle the Moose-Cous." That's Tony, grinning. He's moved into en-emy territory. I'm staring right at him but I don't see his face anymore—the gor-geous eyes and smile I dreamed about. He's with *them*. And he's got bad teeth.

"Bruce-cous."

"Couscous on the cob."

"I had an Uncle Couscous once."

This one actually makes me smile. Any other time all this could be funny. It *is* funny. But with each couscous variation they name, Zizou's eyes darken and widen.

"How about couscous a la mode?"

"No, I got it. Couscous pizza."

"Couscous pot pie."

I stand, feet rooted to the floor, watching the three of them laugh hyster-ically. Laugh with them, I command myself. Laugh at this crazy Couscous Café and your whole crazy life. Zizou watches them, bewildered. She's not stupid: she feels the kicks behind the laughter. Her eyes meet mine in deep aching sorrow.

Pete gestures to me. "Look at Elmo-lay. I think she's going to cry."

Billy sneers. "I'd cry too if I lived here."

6. Go ahead, cry. Water it with your tears. There is no House on the Hill, no dream that comes true, your name isn't Nancy it's Sophie, and you're not eighteen you're not even fourteen yet, and whatever Josette says, big breasts are more than a state of mind, and you'll never get Tony Rivers, never ever...

My chest grips tight as I wait for Tony to deliver the final blow. I know it's coming, the way Julius Caesar knew—warning upon warning, omen upon omen. Beware the Ides of March! I meet his dark blue eyes.

"Hey, this couscous tastes stale. Someone oughta tell the Board of Couscous."

Et tu, Tony. You can do better than that. But I don't want to hear anymore. I can't bear his voice, or Pete's, or Billy's another second. I clear my throat. "I think you guys should leave."

All three look at me, astonished. Pete flicks his tongue like a snake. "You telling us to leave? *You?* What the fuck?"

Tony looks me up and down, then kicks back his chair and gets to his feet. "Yeah, what the fuck." And the dream of a happy ending of Tony falling in love with me forever after, splinters once and for all into a thousand pieces.

"Look, it's Tonto," says Pete with a jerk of his narrow shoulder. "Hey Kimosabe, where's the Lone Ranger?"

I turn and see Carlos sauntering toward us, casually swinging the hammer at his side. His eyes squint in the fierce look that turns his face into a wood carving. He ignores me and glances at my aunt. "Zizou, you okay?"

"Carlos," she says happily.

His eyes gentle, and he folds his arms across his chest, hammer still in hand, and whistles a low tune as if he's on a street corner waiting for a bus.

The guys look at him for a minute, measuring themselves against his broad shoulders and the hammer in his hand. And behind him, the musicians and neighborhood men, none of them lightweights.

"This place is some crazy shit," mutters Pete.

"Yeah, let's blow this joint," says Tony, probably the wisest one after all.

"Why?" whines Billy. "We didn't do nothin."

Pete snarls like the mad dog in the alley. "We ain't paying."

"Don't pay," I say quickly. "Just go."

Billy shrugs, and Pete gloats, "No tip for you, Elmo-lay." The two of them swagger to the door but Tony looks from me to Carlos and back to me again. "That didn't go right…. Maybe I'll come back on my own."

I don't say anything.

"Hey, I'm sorry. Those guys get out of hand sometimes. Like family. You know." He glances at Zizou and holds out his hands.

"Yeah, I know."

"We cool?"

"We cool."

7. Stare into the red-hot heart of the oven, don't step back even when your cheeks burn and your heart hurts from the knowing…

Carlos watches me, arms still crossed. *Tonto.* My eyes blur, my throat aches. I picture him laughing in the Spy Shed, wiping the tears from his eyes and groaning, "Oh Sophie," and on the way home, swearing, cross his heart or hope to die, that he'd never breathe a word to anyone about what we found. And I remember farther back, the very first day he entered our kitchen two years ago. We watched him open his large canvas sack and turn it upside down. The shock of the cascade of instruments scattering across the black and white tiles and the shivering waterfalls of sound. Hand-carved rain sticks, tiny clay horns, wood flutes carved in the shape of turtles and birds, drum sticks, castanets, ice-sharp stones and acorn bracelets and anklets. A world he'd created with his own hands. That night he moved in with us and became the drummer in Dad's band.

He clears his throat. "He's still yours, brat. *If* you want him. He's probably not so bad on his own, away from his friends."

"Will you tell me just one thing? Are you leaving because of me? If I promise never to spy on you again, will you stay?" I squint at him through a wet blur. Without warning the shock hits me again: the flashlight aimed into the mouth of the dark cave.

Shadows flicker in his eyes—no hint of laughter now, no sign of sun. The orange smudge looks like a tiny flame. We're in the dining room surrounded by people, lights bright, music blasting, but at the same time we're in the cave, just Carlos and me, and I dropped the flashlight and suddenly everything is dark except for his eyes. That's why I can't look away or even blink.

"You know, I could be your big brother or your uncle."

"My *uncle*?" I imagine the mythical Uncle Couscous and snort.

He has the grace to grin, but he lowers his eyes, and suddenly I *know.* The way Josette said a woman knows. But Josette, an hour ago I thought I was in love with Tony. And now I'm all confused. Shouldn't I …?

I hear her voice in my ear: *Ah, Sophie, love has nothing to do with should.*

8. Smile smile smile, and when he smiles, turn three times and go back to being thirteen when you had a secret true house and a secret true love…

I cross my arms just like him and smile brilliantly. At least he's not leaving because of Angela. And I am a woman, not a child, no matter what he thinks. And maybe I can convince him to stay so we can at least talk like friends, or like uncle and niece. I smile till my mouth aches with the effort. I wait for his smile to return us to yesterday, but when he slants his eyes to meet mine, he doesn't smile and doesn't smile, he won't smile, and in the split-second before my smile collapses, I see poor Madame Bensibal trying to return to yesterday, before everything changed and she became a marked woman (you can't go home, Madame Bensibal, you can't go back to who you were even an hour ago) and for the first time I wonder if that's why Tata Zizou tells that story, trying to return to the moment before the madness hit, and I realize I can never go back either, and my smile crumbles, it was brittle and broken anyway, and it's too late, something terrible and scary and beautiful has entered me, and while I'm staring at him, he makes a strangled sound deep in his throat, and without a word, stalks away and leaves me standing alone in the dark.

9. Don't move, don't breathe, something's about to happen, it's almost ready, just wait for the timer, any minute now he's going to turn around…

Warren Alexander

Wrong Train

Unkle Traktor and Aunt Georgia took me to the old Penn Station, a new world imitation of the Baths of Caracalla and the Gare d'Orsay. Hundreds of kids bound for summer camp appeared and disappeared in the shafts of sunlight as they waved good-bye and traipsed down the platforms to their trains. I threw my duffle bag over my shoulder, grabbed my guitar case, and joined the herd. Some children cried, others never looked back. Some parents cried, others planned lunch. Anxiety, excitement, and unclear track assignments filled the terminal.

From the beginning, nothing on the train seemed right. Many of the girls sported bobbed noses and the boys' haircuts were measured and fashioned, not just mowed short for the hot summer. I had never heard socialists laugh so much. Their pastel shirts seemed far too happy and crisp. Even at my age, socialists were required to bear the weight of the world on their shoulders and faces, if for no other reason than to prepare us for being adults. And no one, but me, brought a sandwich and an apple. A salami sandwich designed to withstand hours of inattention and lack of refrigeration sat next to me identified by the spreading grease stain on the brown bag and the pungent smell of fat and spices.

As the train inched along the Hudson River, counselors called out the names of the campers. My name was nowhere to be heard. If there were any Jews in the crowd, they had crypto-Jewish names like Brown, Stone, or Rose. I continued to listen for my name. Two hours later, when we alit from the train, I approached the oldest adults. They furiously scrutinized their lists.

"Where are you supposed to be again?"

"Camp Emma Goldman. Sacco and Vanzetti Cabin. Rifton, NY. Where Sojourner Truth was born."

"You're in the wrong place. This is Camp Sunshine."

"Camp Sunshine?" I said. "Sounds like one of those the Fresh Air camps."

"I can assure you that we are not a Fresh Air Fund camp," said one of the adults with the borrowed contempt of a salesperson in an expensive store. They huddled and murmured among themselves.

"What are we going to do? We never make mistakes."

"Of course not. It's the boy's fault."

"But what to do? We can't just leave him here."

"We must make lemon poppy seed cake from lemons."

They turned to me.

"How old are you?"

"12."

"12. 12. Well, a 12-year-old boy should be with the Noble Savages."

"But that doesn't solve the bigger problem."

"I got it. We'll make him a pet. A mascot. A project. He'll be the first 'Camp Sunshine Fellow'."

"Excellent."

"Would you like to be the first 'Camp Sunshine Fellow'?"

"I guess," I said.

"We'll give you ¾ privileges."

"Does ¾ privileges include lunch?" I asked.

"Yes."

"Every day?"

"Yes."

"Ok."

"Get on that bus."

The buses were not the standard yellow buses owned by companies like Ed-Deb Trans with hardened lumps of gum under the seats and young love carved into the seat cushions. These buses were benevolent whales with air conditioning that formed a hump on the roof and individual reading lights that glittered as eyes.

It was clear now. Not only did I get on the wrong train, but I was going to a camp for socialites, not socialists. Not a common error and one for which I had no excuse.

When we arrived at Sunshine, I said, "I have to call my guardians."

I was led to a phone where I called Aunt Georgia and Unkle Traktor to explain the situation. I imagined them sharing the receiver.

"How did you get on the wrong train?"

"They all looked alike."

"Are they treating you well?"

"The offered me ¾ privileges. It's a fellowship."

"What does that mean?"

"I'm not sure. But it includes lunch."

"Do they know you're Jewish?"

"They know that I was supposed to go to Camp Emma Goldman. Sacco and Vanzetti Cabin. Rifton, NY. Where Sojourner Truth was born."

"So they know you're Jewish. And that ¾ thing means the camp is restricted. They will exclude you from what they want and hide behind that phony fellowship. Dirty bastards. Let's figure out a way to get you to the right camp."

I felt awful and stupid about the entire situation until Aunt Georgia said, "Wait. Maybe you can stay and you can be a Margaret Mead in reverse. You can observe and verify what we suspect already and, when you return home, you can write about it."

"Yes, yes, maybe that's a better idea," said Unkle Traktor. "What an opportunity. Then when you get home, you can write 'How Those Dirty Bastards Really Live.'"

"We'll work on the title later," said Aunt Georgia. "But remember, while you're there, don't write anything down. Just take mental notes. Written notes can be used against you. Remember Alger Hiss and the Pumpkin Papers."

The more we spoke, the less guilty I felt and the more enthusiastic I became about my mistake.

"OK, stay. But be careful. Those dirty bastards," said Unkle Traktor before they hung up. Aunt Georgia then called Emma Goldman and told them that I would not be coming for lunch.

The Noble Savages cabin had only five other boys my age and they all knew each other from previous summers: Biff, the twins--Tad and Trey, Ed, and Mellon, who bore his mother's maiden name as his first. My bunkmates tried the usual pranks, short sheeting the beds, Saran Wrap over the toilet bowl, and passing off Ex-Lax as expensive chocolates sent from home. It was done more from tedium and a lack of imagination than malice.

Because a caste system existed within the caste system, I was co-joined with Mellon. His father had been accused of some sort of fraud. If he had swindled only the poor, I assume his son would have been welcomed and I would have been assigned to someone else. But père Mellon had crossed the line and stolen from the wealthy. When a crime is committed, small or notorious, by someone from a minority, every person of that group squirms with the fear of repercussions beyond and out of proportion with the crime. But at Sunshine their grievance was internal and the result punitive.

Linking us didn't create friendship; official pairs were required during activities such as canoeing, tennis, and deep-water swimming. Mellon is a horrible name for a child who is well-liked, let alone someone who is ostracized. At Sunshine, they called him The Lope, as in canta-Lope. Even our counselor, Ned, called him The Lope.

Ned, a former camper, possessed a perennial squint which betrayed his anxiety about what people above and around him might be saying. If there had been an organization of Junior Sycophants, he would have been the first to say yes and join. It must have been hard to go through life always frightened. Ned deeply wanted to inculcate us in the traditions of Sunshine. He did so by repeating his version of the Sunshine motto, "Liberté, égalité, fraternity." Not fraternité but striped polo shirts fraternity.

Ned was most serious when completing the nightly KYBO report. Although I never learned the exact meaning of the initials, I thought they stood for "Keep Your Bowels Open" because every night after dinner, Ned would dutifully record our responses to the following questions:

"Did you write home today?"

"Did you excel at anything today?"

And "Did you KYBO today?" referring to a crap.

Just exactly how these activities were related remained unclear to me. Tad and Trey, who were quite regular, took an unnatural interest in each other's bowel movement, which was instructive as to why Mengele and others liked to study twins. Fortunately, they did not keep an official accounting of how often Mellon masturbated, for which he had a distinct aptitude.

I found it useful to masquerade as a street-tough in order to intimidate Ned and the others. On the days I did not wear my junior wife beater, I rolled cigarettes in the sleeve of my T-shirt. I always carried my pocket knife and played basic schoolyard basketball by going hard to the hoop no matter who came between me and the bucket. I did not want to get close to anyone and have them ask how Unkle Traktor's and Aunt Georgia's became my guardians following the sequential and unexpected deaths of my real parents. I certainly did not want anyone to learn about my guardians' Communist ties. Or Unkle Traktor's ideological quirks, such as getting unreasonably irritated when someone called him a Trotskyist instead of a Trotskyite.

The true benefit to my association with Mellon were the meals. Since his father was still out on bail, his parents often came to visit, and would take us to expensive seafood restaurants with French names. At first I was intimidated. I, a 12-year-old, was the representative of an entire religion. How was I going to explain why Jews cannot eat this or that, or worse, unravel the logic and history behind Jewish dietary laws? Why, for instance, is the waiting time between eating dairy then meat different than the waiting time between eating meat then dairy? Or if we are right, how come the entire non-Jewish world is not dead of shrimp or pig poisoning? All Jews, including the ones who do not keep kosher and those who barely know their home address know the spelling and dangers of trichinosis and crustaceans and are imbued with the horrors of eating pork and shellfish.

Add to this, Jews never eat fish in its natural state. It must be smoked, mashed, mushed, pickled, salted, peppered, creamed, or transformed into gefilte fish before it can be served. How do you rationally explain that?

I did not recognize the names of any of French fish on the menu, so I ordered something I hoped was not shellfish. I was quite fearful of appearing hypocritical and eating prohibited food that was not Chinese. At least back home, seafood restaurants had Landlubber's Menus, offering something chicken acknowledging that the neighborhood had not been red-lined. My fish arrived ovate except for the tail. It was accompanied by a lonely lemon wedge enrobed in mesh which I removed as being unnatural. From then on, wherever we went, I ordered sole, which everyone naturally assumed was my favorite. And in a way it was.

Sitting across from the dour parents of Mellon, I was so uncomfortable that I passed up a family joke. "I don't see herring on the menu. I guess it is too early for young kippers." Yet Mellon's parents had no inkling of my apprehension. In fact, based on our hesitant and dislocated lunchtime discussions, they seemed to believe we shared common interests.

"We sent Mellon to one of the finest public schools in England, Eton," said Mellon's father.

"Me too. I went to Public School 225 in Brighton Beach. Very good reading and math scores," I said.

"We spent last summer at the beach in Brighton," said Mellon's mom.

"Me too," I said.

"Have you ever been to England?" asked Mellon's dad.

"Just the New one," I said.

With my ¾ privilege caveat and, as was the wont at Emma Goldman, I thought I would have to wait on tables and wash dishes. But at Sunshine, young men dressed in white outfits with black belts, pretending to be professional waiters, served our meals on matching plates without any chips. And the Sunshine campers ate with their spines parallel to the backs of the chairs. Seemingly, they took no pleasure in their food, spooning it into their mouths at a swift 90 degree angle. Although impressive, it was more like a gesture of obedience, like dogs sitting quietly by their bowls until given the signal to eat. We also had people who did our laundry. Everyone had name tags in their clothes, except me. Any piece of clothing without a label became mine, no matter the size or sex.

The baseball fields at Sunshine were an exuberant green and limned every morning. They fanatically measured the height of each tennis, volleyball, basketball, and badminton net each day to conform to international standards. The wooden canoes seemed polished and unused. And I imagined they drained the lake every night and scrubbed the ring around the shoreline to get rid of the scum left by the nearby bungalow colony.

The only time the ¾ privilege was invoked was when everyone, save myself, went horseback riding. I was not totally ignorant of horses. Amid the eight-lanes of traffic on Ocean Parkway in Brooklyn, was a bridle path used mostly by people to walk their dogs but, on occasion, a horse and rider would pass. I always liked to see the horses waiting for traffic lights as if they were pedestrians or cars. This was not life as seen in westerns or English movies but Brooklyn-style, where everyone had to stop for people actually earning a living, like driving a cab and truck.

While the others were riding, I spent that time in the infirmary with the nurse and the official designation 'Under Observation.' Despite Aunt Georgia's admonition about not leaving a written record, I often sent letters to Aunt Tillie, her older sister. I always felt confident Aunt Tillie would not share my secrets and adolescent idiocies. I was also pretty sure none of my letters, outgoing or incoming, were steamed open to reveal their contents.

Dear Aunt Tillie:

As you probably know, I am at the wrong camp. I am not at Camp Emma Goldman. I am at Camp Sunshine. It is filled with very rich kids. Some are from important families they tell me. Prominent is what they call it. They tell me prominent is good. It seems that stupid and lazy children from these prominent families are set for life. Another term I just learned. Please send any Jewish food you think will make it through the mail.

PS: I think I found what I want to do with the rest of my life. I want to observe the lives of others and then tell them what I think of their lives.

Within a week, Aunt Tillie sent me three dozen *mon* cookies, sugar cookies, but not too sweet, and dotted with thousands of poppy seeds. She attached a note.

"Be careful with your observations. Remember what happened to Michael Rockefeller."

That summer, I auditioned for *Guys and Dolls*, Sunshine's main production of the summer. I desperately wanted a role. After all, Abe Burrows, one of the writers of the play, had been denied the Pulitzer Prize because of his troubles with HUAC. A motivation I kept to myself.

Monte was our dramatics counselor. His real name was something like Davey O'Brien, but he chose Monte because he thought it sounded more considerable. He pronounced it "Mon-TAY" to heighten the affect and called himself the Theatrical Director. It was rumored that Monte had once been a prominent director of Broadway musicals or movies or something. But, after he told Gene Kelly that dancing in puddles was stupid, he was relegated to directing people like myself.

It was at these auditions that I first saw Patrice Anne. The sun bounced off her skin like a nomad's white kaftan reflecting the heat. She was as elegant as any 14-year-old could be. She parted her strawberry blonde hair just slightly off center, so as not to look like a poet. Patrice Anne was exotic. There was no one like her where we lived.

Monte selected me to play the part of Nicely Nicely and I would sing *"Sit Down You're Rocking The Boat."* He chose Patrice Anne to play the lead, Adelaide.

Every day at rehearsals, I took the opportunity get closer to her, to sit near her, by her, next to her. At our age, this constituted a relationship. A few of the others would pass by and warn her in a stage whisper, "Watch out. He's not one of us," or "I heard he's a Commie." She cared little what the others said and she saw through my tough guy façade. I slowly came to trust her. She was not only amused by my Brooklyn upbringing but even intrigued. And, as for me, her stories of the Upper East Side of Manhattan were just as alien, a world like Sunshine but with concrete underfoot.

My value as a mascot was never higher as when Monte realized I could play the guitar and knew enough songs to lead a campfire sing-a-long. Of course, I had to submit a play list for approval but I knew my audience.

I was introduced as a Noble Savage and the First Camp Sunshine Fellow. Though I doubt there was ever a second. I played *Greensleeves, Tom Dooley,* and *Michael Row Your Boat* and planted a few mildly subversive songs, *If I Had a Hammer,* and *Puff, the Magic Dragon.* Two counselors thought they were cool by putting two fingers to their mouth and making a sucking sound. Nearly everyone sang with a dazed indifference, except Patrice Anne who sang loudly and beautifully.

Someone called out, "You know *'Ain't I Right'* by Marty Robbins?"

"Sorry, don't know it," I said.

"Of course you don't," responded the voice.

"Sorry."

"Well, I'm going to sing it and you can figure out how to play along."

The older brother of one of our Noble Savages, Biff, emerged from the darkness. He walked to the edge of the campfire, his face glowing eerily from the chin up, and he started singing, and not very well. It was more country than anything but I gamely tried to play along. No one sang with him.

By the time he got to the end of the second verse, he was glaring at me, hoping others would get the message. *"Ain't I Right"* was not about a wayward grammarian but a gleeful anti-Commie ditty.

I thought this needed a response but did not play *Joe Hill.* Woody thought *God Bless America* was exclusive and unrealistic and wrote *This Land Is Your Land* as an antidote. Another bit of leftist history I did not share and added the rarely sung verses:

As I went walking I saw a sign there
And on the sign it said "No Trespassing."
But on the other side it didn't say nothing,
That side was made for you and me.

In the shadow of the steeple I saw my people,
By the relief office I seen my people;
As they stood there hungry, I stood there asking
Is this land made for you and me?

Biff's older brother and two of his friends waited for me after the sing-a-long. Apparently, their parents were landed developers. They started to shove me and shout, "Commie," "Pinko," and "Jew bastard." Not too bad. Only one Jew bastard the entire summer.

All three were bigger than me. I could have sworn I saw my counselor Ned lurking in the shadows. He knew from which pockets his tips would come.

One aspect of being street-wise is knowing when to fight. Sometimes, you have to fight even when you're going to lose. I considered kicking two of them in the balls and gouging the third in the eyes. I could have run and hoped that someone from senior staff would intervene. Then I had a better idea. I pulled out my wallet and managed to find my Republican voter registration card, an ironic family heirloom. Unkle Traktor had found it lying on the ground after a melee at Union Square Park with some outside agitators. He decided that the youngest person in the family should carry it around as a reminder of what not to become. And when my next sibling or cousin turned ten, they would become the temporary holder of the card and so on from generation to generation.
"See, I'm one of you," I said, holding up the card and concealing the real person's name with my finger.
Fortunately, it never dawned on them how or why a 12-year-old had a Republican voter's registration card. All they saw was a tangible representation of their culture.
One of the boys said, "OK. But I have to hit you. I have to be able to tell the others I hit you."
"Ok," I said. "But not in the face or the nuts."

Nothing was mentioned at the next rehearsal and Monte acted as if he was not aware of the fight. But did I share some of Aunt Tillie's constant supply of *mon* cookies with Patrice Anne. She, in turn, invited me to visit her that very night.

The girls' camp was across The Lake. The Lake was named after an unknown and unpronounceable Native American, so everyone simply called it The Lake. There were three ways to get across The Lake--swim, take a canoe, or use the footpath along the shoreline. The inherent dangers in swimming or taking a canoe in the dark allowed for the possibility of death by romance. But, everyone used the footpath but never admitted it. Still apocryphal tales, shrouded in death, arose about crossing The Lake at night. Supposedly, a head counselor drowned while heading for a night of debauchery with an underage camper. All of which allowed the kids to say, "Sex kills."
I arrived at Patrice Anne's cabin and tried not to wake the others. We spoke in hushed whispers, smelling of mouthwash. We, of course, discussed how I got across The Lake and I lied and said that I had taken a canoe. We gossiped about Monte and the other Guys and Dolls cast members and we laughed at things that weren't funny. I wanted to touch her but her pajamas seemed too expensive. Then she suddenly asked, "You're Jewish, right?"
"Yeah, why?"

"Just curious."

"I am."

"Can you prove it?"

"Sure. Do you want me to recite a blessing?"

"What kind of blessing?"

"Well, we have all sorts of blessings. Mostly about food and death."
She saw my hesitation and said,   "You know what I mean."

"Not really." Really I didn't.

"I've never seen a real one."

"A real what?"

"Well, except for my brother's. But that was an accident. And never one with missing pieces."

I was confused for a while and then I realized what she was saying, "That? You want to see that?"

"Yes, 'that.' Jews have missing pieces, right?"

"Well, some. But not big pieces. I never saw the original. That took it away a long time ago."

"So, can I see it? Just once. Please."

Until that moment, I did not think that rich boy's were different than mine. In fact, I had never seen anyone's original. Sex is confusing for many, especially adolescents. And uncertainty can be an effective and primary form of birth control. Patrice Anne was genuinely curious. Maybe I could foster a better understanding between Jews and non-Jews, so as I began fumbling with my pants.

All at once beams from flashlights appeared from every angle all aimed at me. It was as if a prisoner had broken out and the guards turned on their searchlights and unleashed the dogs. The dark filled with tittering and laughing and random comments.

"Is that what it looks like?"

"I've never seen one like that."

"It is different."

"Kill it, before it grows."

"I must find one just like it."

"Let's call him 'Sir Cumcision.'"

I was totally humiliated and felt betrayed by Patrice Anne. I leaped up and ran from her bunkhouse, pulling up my pants, stumbling along the footpath back to the boys' side.

I avoided Patrice Anne the next day but she insisted I speak with her. She told me over and over that she did not know what the others had planned. She admitted, however, that she had told them that I was coming over but repeated her sincere, teary, and profuse apology. I wanted to believe her but remained unconvinced until that day's rehearsal. Then Patrice Anne had to sing *Adelaide's Lament.* From the emotion in her voice and her watery eyes, I understood she was singing to me, the boy with the missing pieces.

For the reminder of the summer, Patrice Anne and I spent as much time together as possible, surreptitiously meeting at the boat house whenever we could. Our time together and our relationship was frightening, enthralling, confounding, physical, and emotional. I was unprepared in every way and that made it even more memorable. For all of Patrice Anne's attentiveness, it did not stop the entire camp from calling me Sir Cumcision, or more the terse but ironic Sir.

We only saw each other twice after camp ended, under watchful and disapproving parental eyes. Of course, she has a special page in my life and I would hope the same for her.

And before I returned home, I wrote one last letter.

Dear Aunt Tillie:

When I think about the summer, I think the biggest difference between us and them is that we are darker. Jewish people are not exactly white. I don't mean skin color. Our hair is darker, our eyes are darker. When I lay in my bunk in the pitch black, the others seem to glow. You cannot find me. They are confident about the future, but you taught us the Yiddish proverb, "Men plan and God laughs." We also laugh at different things. We laugh at things we are not supposed to, like death and failure and that only makes it funnier. Our food is darker. They eat white bread, we eat pumpernickel and rye and dunk it in soup. We live in neighborhoods with dark haired neighbors with heavy woolen coats and we have beauty parlors that turn dark hair into blondes. Even the covers and spines of our most important books are black.

Nobody really wants us because we are just different. We read different books and have different heroes. When we pray, we do not kneel. You always use the word shanda, *but there is no such word in English or here. Here they speak about their clothes a lot and they have many words for the same color-taupe, ecru, shell, off-white, and beige. Kind of useless I guess, but then I thought Jews too are not exactly white but off-white. But I don't think we are taupe.*

HONORABLE MENTION, 2016 RICK DEMARINIS SHORT STORY PRIZE

Megan McNamer

The Aliens Among Us

It happened on her last day of work, although she didn't know it was her last. She was talking to Tommy Boy, who was mooning around the cash register, right at the start of the shift. She was trying not to picture his teeth. He had a problem with saliva. He didn't seem to feel the need to deal with it. I can't think of the words, he was saying. I can't think to say it. Are you?… Um… What's that ring you're wearing? He finally blurted this sentence out, his voice buzzing through his mask. Is it from your boyfriend? Is it from Jimi?

No, she said. Anita wants you, she said. Go talk to Anita.

She pulled out the mirror she kept under the counter and checked her lips. The beauty consultant at Nordstrom's gave Denise an extra set. She drew them right around the lips she already had. They were supposed to make her own look fuller, but they looked instead like she was wearing two pairs. It looked like she had a mouth within a mouth.

Jimi said a mouth within a mouth was a sign you were an alien. He showed her a flyer a guy was handing out over near the community college. The aliens among us, the flyer said, can be detected by the fact that they have a mouth within a mouth. The flyers had blurry photos of sample aliens. One was Dan Rather and another was Martha Stewart. You could sort of see it.

She blinked at herself in the mirror. Sometimes her eyes stung and she had to blink a lot. Tommy Boy would ask her then why she was crying. I'm not, she said. I'm just wearing mascara, which can give you pink eye.

People might describe a woman or girl as not pretty, but beautiful, but she was neither. Maybe she was cute. That was possible. She examined the back of her head from time to time in a mirror. Or she looked at herself face on, quick, trying to get a fresh perspective. But in the end she didn't care about cute. Cute was a quantity. You were more or less cute. On a scale of 1-10. It could be graphed.

She wanted to be beautiful. She wanted to be touched by beauty, marked by it. Imbued. Stricken. She wanted to be like Snow White—dead, when the prince first meets her. Beauty embalmed. She wanted it out of her hands.

Tommy Boy always told her she was pretty. She was not. She felt his wistful gaze. She was the only one from the regular staff who ever listened to him talk. The pizza boys just snorted and laughed and filled the orders. Sixteen pepperoni on a medium, twenty-four on a large. They had to count it out each time, they couldn't tell by looking.

Tommy Boy showed up for work on foot carrying his costume in a paper sack, mouse ears sticking out the top. He rode the city bus. He had his schedule all worked out, he'd repeat it to you. He came plenty early to get ready. Denise figured he thought they were stars, he and Anita, when they put on those masks and danced out under the pipe organ, Mickey and Minnie, all the colored lights whirling and the bubbles spewing from the bubble machine. It was the pizza boys who started calling him "Tommy Boy." They'd zing an empty pizza box at him, which he'd catch in the stomach. And then it was like the smile on his mask went slack. His teeth, Denise could just guess, were bared and wet.

The pizza boys talked to each other through Tommy Boy. They said How's it goin? What's happenin? Whadaya say? Gettin' any? Okay, nothing, not much, no, he answered. Then he searched the words for the meaning. The pizza boys screwed up their curly lips and talked sideways. Or they managed to make their lips not move at all.

Brittany, Bethany, and Brianna never talked to Tommy Boy. They stood stoic at their cash registers, each in the droopy, red corduroy cap, the big, red bow tie, the striped smock with the monkey applique on the back. They were high school seniors who only talked amongst themselves. There'd been another "B" – Bridget, Burgundy, something, but she became "with kid" (as Jimi called it) and quit.

The three B's punched in the orders, took the money, and said "Thankyew!!!" like somebody pulled a string.

Mr. Mancey walked through the work station every night nodding to the B's and the pizza boys, saying – How's it going? What's happenin? Whadaya say? Everyone answered: Okay, nothing, not much. Then the pizza boys snorted and laughed.

Mr. Mancey wore a green suit jacket and a maroon tie and tight pants over his ample tush and a thick wedding ring and a name tag bigger than anybody's, with a bigger organ logo. He had an old permanent in his dirty red hair. He played the big guy to Denise. He tapped her resume with a pencil when he hired her and said: What's a facilitator? Like it was French. He wanted to know about the "Shoot for the Stars" workshop ("Shoot the stars!" Jimi called it), like maybe he thought Denise was making it up. He said: What's a Care Co-Aide? about her month with Mr. Simms. He said What's this three-year gap?

She got one dollar above minimum wage and no tips. Head cashier, big fucking deal. BFD. Thank god for her mom, good old mom. And her dad, ol' deadbeat. But not that *ret*ard Jimi, the person she was supposed to be escaping from on her trip, her fabulous **Orient Escapade to Amazing Asia!** (per the signage and brochures).

Denise's mom worked for TruTravel in the Portland office, downtown. She set up the tours, the **Amazing!** whatevers. Every time Denise's mom heard Jimi was hanging around again looking evil (his specialty), she sent Denise somewhere warm. She gave her vitamins. She said Denise did not want to compromise her future. She gave her herbal remedies. She said the company we keep says a lot about ourselves. She said Denise should take notes. On the tour, not on Jimi! She wanted her to go to tour school or whatever. Forget it, Denise said. I am nowhere near **Amazing!** enough.

Mr. Mancey said, being real friendly, that they were all Grinder People, the pizza boys and her and Tommy and Giggles, which is what he called Anita, who always did then, she giggled, like clockwork. But he wanted to make them pay for the fact that he wasn't a doctor or lawyer or a stockbroker at Piper, Jaffray, and BFD. He was just the manager at the Organgrinder, the pizza parlor with the two-story pipe organ. He wasn't **Amazing!** at all.

~

Jimi was named for Jimi Hendrix. (Scuse me! while I kiss the sky!) His mom was a biker. He'd been a biker baby. His dad was dead. Viet Nam. Ka-powie. The last year of the war, the last month, maybe even the very last day. Maybe even the very last bullet, the last piece of shrapnel. It had to be someone, didn't it? The last casualty. The only proper way for a professional soldier to die! Jimi jumped up on the coffee table and saluted. Shit happens.

Jimi's mom would show up, then she'd go away.

"She comes and goes with the buffaloes," said Jimi, who claimed he was part Cherokee. Mostly she'd go. She'd be totally gone, "in every sense of the word," said Jimi, who was pretty smart, even if he didn't always act it. Pretty smart and pretty old to be still trying to figure out how to eat.

He hung around a lot at "the Organ" (his term) before Denise became scheduled to escape on her **Escapade.** See you at the Organ, he'd say. I just love the Organ, don't you? That's what he'd say. He pretended to be thrilled when Mickey and Minnie did the Disney Dance-through every hour at quarter past. Denise thought that maybe he really was sort of thrilled.

It was certainly a big deal for Tommy Boy and Anita. They waited in the wings, which just meant they stood against the wall by the cash registers in full view of the customers filing in, but out of sight of the customers eating pizza out on the floor beneath the giant organ. They'd stand there by the customer line being Mickey and Minnie and waving back and forth, back and forth, while hand-ing out flyers for delivery specials. When the time drew near, Tommy Boy would straighten the flounces of Anita's frock, per her muffled directions, and she'd fuss with her gloves, they would really get into it and act nervous. Then at a quarter past the hour organist Terrance Tawney would play a big "Tah-Da!" chord and they'd do the Disney Dance-through, skipping out among the tables as if they'd found their long lost playmates. Even though everyone eating pizza had already seen them.

Anita arrived at work in her full Minnie getup, including the large white gloves and the little black purse and the shiny Minnie shoes. The van from Living Alternatives dropped her off. She even wore her mask. She looked like a large trick-or-treater, sitting there in the way back seat. No one knew what all she kept in that purse. Nothing, maybe. It was just part of the costume. It was Minnie's. When Mr. Mancey's wife Melinda came in (who Mr. Mancey called Belinda and

the pizza boys called Beluga), looking large and sleepy because she was preg-
nant, she and Mr. Mancey would eat a pizza out at the tables, and Anita would
hang around them, her masked breath heavy and moist. You're eating for two,
Anita would splutter. Make sure you feed that baby! Mr. Mancey teased her
about getting a baby of her own. He said Go for it, Giggles! and she giggled, the
sound a big gulp behind the happy Minnie face.

~

The extra lips were drawn on with a Rosy Quartz 06 pencil, then filled
in with "Moon Glow." All of it *Quintessence*. She could only afford the lipstick
because she was saving up for her tattoo, which Jimi said he would do at a dis-
count. Plus, she wanted to get some of the Body Balm. Either that or the Mois-
ture Lush face cream, designed to smooth out fine wrinkles and marionette lines,
according to the beauty consultant, who pointed at invisible vertical indentations
on her own face. The Body Balm came in a pink frosted jar with a lid shaped like
a big seashell. When the beauty consultant screwed open the jar it made the
slurping sound jars with expensive stuff make.

A man with long, pale fingers and a leather bracelet smoothed the lotion
on the back of his hand while Denise was having her makeover. She couldn't
move her head, so she only saw his fingers and the bracelet. Does it plump up?
he asked. He smelled good. Denise wanted to look at his face but couldn't, be-
cause it was time for her eyes.

She wanted the Body Balm because of the jar, and she wanted the tattoo
to affix herself permanently in youthful beauty (as Jimi so fancily put it), as well
as to exile herself forever from certain kinds of lives (as Jimi proposed), lives that
required a totally normal appearance. Plus, she just thought it might look good,
a little spider on her neck, just below her earlobe. Jimi said he could do that. He
said it would be like an accessory. Set off her features in a very cool way. You
could tell he was practicing his tattoo talk for his customers, once he ever got
any.

Organist Terence Tawney didn't appear to have a tattoo, but he had a
full-on mullet. No one saw him up close, because he never took his breaks. He
just scooted into the men's room and returned all slicked back. He never col-
lected his allotted Little Monkey's pizza or salad. He didn't even swipe a cracker
from the salad bar and this was in a six-hour shift, three to nine. Yet he was very
pudgy. He bounced around on that bench and did his tap dance on the pedals,
but other than that Denise guessed there wasn't much exercise playing the or-
gan.

When organist Terence Tawney first got to work he walked directly from
his dented Mazda in the parking lot to the front doors of the building, passing the
poster that showed him baring his teeth. He glanced at the poster, checked to
see if that was still him, and then he hustled straight to the high, polished organ
bench, nodding right and left to nobody in particular. He wore the same mus-
tard-colored suit jacket every day, with a striped tie and a dingy old white shirt
pulled tight over his paunch. If there were people already on the floor eating their
pizza, he gave them a bug-eyed stare that possibly was supposed to be a pleas-

ant hello, before he slid around and pulled out the stops.

Once Denise saw him coming out of the McDonald's on 82nd late in the evening. She was on the bus, the 10:20. He stopped on the sidewalk with his hands in his jacket pockets and just stood there, angled out toward the street, his head illuminated in the glow of the golden arches, his face cocked sideways and up, like he was listening to some terrific story. His pug nose and those round cheeks were all red and sweaty between the retro sideburns. He was smiling and nodding, all by himself, and his mullet was getting all matted from the rain.

Another time she spied him arranging his face in his car out in the parking lot. He had the rearview mirror angled and was choosing his entry expression. Pleasant, yes, and slightly surprised. Rushed, pressed, many engagements. But pleased to have been asked to play.

When organist Terence Tawney played "Take Me Out to the Ball Game," no. 12 on the Old Favorites list, that was the cue for Tommy Boy and Anita to get ready. They gave themselves plenty of prep time. They stood still and thought about their characters. "Take Me Out to the Ball Game" was the only Old Favorite that no one ever requested, but it was always right before the Disney Dance tune, which was always "It's a Small World, After All."

It's a small world, after all. It's a small world, after all. It's a small world, after all. A small, small world.

During the Small song, Mickey and Minnie were supposed to shake hands with the customers. This was something that Tommy Boy and Anita could really get worked up about. They'd stop on a dime, mid-prance, clap their heels together and bow like robots, elbows clamped to their waists, hand-shaking hands jutting straight out. They only did this for the little ones, though, the real little kids, like two-year-olds, maybe, or any nice-seeming grandmas. Because older kids sometimes made fun of them. Even grownups.

~

That day, the day she didn't know was her last, they were getting ready for the Disney Dance and Anita was bowing her head like she was praying, and Tommy Boy was squaring his shoulders, pulling at the chin of his mask, positioning it over and over, his nervous tic. There was a lull in her line of customers, three large families were shuffling on to Brittany, Bethany, and Brianna. Denise decided to straighten out and bundle her bills, which were piling up, it had been a super busy day. All of the bills had to be face up and the heads of Washington, Lincoln, or whatever had to be pointing up and down the same way. When she got them all organized, she'd take the little key from underneath the money tray, unlock the drawer below the register, take out the canvas Seafirst Bank bag, deposit the bundle o' money, zip it back up, put it back in the drawer and lock it, put back the key.

Usually she had this down to a one-minute motion, but that time she wasn't finding the little key. Jimi was distracting her, hanging over the counter and punching buttons on Ye Olde Cash Register. They had to use old-timey, brass contraptions, like everyone stuffing their faces with pizza in front of a two-story pipe organ with big, dancing rodents was quaint as hell.

So she was sweeping her hand underneath the cash carrier, but only getting paper clips and rubber bands and personal checks with all those different designs on them, scenery and ducks and shit. Some teenage boys came up to the register while she was riffling around this way, hoping Mr. Mancey wasn't looking at her clutching that big wad of cash. And the teenagers were all ordering at once and she said One moment please, and they kept on ordering. They said Gimme the Orangutan, like it was a big joke instead of just the menu. They turned to each other and said Gimme the King of the Jungle and hooted like morons. Denise said I'll be right with you and they sang "Taaake me out and let's ball, babe," tossing crumpled-up flyers onto the half-finished pizzas of the pizza boys, who snorted and laughed.

Finally, she found that goddamn key down in the pocket of her monkey smock where she kept her Calms Forte bottle. It was caught in Kleenex, she couldn't believe it. She couldn't believe she was almost crying. What was _wrong_ with her. Lately like this, weepies at the drop of a hat. She should just smack those little piss-ants.

She unlocked the drawer and grabbed the bank bag, and then she couldn't find the bunch of bills. She must have put it down somewhere, holy shit. She said to the idiot boys I'll be right with you, using her best fake voice, and they milled around, slamming each other into the wall. Then Jimi, who'd been lounging all over the counter laughing, got the good idea to tease Anita, showing off for the youngsters. Anita came out of her prayer state just in time to see Jimi's hand heading for that polka dot bow on her head. She clamped both of her hands over the bow, and over his hand, too, and their hands tussled up there on her head for a bit, becoming all wrapped up together. Anita couldn't seem to let go. Finally, one of her white gloves came off in Jimi's hand. Tommy Boy was just standing there, holding his mask by the chin, the tips of his fingers on that big, insane grin.

Jimi got real embarrassed then, everyone seeing him tangling hands like that with Minnie. And Jimi embarrassed was sort of ugly. He swore at Anita and yanked his hand away and threw down the glove like it was infected. Then he headed out the door and the pizza boys were hooting and Denise could hear Anita crying with big, coughing sounds behind her mask, just as the Small song began.

_It's_ a small world, after all. _It's_ a small world, after all. _It's_ a small world, after all, small, small world.

~

When Jimi skedaddled, he called back "Later!" and "Tattoo night! Don't fergit!" He had some stuff he'd been all cagey about, too, something or other they were going to do, good shit, he said, expensive as hell. He'd made her pay half and she didn't even know what it was, what kind of big treat she was in for. That was Jimi. Half her paycheck seemed to go to Jimi. He'd say something was all whoop-ti-do, and they'd take it and—nothing. Expensive as hell, every time, could she pay half? Denise suspected they were tripping on vitamins.

Anyway, that was the end of her career as a Grinder Person, as it turned out, in a week that involved the police coming to the house along with Mr. Mancey, who accused her of stealing from the till and then the police wanting Jimi's full name and address, and her mom getting all freaked out, and Denise puking all over her mom's new couch from Ikea. Then there was the hearing, plea bargain, whatchacallit, and then there was a no-nonsense, first trimester abortion, mommy-paid, in and out, here today, gone tomorrow. And then there were the first exciting preparations for a glorious SuperValue **Chartered Quest** to parts unknown. Denise's mom drove her up to SeaTac just to make sure Denise got on the flight, and even ol' deadbeat Dad came along, telling his department chair he had jury duty. Everything, except the puking and the police, so very familiar.

~

Anita's bow ended up crooked on that eventful day, but by God she had it. When she stopped crying, she slid an old compact and lipstick out of her pinafore pocket. She pulled her mask out to a 45-degree angle and did a quick check on her lips. She liked to keep them smeared with bright red lipstick, even though no one saw them. Mr. Mancey came over, wiping his mouth with a napkin. The teenagers had moved on and were sprawled up and down the big table right under the organ. Mr. Mancey told Anita to keep her white gloves on at all times while on the floor. She nodded and nodded, her mask going up and down, then she and Tommy Boy held hands and started waving, waiting for the umpteenth verse of the Small Song so they could start out just right for the big prance.

Denise's eyes were getting pretty blurry by then. Her eye shadow, right on schedule, was making her lids itch. The Small Song churned away. Sometimes she liked to keep her brains straight by punching out the orders in tempo. She'd take a pill from her Calms Forte bottle and then she'd punch away. (*It's* a small world, after all. *It's* a small world, after all.) Except for the on-the-hour "Theme from 2001 Space Odyssey," organist Terence Tawney played every song at the exact same speed and all, especially the Theme, *fortissisisimo ffff!* He played that giant two-story organ like it was a John Deere tractor and he was working his way around the field, getting in the crops. When the songs were ended, that was that, hop off the seat, out the door.

The soggy light in the parking lot began to fade at the last playing of the Theme. *Keep your future wide open.* That's what her mom loved to say. Denise could see her reflection in the far window, moving here, moving there, like a puppet. *Don't do something you will later regret.* Rain made the pavement shiny. It was warm inside the Organ, incubator warm, yeasty-smelling from all that dough, everything a bright orange. The parking lot began to disappear and her reflection grew clear. She could see her big, red, corduroy hat bobbing around like a poppy.

She'd get another makeover, get some *Quintessence shit*. Body splash, maybe. Because skin can forget to function. Cosmetologists will tell you that. They'll give you pamphlets. Note your skin's behavior, the pamphlets say. Is your skin sluggish? Overstimulated? Does it need comforting? Irrigation? There's a cascade of ongoing negative effects. You must hydrate, feed, firm, and protect your skin, while refreshing its moisture memory. Underneath the skin you see is the skin you want.

The glow outside turned fast to black. Behind their masks, Anita's lips were brilliant and Tommy Boy's teeth were glistening. Mr. Mancey and Melinda wiped their mouths and just at that moment the pizza boys burst out laughing. Denise blinked and said "Thank yew!!!" like somebody pulled a string.

1ST PLACE, 2016 BARRY LOPEZ NONFICTION PRIZE

Natasha Singh

Edmonton Uncles

They arrived unannounced, the two of them. Drunk and teetering, all the way from Edmonton. "We came to visit you," Uncle Number One slurred, as my parents let the men in. It was pitiful sight, but not an uncommon occurrence. My mom ushered these uncles towards the dining room table. "Eat something," she insisted. "Please eat." They shook their heads and remained silent, so she served them chai instead. "Drink this then," she instructed. Clumsily, the two men brought the cups to their mouths and drank in quick, furtive sips.

Hidden behind the basement door, my sister and I giggled into our palms. Though we'd been raised to call all our elders "Uncle" and "Auntie," including our white Canadian neighbors who were initially baffled by the quickness with which we'd claimed them as relatives, we didn't relish the constant stream of Indian visitors who made our mountainous town their favorite holiday spot. Some were too nosy or rude, we thought. Whenever they visited, the wives would say, "Look at what a fattie the older girl is now," or, "She is so dark, that skinny one." Not caring if we were listening. Others, like these drunken uncles, came at odd hours and didn't bother to phone in advance. Then there were the Indians we didn't know. When passing through Jasper, they'd find our last name in the phonebook—the only Indian name—and call to ask if they could spend the night. When they arrived at our doorstep, my mother would cook and serve these strangers so often that our home seemed more like a hotel. A place where the door was always open, and my generous, exhausted mother never said, "No."

"Natasha! Manisha!" she called out. We considered pretending we hadn't heard her, but then she called our names again—a singing sound on her lips— and we rose from where we were perched and flew upstairs like two pretty birds. Wearing the matching shorts and rainbow coloured tank tops my mom had ordered from Woodward's, we smiled politely upon entering the dining room where the uncles sat and where my parents were speaking with them in hushed tones. The men glanced up. "Hello, Uncle," we said in unison. At eleven and thirteen, we were just beginning to develop breasts. Manisha's jiggled when she walked and mine were two soft nubs, but we'd barely noticed their respective arrivals.

"*Array,* your daughters have grown," one of the uncles observed.

"Come give me a hug," the other one said. Rising unsteadily to his feet, he encircled both of us in his arms. Pulling us close, he ran his hands ran up and down our backs and then over the curve of our bottoms, as if unsure of where to rest them. We wriggled out of his grasp. Patting our shoulders, he sank onto his seat while my sister and I exchanged tiny tight-lipped smiles.

When we became older and began attending parties in Edmonton, these kind of uncles would gather round clapping and urging us girls to dance while women our mother's age—all our aunties—looked on in silent disapproval. My father was never among these men. He did not dance or drink, and tended to stick close to my mother or to the older men who could barely rise from their seats without the help of a cane. Into these elders' ears, he poured his monologues about health, diet, and loose morals. Once I saw one of these elderly men slide off his hearing aid and slip it into his pocket. Only then did he lean back and surrender his ear to my father, who was as oblivious to this slight as he was to those uncles in the room who were undressing his daughters with their eyes.

With a stern nod, my father signaled to the kitchen and dutifully we went to the cupboards, looking for snacks—little foodstuffs to pile onto plates and pass around. "Eat, eat," my mother would say to each of her guests, until eventually they succumbed to her persistent pleas. As we balanced the plates in our hands, we heard my father begin to complain. "My children, not listening anymore," he sighed. "This culture is ruining them."

Manisha and I studied the floor in embarrassed silence. My father, we knew, could have been referring to many things. In my sister's room that week, he had discovered black eyeliner; and I had failed to bring home top marks again. My little brother, Ravi, was getting into frequent fights at school, and the neighbors were now referring to him as that "lippy little shit." At home, we weren't quiet enough when my father wanted to watch the six o'clock news, and we constantly argued over TV shows. *Fantasy Island* or *The Love Boat*? *Charlie's Angels* or *Happy Days*? *I Dream of Genie*, *Spiderman*, or *The Flintstones*? There were many more things that could have been on the list that my father kept inside his head.

These uncles had children as well, but theirs were much younger. Inside their circle of friends, my parents were the earliest immigrants to Alberta, so we were supposed to be role models, older siblings to numerous youngsters in Edmonton who just happened to be Indian, too. My mom was called *Jasper Auntie*, and we were known as the *Jasper cousins*. But it seemed to me that we had so little in common with these kids who, when they grew older, worried constantly about what other Indians thought of them. Since we were removed from an Indian community and its concomitant policing, my parents couldn't get reinforcement for their views, so ours was an upbringing that marked us as unusual, maybe even wild.

As my father continued complaining about us, Ma remained quiet, listening as the men exchanged words. I stole a look at her to see if she was bored, but she appeared interested, maybe even pleased to have their company because, without visitors, our house plunged into a quiet that frightened her and made her sad. She craved company, phone calls, and letters, all of which for brief but precious moments cut through her loneliness in Canada and connected her to the life she'd led in India.

As Manisha and I made the rounds with the plates, my father continued his grumbling. "Children in this country, they have no respect for their elders." "Here you go, Uncle," my sister said in her best grown-up voice.

"Would you like anything else, Uncle?" I added, trying to outdo her. We bumped hips, my sister and I, in our efforts to be the hostess-with-the-mostess. One of the uncles looked up in surprise. Blinking his eyes slowly, he leaned back to appraise us. Licking his lips as if thirsty, he tilted his head to one side and sighed. "You girls," he said, his voice trailing off like a whisper in the wind.

Suddenly stiffening, my mother sat upright in her chair as if shaken by something we couldn't yet see. "You girls go from here!" she hissed. Waving her arm in front of her face, she said it again, her voice now shrill and indignant. "Hide yourselves! Just go from here!"

We stopped smiling and put down the plates. As we hurried away, the same uncle cleared his throat and said loud enough for us to hear, "Your two girls, how old are they now?" Without waiting for my parents to answer, he added, "Those two. They are looking like sluts." Stopping in our tracks, we waited for what seemed like forever for our parents to stand up, to shout at them for saying such a thing, to tell them they were no longer welcome in our home.

But when I looked back at them, my mother was staring at the wall, her eyes filled with shame and quiet fury, while my father put his head in his hands. "What to do?" he merely said in a defeated voice. "What to do?"

"Can you believe that?" Manisha whispered over her shoulder as we crept down the stairs, back to her room in the basement. "Mom and Dad didn't say anything to defend us." Once on her bed, I hugged my knees to my chest and leaned against the wall, which she'd decorated with posters of Michael Jackson, her favorite singer. In the dim light of her room, her skin seemed paler somehow, our tank tops no longer as colourful. "I just can't believe it," she said again. Shaking her head, she turned her back to me. Bending over her papers and textbooks, she began flipping the pages as if she'd forgotten the whole matter. Upstairs the low murmur of adult voices continued to fill the house, like a humming that grew louder and louder. *Slut.* I rolled the word around and around in my mouth. That night after the uncles had eaten and left, I tried to spit it back out.

But it was too late. I had swallowed it.

Christin Rzasa

Leading The Blind Mare Home

The owners had dropped off the grey mare at our clinic the night before, leaving her with grain, apples, and the best hay they had, but when I drive up the next morning, she is visibly agitated. We're getting new neighbors: a dental clinic is under construction and the landscaping crew is already at work, the tamping machine where the walkways go, a ditch-witch for irrigation lines. The mare paces along the front of our barn, her ears erect, head swinging from side to side as staccato and strange sounds assault her. She is 28 years old and essentially blind – one eye nearly overwhelmed by a nasty, painful tumor, the other clouded by cataracts. She can probably see shadows on the one side but nothing definitive. I try to soothe her by greeting her softly, and she approaches then backs off warily, her ears again swiveling toward the machinery. The landscape crew is oblivious.

This is Friday morning, and that means it is the mare's last morning: Fridays are when the truck comes to haul euthanized horses to the landfill in Spokane. Since the government closed down horse slaughtering in this country, owners are limited in their options for disposing of old animals too sick or too costly to keep going. You need a backhoe and a good distance from your (or your neighbor's) well. For some, it's easier to drop the horse off at the veterinary clinic.

My boss arrives an hour later, heads out to the corral with the other technician to sedate the mare, while I get ready to clean a dog's teeth. After ten minutes, my boss is back, carrying a lariat and the mare's halter.

"Will you go out there, please?" she asks. "We can't get near her."

I head out the back door with the blind mare's halter, and she turns my way. She is standing in a back corner of our corral, as far as she can go from the veterinary clinic and the din of machinery. Her back end to the corner, she raises her head defensively, her breath in steamy puffs from flared nostrils. She's on the fight now. A cold fog is lifting and the sun slips above the mountains, sifting anemically through the haze. The mare is trembling with the chill and anxiety. I address her softly, keeping up a constant chatter so she knows where I am, my voice taking the place of a visible form. I climb through the rails and approach her, but when I'm only about 15 feet away, she wheels and trots off stiffly, a pronounced limp reminding me of the arthritis in her hips. I move to the center of the corral and urge her forward, kissing and clucking, swinging the halter rope she can't see but knows is there. She can't see the corral fence, either, but she had all night to memorize the dimensions: 15 paces south, ten east, 15 north, ten west. She turns flawlessly.

After a round, she slows to a walk, then stops in her far corner to await my next move. I approach, she moves off, I go back to the center, then urge her back to a trot. After three rounds, I step in, still talking, and turn her 180 degrees, send her off again at a trot. I can see her relaxing. At last, there is something here she recognizes. This is primary school stuff – "Dick & Jane" for horses. This is what her first humans taught her – the first 'words' she understood: pressure and release, action and reaction. The human moves in, the horse moves off, until the horse recognizes that her movements are being designed by the human. Here in this foggy, chaotic darkness is finally something familiar.

She stops again in her corner, winded. I give her a minute to rest then ask her to move off at a walk, and she goes calmly, ignoring the clattering machines. I keep up my soliloquy, my oral footprint. After two rounds, she stops and lets me approach. I pause a nose-length away and let her explore my jacket front and my jeans. She finds the pocket where I kept treats for my gelding this morning. I pet her on the neck – the side of shadows, not darkness – and tell her what a good mare she is. I slip the halter on her and continue talking to her there in the far corner, her safe place. I tell her we're going to help her go where the sun is warm, the green grass is belly-deep and there is never winter. And when she gets there, her old pasture-mate will be waiting. He'll call to her and her eyes will see him clearly, and she'll run to him without the pain in her hips.

My boss comes out of the clinic and motions me over to the near end of the corral, closer to where the truck that will take the mare's body to Spokane can back in. The mare pulls back suspiciously, but when I pat her neck and speak to her, she ducks her head trustingly, nuzzling my jacket, keeping me close. I promise her I won't leave, direct the vet to her shadow side – the less scary side. The vet gives her an IV sedative and the mare droops and sighs, leaning into me. I keep up my soft chatter, knowing my voice is more and more like white noise, like a breeze sweeping down the valley through the long grass and from far off comes the call of an old friend.

HONORABLE MENTION, 2016 BARRY LOPEZ NONFICTION PRIZE

Manasseh Franklin

Finding the Small Ones

In the dirt parking lot of Kintla Lake, Glacier National Park's most remote front country campground, Matt and I asked Lyle, the 94 year old ranger, about nearby glaciers. On our map, we'd spotted two white blips in the peaks off the southeast side of the lake. We showed him the map.

"Do you think we could bushwack to these glaciers?" Matt asked.

Lyle, standing thin and wrinkled beside an old van with shovels and picks propped alongside of it, laughed and shook his head. "That's bushwacking alright," he said with a slow drawl, "that's bushwacking double."

If any one knows about glaciers on this side of the park, it's Lyle. He's been the ranger at Kintla Lake for over twenty years. "You're best off just taking your boat out around here," he suggested, "and head on down to St. Mary tomorrow." St. Mary, the name of a lake and a ranger station near Glacier's most visible glacier, Grinnell.

Matt and I had driven from Alberta to Montana the day before. Fresh out of Canada's glacier country, we were excited to see what the Rocky Mountains of the U.S. had to offer. As the red Mohawk canoe we'd brought along cut silently through the calm lake water, I scanned the valley sides that flanked the lake, hoping for a glimpse of ice. I saw only thick evergreens and silver mountaintops. A few fading snowpatches. Maybe we could have found one of those white blips tucked into a cirque or valley that we'd spotted on the map, but the vegetation we'd encounter en route looked impenetrable.

We steered our canoe toward a wide U formed by rock walls at the far end of the lake. Two mountains met there, each granite side cascading down to an invisible point at the lake head. The water around us was vibrant green and blue. The U had once been filled by ice; the ice had once stored the water. Alpine glaciers—those that form in high mountain cirques—leave behind signature U-shaped valleys. The majority of glaciers in the park are of the alpine variety. Those that still exist are remnants of the larger alpine glaciers—and an ice sheet—that molded the signature vertical peaks of the area.

As we paddled across the silky smooth lake surface, I realized that we were surrounded by the enchanting ghost of a glacier that once was.

People didn't really talk about glaciers until they started changing and shrinking. But in the continental U.S, glaciers have been shrinking for thousands of years. The glaciers of the intermountain West were once encased in the ice sheet that extended down from Canada—the Laurentide—or the one that covered the Yellowstone Plateau and surrounding mountain ranges during the more recent Pinedale glaciation. Since that last glacial maximum between thirteen and twenty thousand years ago, the glaciers have steadily declined, leaving behind fertile plains of Wyoming, Montana and Idaho, and plenty of high alpine cirques.

This deglaciation happened quickly, long before people started to keep record of such things as ice extents. By the time settlers began exploring and recording glaciated regions of the West in the late 1800s and early 1900s, the glaciers had already been reduced to the cold comfort of high alpine regions in the Tetons, Wind Rivers, Absorokas, Swan and Livingston ranges and more.

Perhaps this is why most Americans don't realize the West still has a formidable collection of ice. The general public knows Glacier, of course, but the glaciers that linger in other areas of the West? They are far out of site, hard to reach and therefore, out of mind.

In Alaska and Canada, I'd traveled to glaciers and landscapes that I knew were shrinking and shifting, but the glaciers themselves were still present. Those I'd encountered in both places were relatively massive, sometimes unfathomably so. I knew they were shrinking because I'd combed through the scientific papers and detailed measurements, looked at the time lapse photographs and read written accounts and newspaper headlines—but not because I could watch them shrink, not because I saw before my very eyes the melting that would mean the end of them. There are decades of life left in those glaciers; in some, centuries.

In the Rocky Mountains of Montana and Wyoming, the story is different. They've been on the decline for thousands of years, and by most scientific estimates and models, have only few years left. In Glacier, scientists estimate the ice will be gone by 2030. In the Tetons, it's the same story. In the Wyoming Bighorns—you didn't know there was a glacier in the Bighorns?—maybe the one remaining glacier will last until 2025.

Approximately 2 million people visit Glacier National Park annually, and in late July, there were easily thousands of them. Matt and I discovered this as we drove toward Lake MacDonald, St. Mary and most accessible glaciers in the park. Cars lined Going-to-the-Sun road, a roughly 50-mile stretch of winding road and hairpin turns that connects West Glacier to East Glacier. Trailheads overflowed with cars. People spilled into the road, cameras raised and pointing at anything, really, not even glaciers. Mountain tops, clouds, the sky, themselves.

If there were glaciers to be seen, I'm sure the camera lenses would have focused on them, but in Glacier National Park, it is in fact increasingly difficult to see slowly moving ice. When the park got its namesake in 1850, roughly 150 glaciers were visible, but 175 years later, only twenty-five remain. That number dwindles each year. Of those that linger, a handful sit within reasonable hiking distance on a maintained trail. The rest are like those near Kintla: they require bushwacking, alright, bushwacking double.

Matt and I didn't expect it to be so difficult to find glaciers in Glacier. But our difficulty wasn't so much in the remoteness of them but in the bureaucracy of the National Park system. As we stood in the St. Mary's Visitor Center and attempted to plan our glacier hikes, we discovered that the most accessible ones—namely Grinnell and Sperry—were impossible to access. The trail to Grinnell was closed for maintenance and trespassing carried a hefty $500 fine. The two campgrounds en route to Sperry were closed due to flooding.

"What about zero impact camping?" I asked the ranger behind the counter. Because the hike to Sperry tallied fifteen miles round trip, 5000 feet of elevation gain and there was a chance of wintery weather, we didn't want to risk pushing the trip in one day and not having a place to camp. Getting a zero-impact permit would allow us the flexibility to bivy if needed and leave no trace, hence the term zero impact. Plus, I wanted to spend time on the glacier. I needed to explore it, and I needed more than a single day to do that.

The kind-faced ranger with a long grey braid didn't even consider. She shook her head gently. "Sorry," she replied, "we don't allow that here."

"But I'm writing about glaciers," I insisted. "I can't come to Glacier and not see a single one."

She wouldn't budge. "Well, you'll have to convene with your glaciers another time."

We had one last option: to hike the Highline trail—a long, exposed alpine traverse with expansive views of Glacier's mountaintops. From it, we could see glaciers at a distance, if not up close.

There are two trailheads: one at the top of Logan Pass—the pinnacle of Going-to-the-Sun Road—and another a few miles further down the west side of the road at a parking area referred to as The Loop. The trail itself is a one way through high country, and most people park at one trailhead and take a Park Service shuttle to the other. Matt and I parked at The Loop and shuttled to the top of Logan Pass. The parking lot at the top of the pass was jam packed with cars pulling in and pulling out, and with hoards of people entering the visitor center or snapping photographs outside of it.

Despite the number of vehicles in the lot, we saw relatively few people on the trail. Within the first few miles we met a bright white mama mountain goat and her kid, who calmly stared at us from a rock bench three feet above our heads. For roughly eight miles we soaked in unrelenting views of jagged peaks. MacDonald Creek threaded a thin line through a lush u-shaped valley more than a thousand feet below. We spotted ridgelines with snowfields smeared beneath but from that distance, it was difficult to determine what was a glacier and what wasn't.

Eventually we reached a trail junction. The small wooden sign read "Glacier Overlook," with an arrow pointing to a narrow, rocky and barely visible trail.

"Huh, I didn't see this on the map," I commented to Matt while fumbling with the folded paper.

"Well, it looks like what we're looking for," he replied. "This might be the only glacier we see in Glacier." He disregarded the map in my hands. "Let's go."

The slight, sharply inclined trail traversed a loose, exposed valley side. *What glacier is this?* I wondered while my heart pounded in my ears and my chest heaved. The trail was steep, really steep. Matt and I trod on the balls of our feet, boots slipping on the loose gravel beneath.

What is it going to look like? After all the hype about the glaciers in Glacier, I realized I had never actually seen a little glacier. *Will it have crevasses?* I wondered. *Or will it just look like a snowfield?*

The trail gave way to a rocky saddle. We stood on the saddle, panting, and looked down.

At first, I wasn't sure exactly where the glacier was. In a wide cirque below, there were two long strips of snow and ice hugging the sheer sides of the Garden Wall—a narrow vertical rock face that extended skyward beside us.

Which one is the glacier? Are they both glaciers? I pulled out the map again. Indeed, there was a cluster of glaciers in that cirque, a collection of three that had once only been one. That single one had shrunken and fractured so much as to make three. The third I realized, Grinnell, was out of sight. Of those I could see, only one actually looked like a glacier—as told by glacier blue stripes that could be crevasses—the other looked like just a strip of lingering snow.

I checked the map again. Salamander Glacier sits at the base of the Garden Wall, in a shallow basin above its better-known counter part, Grinnell, which was out of site. Gem, the smallest of the three, sits along the Garden Wall beyond the Salamander. Yes, I realized gazing at the larger snow strip with faint blue stripes—the Salamander—I was looking down on a glacier.

"It's so small," I breathed the words without realizing I was speaking.

"Are you sure that's a glacier?" Matt asked.

"Yeah," I replied softly, pointing to the map. "Check it out."

We hopped delicately between the rocks on the saddle, trying to find the best angle to see the Salamander's miniature features. The loose mountainsides bordering the ice were so steep and filled with unstable scree, we couldn't stray too far from the safety of the trail. Actually reaching the glacier was impossible. Not long after arriving, we turned around.

The Salamander's image stayed in my mind during the four long miles to the end of the trail. We'd run out of snacks a few hours prior, and were each on our last drops of water. After hiking nine miles earlier that day, the last miles stretched interminably, despite the gorgeous warm sunset that filled the valleys and poured golden light on the mountaintops around us.

The glacier's form stayed imprinted in my mind while we drove in slow traffic along Going-to-the-Sun Road. It lingered still as Matt and I cooked baked beans and sausage and listened to the noises of the Rising Sun Campground overflowing with summer tourists. After dinner, I sat at the campground picnic table sipping wine from a tin cup. I thought again of its blue crevasses. Later that night after the campground had quieted and Matt had fallen asleep beside me, I stared at the ceiling of my truck cap and tried to sleep, but instead thought about the Salamander.

I wrote in my journal: *as much as inanimate objects can die, that glacier is dying.*

What determines the threshold when a glacier ceases to be a glacier? Size, movement, characteristics. Glaciers are cyclical. They form, grow and move when snow accumulates in winter, they shrink when ice melts in summer. More ice must accumulate then melt for the glacier to maintain its mass. If more ice melts than accumulates, the glacier shrinks.

A receding glacier is not receding into itself. The glacier always moves as gravity designates it to. A receding glacier is simply losing more ice off its toe than it is making at its snowline. And so as it shrinks it keeps moving forward, but to a shorter and shorter terminus.

By definition, a glacier must measure .1km by .1km, or approximately twenty-five acres and 100 feet thick or more to be considered a glacier. These measurements are not arbitrary, but the mass necessary for the glacier to maintain its movement.

Of the glaciers that do remain in the West, Wyoming has the largest concentration, the majority of which are situated in the stunning and secluded Wind River Range. Montana is in close second. Colorado, Idaho and Utah trail behind. There were glaciers in New Mexico during the Pinedale Glaciation, but they are nowhere to be found now. Not in physical form, at least.

As these glaciers dwindle, more than ice is lost. During my short time in Glacier, I met with Dan Fagre of the United States Geologic Survey. His twenty years of glaciology and ecology research in the park provide a steady record of changes not only in the ice but in the ecology of the mountains.

Each year, spring arrives sooner in Western Montana. Within the park, Fagre and his research team have documented fewer and fewer days with snow on the ground per year, a change that has spurred wide-reaching ecological alterations. Wolverines—a species that relies on year-round snow habitats—are forced to den earlier and earlier in the spring, which puts their offspring at risk (not to mention, the snowy habitat relied upon by the entire wolverine population is quickly declining). Early springs cause fauna to peak before migrating animals—who depend on seasonal consistency—can reach it. Treelines, in response to shifting ice extents are crawling higher in altitude, which has the effect of creating habitat for some, while taking away from others.

The most visible creature affected by glacial melt is one most people have never seen or heard of. The western glacier stonefly is a small, dark colored insect that exists only within the glacial meltwater in Glacier National Park. Despite its seemingly insignificant size and stature, this bug has prompted a fiery lawsuit between the national Center for Biological Study and the U.S. Fish and Wildlife Service.

Environmental groups claim that the insect is under immediate threat of climate change, and that the U.S. Fish and Wildlife Service has not done due diligence to protect its habitat: the quickly melting glaciers of Glacier National Park. They seek protection for the insect on the Endangered Species Act, citing that its diminishing habitat is a call for the immediate reduction of global greenhouse emissions in the U.S.

This isn't the first lawsuit calling for the protection of a species under threat of climate change and as glaciers continue to diminish, it's unlikely to be the last.

From Glacier, we headed south to Wyoming's Big Horn mountains. The range runs from the northwest to the southeast of north central Wyoming. It is home to several of the state's highest peaks, including Cloud Peak, the tallest in the Big Horns and 7th tallest in the state at 13,167 feet. Beside that peak lays the last remaining glacier in the region.

From the start, the glacier was a mystery. I found little literature on it and few scientific studies. I uncovered no news articles, only a small write up on a website out of Portland State University called Glaciers of the American West, and a smaller website with a few photographs taken over subsequent years. There were no trip reports to be found, just a climbing forum discussion about summiting Cloud Peak that included mentions of seeing the glacier from above.

Matt and I started at the West Tensleep Trailhead in late afternoon and hiked six and a half miles to Misty Moon Lake. Purple lupines and crimson Indian Paintbrush burst from the edges of the trail until we reached, and passed, treeline. We set the tent in a depression among tundra grass. Plumes of mosquitoes hovered around the tent and around our heads each time we made a mad dash away from the nylon cover. The evening was hot pink—on the horizon, the peaks around us, the clouds reflected in still lake water.

The mosquitoes still swarmed the next morning. They bit through hiking pants and wool shirts. Matt and I walked through miles of alpine tundra until the soft grasses gave way to valleys of crumbling rock interspersed with grass, and then only rock. Cloud Peak isn't a technical climb—we didn't need ropes, harnesses or other climbing gear—but it is a trying one. Once we left the tundra, miles of rock piles lay before us.

Talus. Calf-aching rock hopping. It was the kind of rock hopping that makes you measure your steps because if you don't, a sprained ankle might be the best consequence, a broken leg the worst. Contrary to the crowds of Glacier, we saw few other humans en route to this glacier. In fact, once we left the tundra, we saw none.

As we approached the peak, I tried to orient myself. The summit was roughly northeast of where we scrambled, which meant the glacier itself was in the valley beside us. Clouds gathered to the west. Some dark and ominous, others fluffy and harmless. They brought to mind a close encounter with lightning on an exposed ridge like this in the Uncompagre Wilderness in Colorado a few years ago. I'd heard a buzzing sound and felt ants in my hair. The buzzing was the electric current through the rocks, the feeling of ants was an electric current in my scalp.

I did not get struck by lightening then, and did not want to get struck by it now. A tip I'd read about Cloud Peak on the climbing forum kept nagging me:

"The biggest thing to consider while on this mountain is that it is difficult to get off the very long summit ridge if a thunderstorm comes up quickly (as they tend to do here, sometimes as early as 10:00 a.m.)."

It was noon, and there was still no summit in sight, only rocky false summits that led us on.

We climbed higher. "We have to be getting close," I said to Matt through a half-chewed Clif Bar. He nodded, seemingly unfazed by the clouds or difficult travel. We continued. We hit snow that straddled the rocks. We scrambled up with hands and feet on rocks that sometimes moved beneath us. I swung tired eyes over the surrounding rock pile. Wind gathered, kicked across the rocks, tugged our shirts and hair strands. "I'm not going to go," I yelled over the wind.

"What?!" Matt yelled back. I waved him ahead. "I'm just...I'm just tired!" I yelled. "You go!"

I watched his coat shrink smaller until he was a blue ant crawling among the rocks and then he was out of view. I sat down on the cold granite and fished my shell, hat and gloves out of my pack. *What is wrong with me?* I thought. I waited. I stood up and picked my way to the edge of the summit ridge, hoping to grab a glimpse of the glacier. No luck. I found only concern that I'd lose track of Matt among the talus or he'd fall and I'd not be able to find him, or I'd fall and he'd not be able to find me.

Part of me was tired, my body worn thin from a summer spent carrying heavy packs in hard, cold alpine spaces. Part of me was weary of the dense, dark clouds moving closer to the peak. But most of me, I realized, simply balked; I didn't want to see another dying glacier.

A half hour later, Matt returned. He pulled out his phone and swiped photos of the glacier into view. It appeared as a broad flat snowfield with dirty crevasses carved in its side. The bottom gave way to a glittering emerald lake surrounded by loose rock.

On the one website where I'd found a few paragraphs of information about this glacier, the authors had posted Google Earth satellite images of the ice. In the first, taken in 1994, the lake was half its current size. In the next, from 2006, the lake had increased by a quarter, and the glacier had visibly shrunk. By 2010, when the last image was collected, the glacier had lost mass from the bottom and from the top and the lake had grown larger still. The authors of the website concluded from this rapid retreat that "the glacier will not survive."

I should have gone, I thought. But, what good would it have done? I'd seen it before, those thin crevasses, crumbling sides. In short time, my understanding of the fate of the small glaciers of the American West was becoming inescapable. It followed me like the ominous clouds overhead. How would me looking down on that glacier in any way change the fact that between ten to fifteen years, that glacier will be gone?

Matt and I pulled into the Lupine Meadows parking lot in Grand Teton National Park as the big sky began to grow light. We slowly rolled past long lines of cars parked in the dirt lot. Lupine Meadows is the major staging ground for climbers headed to the Grand Teton, the second tallest in the state at 13,770 feet above sea level, along with a handful of other high alpine trails.

We made coffee on the tailgate of my truck as other cars pulled in and the crunch of gravel under tires cut the morning stillness. Perhaps it's a symptom of National Parks to inherently become zoo-like in summer time. Teton National Park, with its iconic peaks and the chic western town of Jackson nearby, suffers from this symptom.

Despite their being in a busy National Park, the glaciers of the Tetons have received little press or attention. The mountain range was first surveyed in 1926, but the glaciers themselves didn't receive recognition until 1949, when Teton Glacier was first surveyed. The results of the survey went unpublished, and it wasn't until the late 1960's that the glacier was surveyed and studied again. In 2014, there are approximately ten glaciers remaining in the park (the original number is unknown) and some were so small it was easy to mistake them for snow patches, not moving, accumulating bodies of ice.

We headed out as the sun began to warm and the air filled with the sweet smell of sage. Matt's long stride covered ground quickly while my short stride moved fast to keep up. The first five miles blazed by; the full summer of alpine hiking paid off in the speed at which we could hike up switchbacks. The main destination for most people who hike that trail are Surprise and Amphitheater Lakes, two shimmering alpine pools whose mountain-flanked beauty makes the uphill effort worth it.

We paused at Amphitheater Lake among a crowd of other hikers and then, at the direction of the park ranger we'd spoken to the evening before, began to hunt for a faint trail that would lead us up the ridge east of the high alpine lake. In the basin beyond that ridge, the ranger had told us, sat Teton glacier.

We found the path in a cluster of boulders and followed it away from the lake. I felt the eyes of other hikers watching but none followed. The incline increased quickly and soon we were scrambling on all fours past scrubby pine trees. We finally reached the ridge only to be disappointed: there was no glacier in sight.

Instead we saw piles of house-size and car-size boulders strewn along a valley floor. Beyond the valley towered a horseshoe-shaped wall of debris. Rocks, silt, and boulders once carried by a glacier and then left behind, the moraine offered a clue. Maybe behind it we would find what we were looking for.

We carefully descended the steep ridge, occasionally grabbing a scrubby pine trunk for security. We picked our way through the boulder field, pressed our feet and hands between car sized granite and scattered shreds of gneiss. Water rushed beneath us, unseen, hidden by a cluttered rock mess. Deposits. Once imbedded in ice, now exposed.

The boulder field steepened. We climbed with all fours. Boulders gave way to sandy scree and rocks. The fluted moraine glittered in pale sunlight that cut through clouds above. We tipped our heads back to see the top of it 100 feet above us, hunched our shoulders and continued climbing.

We inched. Rocks slid beneath our boots. Slow, steady, slow. Occasionally sliding back as far as we'd moved forward.

Atop the moraine ridge, we still couldn't see the glacier, but we were standing where it had once been. Before us a steep loose pitch slanted down to a large snow patch. We slid down the moraine and followed the snow to a sheer rock pillar. We rounded the pillar and were greeted by a tight amphitheater.

I stopped and put my hand on Matt's arm. The glacier sat nestled against the lower reaches of the Grand Teton, Mount Owen, and Mount Teewinot. It filled a small corner of the amphitheater and spread 2000 feet or so to where we stood. Its bergschrund—a wide seam that forms where moving ice has pulled away from rock wall—sat high above the rest of the ice, a large slit pressed against the rock behind. The seam gave way to a miniature icefall, and to the right of the icefall, a small band of crevasses etched in dirty snow.

The glacier had all of the form and texture of a typical glacier, but in miniature.

Down slope from the icefall and the cracks, water trickled through soft ice studded with multicolored rock and punctuated the air with muffled, steady rhythms. The water slid beneath the debris horseshoe that stretched across the opening of the amphitheater, and far down slope, met a creek that gurgled and splashed through Glacier Gulch to the glittering, rich turquoise surface of Delta Lake.

I gazed up at the glacier and down to the lake and imagined ice filling the space as it did during the last Ice Age. During the massive Bull Lake Glaciation, more than 100,000 years ago, this entire valley was swathed in ice. Back then, the site of the current town of Jackson was buried beneath 1500 feet of it. Other parts of the area lay beneath a 3000-foot thick sheet. I imagined the ice filling the valley, and I imagined it retreating—ice melting, Delta Lake forming, Glacier Gulch carving a path along the valley between these peaks. The glacier eroding into itself, its moraine confining the ice to the coldest, most protected space in the cirque where it currently sits.

I remembered the moment in Glacier when Matt and I paddled the red canoe through Kintla Lake. The water was so richly blue and green. Our paddles splashed ripples as we moved toward the mountain valley from which the water poured. Maybe the best way to see glaciers in Glacier, I'd thought then, is by witnessing the landscape they've left behind.

The thought returned in that cirque, but the glacier was still there. A cold breeze blew off it and touched my neck. The melting ice wet our boots. I reached down and touched the ice. I felt all around me the power of the place, the power of the ice to shape a landscape. In that cirque, Matt and I stood in the past, the present and the future. We stood in the presence of a frozen being that we knew would soon be frozen no longer.

WINNER: THE 2016 LORIAN HEMINGWAY SHORT STORY
COMPETITION

Tony McCasker

All Gone

Out on the porch, the short girl's leg milled up and down from her tall clothes.

She whistled at the stars over the symphony of cicadas in the garden. Not to or for. A little thing like her, a melody someone had made up and held high until she reached for it. Sweet and simple, it slipped through her fingers. It was not then she realised all the stars were dead and she cooed to their bright young ghosts, but now. She practiced looking at things like they'd always been there, laying across the boards under the wavering black of a tree that had been little when she'd been little. Kicking her leg up and down, her lips would not be any other shape but around and around. Through the tunnel of their chapped pout, the sweet, the simple. A fly schemed by the wordless voice in the well. The song was short, like she was, and it wavered with the moonlit echo of the tree.

A tear slid away from her and her mouth shook behind her hand.

-

Cicada, and *Isn't that a funny name?*

I suppose it is. Friend used to call me that. This for you.

Thanks Cicada.

It's fine. Drop you here? That OK?

Yes, thanks and then the other one: *We'll give you five stars. Sic-kay-dah.*

Hey yeah, you too.

You too.

-

She remembered the boy who couldn't stop biting his nails

-

Cicada would sit in the basement that was her room all night with her hood shading her face and sometimes her older sister would come down and see her when the house was too quiet, they lived together. Ever since. Cicada would heave smoke into and out of herself so she wouldn't hear the cicadas in the walls but they just got louder. She covered her ears and sank into her knees and her sister would say her name over and over again until it was just *Cade, Cade, Cade* but only her nose would poke out from her hood and a raindrop would form on the end of it. Her sister would hold her and tell her: *It's not your fault.*

Cicada was barely over five feet tall though she told people she'd been taller before the world shrank her.

-

You? You're the girl?

Yes it's me. You wanted, li-

You are tiny.

The world shrank me.

That's funny, that's funny. Cicada, right?

Right.

That you whistling before?

-

She didn't want to go to sleep, she said, No I won't.

Why Cicada? Her sister bent her fingertips against the hair sponging under Cicada's hood. *Are you afraid of the dark?*

No, she said, No-no. In the voice that was quick and hurried, like she was and did. Looking over its shoulder, scooting. Puffs of dust cloudchasing band-aided heels.

I'm afraid if I go to sleep,

Yeah?

I will kill my imaginary friend.

-

and she had put her hand on his shoulder and said *Hey stop,*

-

So it's $250 for a bag and I got some nice Molly, $50 for two. Trips as well if you like but who takes trips anymore?

Nice little racket you got going here.

Is, hey.

Someone could rat you out real easy.

Obviously.

Yeah?

Buy the ticket, take the ride.

Thompson.

Whatever.

-

When Cicada went to work in the early evening every other early evening, her sister would watch the bumper sticker with the smoking alien saying *High there!* beam away and turn the corner. She'd go inside. She'd lay her legs over each other and swing them up and down, feeling the numb carpet on her heels and the ache of the old couch and counting the bruises on the pearskin of her shins. In the lounge room where no one went, the air pricked her lungs and she would throw her lavender shawl around her and toe rusted echoes from the iron steps down to Cicada's room.

A genie's wish lingered. She'd sit on the edge of the bed that was too big and repeat her quiet mantra of counting wounds she could not account for but they were there, blooming, fading, another one. All colours and rumours of colours the rainbow rejected. Cicada's small pots of makeup and smaller makeup pencils strewn and tipped over by the feet of the full-length mirror that sagged against the wall. Her sister would stare at it for hours. Cicada wore her socks whenever she went near it, and would stoop, always leaving the house with her face a darker shade than the rest of her and eyes sucked under by pits of kohl.

Her sister would hug an old stuffed toy she'd given to Cicada a long time go, dirty and bursting in the shape of a morning cartoon she used to wake up early to watch. Her leg would unstitch themselves and stretch out together. In the yellowed purple mosaic of their shins, Cicada's hands would grip the mirror's edge and smash it into her face again and again until it was not a mirror but a memoir and there were urgent reds and blues on the horizon.

-

and he'd looked at her with wavering ponds.

-

Got some gnarly scars.

Damien!

What? She does.

I do.

They're cool.

That's still rude. Sorry about him, Cicada.

It's fine.

Beautiful girl you don't got to hide under your hood and in your hair like that.

Now who's being rude? What the fuck, Steph.

I said it's,

It's fine.

-

We had this conversation about dreams one night, Cicada creaked under the floorboards of smoke cellaring her.

Her sister listened, crossing, uncrossing. Big book on her lap, she'd taken it from the pile by the bed to feel its weight on her thighs. Sniffing the air and dreaming where she sat.

He didn't dream, Cicada went on, Because he never slept.

They looked away from the air between them, old dye and brittle hair over clouded eyes. Time held them. Cicada sparked the genie's bottle to life again and bubbled another wish from its belly. Up for air. *So I got no dreams to learn from,* she said he said, the words wooling from her mouth, *So I read a lot.*

Her sister nodded and there was writing in the front of the book in her lap, words that curled life through the pages but came after they were born: *To Cicada. Your fingers are not too small. I want to hear that wood sing. Got you this. Peace xx,* and then his name, but she closed the book then.

-

In a year she'd found him asleep on her couch one morning.

-

Hey you're sitting on books.

Yeah. Can't see over the dash without them.

Are you serious?

I'm short.

Shit. What books?

Music books. I study when I'm not driving.

You play?

Yeah. Guitar, like my friend. Was teaching me sometimes.

Seriously.

My band's on tomorrow night at Valve.

Time?

8.55pm.

Weird time.

It is.

-

The boy came to the show later that evening and stood up against the bar next to Cicada's sister, though he didn't know it. *What's your name?* he'd asked and *It's not about me,* she'd said. She watched him watch her and she sighed through her nose, hair bleached to cheap porcelain laying its hands over her shoulders. She felt for them and their ends broke away in her fingertips, trapped in the arches and loops. A boy at the store called her a budget angel. She closed her eyes and listened to Cicada tune her guitar, guru'd in a skirt and hunched at the moth-eaten crowd, the hungry dinosaur on her underwear making them shuffle, crane.

She started to play what she always whistled and her sister lifted her head and could only say her name. Once, only once. After a while Cicada's chin crumpled and her hair draped over the strings of her guitar that she had stopped trying to play. Her chest filled the hollow of its body and that was all. One of the boys in the band leant down to whisper something but another one shook his head and mouthed *No, don't.*

Hands waved over necks and the lights went down. People left. The boy who'd come to see her left first.

-

Hey, can you watch the road?

What?

Getting worried back here.

Oh. Sorry. It's fine, though.

Spend a lot of time checking yourself out.

Something always chasing me.

What if,

Yes?

It's looking for you instead?

Hey?

Small girl?

-

He'd come in through the window in the night.

-

Why'd he name me after those, she'd want to know, and her forehead would collapse her eyes.

Her sister would sit and tell her, *Said they talk a lot all the time, like you used to. You two listened to them every evening, walking in the backyard, and there'd be moon on the dandelions and they'd light your way.*

Cicadas in the night are cute and majestic.

In the morning they're loud enough to make your ears bleed, and Cicada covered her smile with her hand inside her sleeve, too long like all her clothes.

I used to watch you two, you know. She knew. *From the porch, shoulder to shoulder with the doorway, kinda. The cicadas in the reeds, on the trees,* she said, *Seemed to call your name.* Her sister would hold her breath. *I held my breath sometimes, I don't know why. Just you two out there most nights.*

Cicada, fidgeting. Looking around. Her white walls black wherever she touched them.

When he used to hold my hand?

You wouldn't let go because you were scared, her sister would say. *You would say,* I'm so small what if I float away, like a balloon?

Together, then, crescent moons: *Sicki just hold onto me.*

Together, again, crescent moons: Silence for half an hour.

-

Hey everything OK back there?

I can stop?

We've just been to a funeral.

Oh. Hey, sorry.

They said beautiful things about her. Just beautiful.

When Samson spoke, I don't know. Did you know her like that?

I didn't. I had no idea she was like that, did those kinds of things for people.

And to think, she was so sad, she-

Never talked about that.

Never talked much.

We never asked. Hi, driver?

Driver?

Light's green.

-

She shook him until her hand went numb from how cold his skin was.

-

Remember when he wrote BORN FREE on the wall in big letters and some of them were backwards but then they seemed to make even more sense? Do you remember this happening?

Yes I remember.

And then he crossed out FREE so it was like BORN ~~FREE~~ and he told us,

A duet, a chorus: *Girls of mine, it is up to you.*

I remember.

Me too.

I don't want to.

Me too.

Cicada disappeared under her hood again with her wishless genie in a bottle but it shook in her hand so her sister took it in hers and placed it on the carpet between White Ox burns and boxed wine stains. She held Cicada for a while until Cicada's little leg shot out and kicked over the genie and they sat there for even longer, smelling a new stain form between the old ones that had lost their scent but still followed them.

-

How long you been doing the Uber thing for?

Not long.

How long's that?

How long's forever?

You were in that guy's lane before.

He was in mine.

Think you're smart.

I don't. It's just, you don't know. The passage of seconds, minutes, hours, days, weeks, months, years. Is it cosmic maths? They supposed to add up to something, like, is there an answer? Maths only has answers. It is answers. You deal in numbers, you're asking something. Funny, though. You ever think how when an equation is solved, it doesn't mean anything to anyone? Its own questions make its answer music instead of noise, but no one asked. Rules and solutions. I'm gonna whistle, you hear that? Got all these answers and no questions. I aren't asking anything anymore. I don't want nothing. I see a shooting star now, you know what? I wave at it and wish it well, wherever it's going, but it's dead already.

I'll get out here.

Hey you want your stu-

No, changed my mind.

What do you think the return policy on the gift of life is?

-

She remembered his bleeding fingers in the grey dawn.

-

Outside the house of a dying sun, its stone eyes looked inside a cloud forest.
His hand on her hand. Knees itchy with the long grass and scalps itchier still with
the city's dry eyes in the distance, closer at dusk when they could open, unafraid
of the day. Everything closer when the light had died. Her sister's shade in the
doorway of the home their parents had left them, he held her hand like he always
did around this time and they got lost outside under a backlit canopy. He'd poke
more holes in it with his finger. *See that one*, he said, *and that one?* She nodded
but could never be sure the ones she saw where the ones he wanted her to see.
They all shone, some bigger like him, some smaller like her, but they all shone,
and she liked that, and stood on her toes for as long as she could. Closer to
them, closer to him. If only for a little while and *All the while*, he told her, *These
stars are dead.* She'd flattened browning grass under her heels and wanted to
know what he meant. *Yeah*, he said, *Their light takes so many years to reach us.
By the time it does*, he said, and ran his thumb under his lip, *They been gone a
long time.* She fretted and wanted to know if there was anything they could do.
She thought he smiled but it was dark. *Just enjoy them while they're here.*

One fell to earth, then, on cruel cue, and her fingers doughed through his and
he told her *Quick, make some kinda wish.* She did, inside her head, rushed and
jumbled but she thought it made sense and she'd wanted it for as long as the star
it rode on had been dust but she was scared of herself and the scent she left be-
hind in empty rooms. A sigh and he wanted to know why. Every time she sighed.
Oh, she said. I don't think the star would've heard me. *What?* I said- *What?* I said-
Sorry what?

The cicadas were so loud.

-

Your clothes are real big.

Too much?

Naw, just, big. Like, you got no hands.

I look OK, though?

Yeah, for sure.

Really?

You look fine.

-

She'd have salted white trails from the sides of her eyes to the sides of her mouth, broken in the night and dissolving in the dawn. Her sister watched her from the iron stairwell while she slept, peered down over her forearm with a dusty chill on her feet and their bent legs. A painted echo of Cicada sitting in his lap, his arms wound around hers, her arms wound around the guitar, and his fingers pressing her fingers to the wood and his hand showing her hand how to pick at the nylon. To play a song. Sweet, simple. She could play it perfectly when he was there. Without him, it came to stay but would lose its way and then, disappear. The night outside had woken blue and it peered in through the windows at the small girl too. She stirred and her sister noticed, for the first time, Cicada slept in all her clothes and kicked the blankets and sheets to the floor.

No hands. The rosebuds of her nails reminded her of trying to say goodbye and she pulled her long sleeves over them after she got dressed, throughout the day, before she went to bed.

-

His nails, they were all gone.

Fiona Martin

the future is queer

nevermind that my parents
never took me to church or
believed in god

i still hear the words
"conversion therapy"
and think of my future

because i don't know my past.
my family, forefathers and fore
mothers and forequeers

they were all murdered.
by laughter or "therapy"
or the plague ushered in by

that last actor-cum-president.

nevermind that you can
barely clock me anymore,
what with my longer hair

and the guys in my bed.
i still skitter into shadow
and cry in the morning.

they think we have a death
drive because they say our
sex can't create they don't

know how badly we want
a future how we would let
ourselves become monsters

to see what a tomorrow feels like.

Michael Martone

Hat Trick

Color Me Red

I was stymied in my attempt to find the official color of the *Make America Great Again* baseball cap. I think of it as red but what red? There must be an agreed upon Pantone numbered color. I recently discovered that the official crimson for the University of Alabama and Indiana University is the same, Crimson PMS 201. As hard as I looked I could not find an exact numbered shade though on ordering forms for the hat. The customer was given a range of colors, a spectrum of Pantone hues to customize the hat. I think of the hat as red, but I also found an article speculating on the correlation between the mood of the candidate and the color of the hat he was wearing. White, the informant believes, indicates a buoyant mood while red signals that we should take warning. I learned that the hat comes in black too. No speculation on what wearing that color would mean. You can order the cap with special embroidery—a general's golden scrambled egg garland on the bill. My search did discover that many sources attempted to assign a Pantone color to Mr. Trump's skin. The consensus seems to be a Pantone color called Gold Flame 16-1449 TPX. I guess "Red" it is, the cap's color. I am colorblind so I don't really see it, the red of the red. I have to take Mr. Trump's word for it.

The Fit

I like hats. I wear hats. All kinds of hats. I noticed early on in the 2016 presidential election campaign that the candidates were, as usual, hatless, but in the absence of hats there is always hair, or the lack of it, to consider and comment upon. I remember reports of past political seasons posting pieces on haircuts and hair plugs, on the sides of severe parts and on liberal curls and conservative comb-overs, evil widow's peaks and Hollywood dye jobs. So it was curious when the one current candidate garnering the most commentary for his hair (his coiffure a concoction of Brutalist architecture and sketchy Escher-esque terracing) donned a hat. It made me think, that hat. The summer political conventions would soon be here, and I thought how those conventions, in my lifetime, had always featured a certain kind of hat, another kind of hat, the straw boater, not the baseball cap of the moment. True, as time went on, the boater's function as just a hat changed more into costume signifier, straw into pressed Styrofoam, of the ritualized political convention and ossified barbershop quartets. Still the boater persisted as political attire. Its flat surfaces provide in the television age, I suppose, stages for decoration and display of stuffed donkeys and plush elephants and bands of buttons and a stand for flags. But still, through it all, the boater retains enough of a signature to read as a political hat, the hat that hosts political conventions. Strange. The boater was simply popular as summer headgear from the late 1800s when conventions as we know them began, and they continued to be so until the Great Depression where the boater was eclipsed by the soft straw Panamas. The boater then would have been *de rigueur,* then, worn to those un-air-conditioned conventions held in field houses, stadiums, armories, amphitheaters, and "gardens." It is as close as we come to traditional costume, a civic uniform. I didn't have a boater. I do now. I ordered one online from the Gentleman's Emporium. I got the cheaper one, a softer Laichow straw, two-inch brim with a dandy grosgrain satin ribbon of navy and red folded into a bow. They also called it a skimmer, the boater, this kind of hat. As the presidential campaigns moved around the country, I followed the progress of my boater as it shipped, drifting from warehouse to distribution center, all the logistics. It arrived. It arrived in a special box, the boater's crown nestled and suspended to prevent crushing in the transit. The lozenge cloth label sewn into the band reads "Authentic SCALA Classico" wreathed with "Dorfman Pacific Company" and "Handmade Since 1921." A less elegant label is tacked behind it, digitally produced ideograms for "do not wash," "do not bleach," "do not dry," "do not iron." Do not iron? And "100% Laichow/Laichow, XLarge/ X-Grande." The reverse has "Made in China/Hecho en China." I like it. It is like a fossil. A ruin. It is a historic artifact. It doesn't even seem to be a hat. It could be a planter, a wall decoration. It is out of time and space. And, indeed, its provider, Gentleman's Emporium, seems to do most of its business creating clothing and headgear for Steam Punk aficionados and anachronistic re-enactors. Now I know how to see it, this hat. I see now that I possess the crucial piece of my postmodern attire, my post-historical ensemble. The idea of progress is so last season. Going forward is not fashion forward after all. I always thought that a boater had transmuted into the sphere of costume—all tap dance-y and vaudevillian. But if the suit fits, wear it yes? All the world's a stage and all that. Costume consumes us. "History," said the boater bedecked (or was it a bowler?) Henry Ford "is all bunk." Or so we seem to remember. What he really said was "History is more or less bunk. It's tradition. We don't want tradition. We want to live in the present, and the only history that is worth a tinker's damn is the history that we make today." That sounds…familiar. Okay. Today, we have the detritus of costume and customs, scraps of quotations all scotch taped together, straw men and paper dolls. Every day we put on some sort of suit, pieces pieced together. I lift the boater out of its box and flip it by the brim up over my head and lower it down on my crown. It fits. But what does that mean, it fits? And does it? And if the hat does fit how, how will I wear it?

David Mason

Descend

And what of those who have no voice
and no belief, dumbstruck and hurt by love,
no bathysphere to hold them in the depths?
Descend with them and learn and be reborn
to the changing light. We all began without it,
and some were loved and some forgot the love.
Some withered into hate and made a living
hating and rehearsing hate until they died.
The shriveled ones, chatter of the powerful—
they all go on. They go on. You must descend
among the voiceless where you have a voice,
barely a whisper, unheard by most, a wave
among the numberless waves, a weed torn
from the sandy bottom. Here you are. Begin.

David Mason

Head of a Man

The change was what he did not see
and now sees with vacant eyes—

a crowd of strutting minotaurs
whose sentences are lies.

Down by the sea a woman sings
Aman, Aman, beyond the time,

her full voice floating up the walls
where cactus armies climb.

But here the sea lies far away.
A dog barks at a noisy cock.

A man croaks to a mobile phone,
There will be talk.

So many voices hushed in rooms
beyond the shattered colonnades—

the head of a man looks on the works
of women who are poorly paid.

Observe the head from the other side,
fine whiskers carved in marbled stone.

Observe the wordless lips the eyes
have sensed but never known.

Observe the head of a man. Observe.
Whatever it was, the rest is gone.

Leslie McGrath

Luna Moth

I last saw one decades ago.
There were nine or ten that July night
moon-green and big as dinner plates
some affixed to the doorscreen, others hovering
like slow applause at the edge of the sphere of light
cast by the hall lamp. Both drawn and threatened
by what we've made to illumine our human way
they were gone by daybreak.

Yesterday morning we found one poised on the lantern.
A tragicomic beauty: his tiny Nosferatu head ironically
without a mouth
the false eyes on his wings meant to scare predators away
could've been cigarette burns.

As a child I might have said he looked like the son of a barn swallow
and a cabbage leaf, of a fairy queen and a kite.
Ten years ago, the son of a coat hanger and a movie theater curtain
a golf umbrella and pinking shears
or a jet and a twenty dollar bill.

How long before we liken every natural thing
to its technologic spawn? No singleton, no swarm
just a pixelated image
I once saw of a moth—mild, defiant, and doomed.

(originally published in *Devouring the Green: Fear of a Human Planet*, Jaded Ibis Press, 2014.)

Leslie McGrath

Mumblety Peg

And when the truth about the emperor's clothes was revealed
the crowd convulsing with laughter at his flaccid gullibility
you noticed a young man easing the battered patty of a wallet
from a bald man's back pocket. Winking, the young man stuffed
the thing into the denim pouch strapped across his chest
then with two slim fingers tweezed a phone from the purse
gaping at a girl's shoulder. *What?* you sputtered, turning away
to look at something, anything, else.
You crouched to retrieve a pacifier from beneath
your toddler's stroller and found something else down there
like a pocket knife stuck in the dirt:
the word *accessory.* It pegged the pacifier; it pegged you.

(originally published in *Agni*)

Leslie McGrath

Feminists Are Passing from Our Lives

(after Phil Levine)

It's wonderful how they jog
in two-toned gel soled racing shoes
their yoga butts barely jiggling
in rosy spandex leggings.

I was there once. I felt
the brash *I've got it all,* I had
the uncomplicated beauty of the young
before the years peeled it from me

like flimsy wallpaper. In my memories
women's work was pin money
 to pay for ballet lessons, summer camp;
suffering children, suffering filing jobs

suffering their husbands
who poured from the commuter train
gin-flushed and slurring. You who
I raised on *Our Bodies, Our Selves*

believe that feminism's as passé
as the sanitary napkin and the typewriter.
You roll your eyes and smirk
at my pleas not to become housewives.

I've seen that beast
hook its teeth on the cleverest PhD
and take her down for decades.
That won't happen to us,

you say, *we've come too far.*
We're protected under the law
a majority, a force.
No. Not that big.

(originally published in the *Cimarron Review*)

Tyler Meier

Our Century

A man behaving as if the century is all that he has, or

　　a woodpecker pounding the air conditioner

　　as if it could live off just the air. The facts

of the world obsess us. Small blue barrel full of pigeon,

　　also known as afternoon. Life span of a heart.

Each window as a little box of sky, indexing.

　　What there is no such thing as: grief, rootstock,

　　allusion.   What the sun does to a leafback

or tip, the regular theft of momentum,

　　or thrust. I have no crossing branches. I have

no given pitch. I mistake every stone under the tree

　　for a peach. Palisade of fence slat.

You said this is what love makes possible and pointed

　　up, like all the sticks in the tree. The man

across the street calls his dog:

　　Oleander! Oleander! Oleander! Mercy

　　is a place we caution against, then for.

I have begun calling for his dog everywhere I go.

My approach to the wind is to recognize it

　　like the old friend that it is.

Somehow July saved the garden.

　　Somehow a straight line remains the history

　　　　of absolutely nothing.

E. Ethelbert Miller

In Search Of Thomas Merton

There are days when I think about going to live with the monks.
My brother Richard did this in the early sixties. He never discussed
the idea with me. A day simply came and my family took him to the
La Guardia Airport. We said goodbye and then he was gone.

I wonder how many men leave a home each year because of a
spiritual need to either be alone or closer to someone other than a
human being. Richard went away to upstate New York. Growing up
in the South Bronx I never thought about upstate. How many slaves
went to sleep every night tired of picking cotton but never dreaming
of Canada?

Lately I listen to people in cafes or pundits on television talking about
the recent presidential election. I guess this is how our nation felt
after Lincoln's death. What will become of our Union now? Alas, I look
into the mirror and see a wretched freeman.

There is a way a tree will talk to a black man, how it might guide him
out of the woods and towards freedom. Outside my window I look at the
trees, I notice their naked limbs, their leaves gone from too much
weeping. I feel like a lover who wakes before daybreak only to discover
love is gone.

I feel a longing, a need for prayer and fasting. Where is the choir for
my soul to join? We are a people in need of song - it's time to compose
new spirituals. We either dream or die.

Bryce Milligan
Not In Our Name

A song for Standing Rock

Oh, the black snake of progress,
we know it so well:
It's cut down our forests
It's poisoned our wells;
It's killing our children
with lead and with flame
and left us aghast at
what's been done in our name.

Now prophecies tell
how the gathering tribes
will fight the black snake
though it cost them their lives;
and they're fighting for us
though it's we who are to blame
for the pain and destruction
that's been done in our name.

We are the water,
We are the trees.
We stand by the rock
to define our destiny.
Seven generations
who will not be tamed:
No more will we let these things
be done in our name.

The buffalo are coming home
where every tribe will stand.
Come and join the battle,
lend your hearts and your hands.
In the sacred river valleys
on the mountains and the plains:
No more will we let these things
be done in our name.

Darlin' Neal

On The Road To Money, Mississippi

I am in Mississippi. I drive around looking for Delta history.

The highway to Clarksdale and Robert Johnson's crossroads with its colorful and prominent crossing guitar street sign in the center of town, that highway is the Emmett Till Memorial Highway. On another road, driving to Money, Mississippi, I search for a name of the road but cannot find a sign anywhere naming it.

I roll the windows down and smell the fertile earth. The air reminds me of coming into awareness of the world around me, learning what voices meant, my first powerful itch, the smell of Mississippi farms, my maternal grandmother's yellow roses and bell peppers. My other grandmother talked about life being a dream and the sun and air bleached her house cleaner even than she scrubbed it and a rooster woke me every morning. Then we were in New Mexico and a brother became my companion and I found pure communion with my dog Cisco. He knew to fetch our pajamas every night and tug on us, time for bed, making the world wonderful in that tiny trailer each night with my brother Jamie's hand in mine and Cisco beside my feet.

It was a sense as strong and pure as that communion that told me of goodness coming from those voices and images on the television screen. Martin Luther King, Jr. talked about love and the world was filled with hope and then I watched him being shot down on the balcony of the Lorraine in Memphis, Tennessee. I saw pictures of Bobby Kennedy talking to children in the Mississippi Delta and with a child's fervor I loved him because he was in that state I considered home and magic and because he was kind. I still remember the confusion and sadness of watching him fall.

The dirt roads pass and pass.

I see my father unfolding a clean cloth handkerchief, folding it neatly and tucking it inside his pocket. We gather bottles from the side of the road to sell, a nickel apiece. During my youth it took a little while before we understood the importance of conservation, the importance of preservation, in part because so much of it was already a natural course of our lives. Everyone took coke bottles to be sterilized and refilled. You used as little of a paper towel as possible to make them last, if you were so lucky you could afford paper towel that week. You washed things you needed and hung them out to dry because the dryer used too much electricity to afford.

On the road to Money, Mississippi I look for signs. I think of Emmett Till, that child who died before I was born and whose mother changed the decade of my birth, that little boy who must have felt something of the excitement I felt as a child coming to visit relatives in Mississippi. His childhood part of Mississippi differs from my own with its open land and golden sunsets, but we both smelled greens cooking in pots on the stove. We both heard the sound of our cousin's voices that told us we were home. Now crumbled earth covers the cotton and soybean fields as the land waits for new crops to be planted.

I remember money as a child, literal money. I wonder if Emmett Till delighted in the name of that town as I would have, that town where he'd have to drive gravel roads to visit someone, that town so different from his Chicago, the safe country place where his mother sent him. I remember a silver dollar so large in my small hand, how my brother collected two dollar bills. To change money into a treat when there was little of it was a cherished and magical moment to me back then and I bet it was to Emmitt Till, made him brave and handsome and filled him with laughter as he stepped into and out of that store in Money, Mississippi.

Along that road that traces the Tallahatchie River, I listen to the rapid sound of wheels on the railroad tracks that curve alongside. So many little graves dot the landscape, so many dead possums and skunks. I notice wooden crosses and fading flowers in the hot humid sun. I remember a time in New Mexico with the heat toasting my skin. A mother took a wrench and opened the fire hydrant valve and a bunch of us children, white and Mexican, slid and laughed and splashed in the gushing water with no worry about the waste. Back then, Bobby Gentry sang a song I heard first on a record player in New Mexico about Billy Joe McAllister jumping off the Tallahatchie River Bridge and I dreamed of a place from home, far, far away.

On that road to Money, Mississippi the history I find first is the second grave of Robert Johnson in a small cemetery beside a little church where I'm told they don't like people to stop and gawk. This is supposed to be the actual grave, one that an old woman told people about when they finally asked her, and here there is a sign telling a story about the bluesman and about his death.

When I was young I loved Bob Dylan and when coming back to Mississippi I felt I was familiar with a song he sang about Emmett Till, but I've searched my albums and CDs and though I find a record that Bob Dylan did indeed write and sing such a song, I can find it nowhere in my belongings and it's only in my imagining and in the rightness of it being sung that I recognize that tune.

A black hearse passes by and I wonder about the virtue of honoring the dead. Once in Jackson my daughter and I watched an ambulance weaving in and out of traffic and no one would stop. Just moments later a funeral procession rolled down a busy Jackson street and cars pulled over. A black man emerged from one, took off his hat and placed it over his heart while bowing his head in prayer.

When I get to the little grocery where Emmett Till whistled at that white woman I find a crumbling down building. People say they want to forget the ugly thing that happened, how grown men took a child and beat him to death, beat him so hard an eye came out of its socket, and then tossed him in the Tallahatchie River. There's no sign here for Emmett Till that little boy who lost his life for whistling at a white woman who sold him candy.

There are other signs, the shape of a guitar in Tutweiler and the barbed wires of the Tallahatchie Correctional Facility where those men never spent one night.

Kim Nicolini

Where Color Hurts

We never imagined a world where color hurts. To imagine
color toxic, sharp is to imagine now. And now

is frankly unbearable. Blare and glare of lines
and edges. Red, white, blue and orange. Screaming

faces I will not
see. Shouting words
I will not

hear. Reducing atrocities to artifice through repetition
on blinking screens. Videos go viral. Color aborts truth

with sensation. Ugly
fonts repeat ugly
words on a white
scroll. Death toll.

Casualties distanced through quantification of numbers.
The most beautiful moment of the moonrise is the darkness

that precedes light. Sliver of time when star glow mutes
color into shadow. Night wrapped in obscurity
of dreams imagined. Bats ascend in a funnel

cloud. This could be a natural
disaster. It rains urine and bat
shit. Crazy. The wash

breathes a deep dank breath. Lost bodies under bridges.
A bra strung across tree branches. Stories untold

on the white scroll
in colors too bright

to see. We hang

on a thread of light lingering over this dry river
bed, this bed of sand, bed of drought, bed of dead
trees and waste. Bed where the man waits his face the color

of rusted coils. Grudge in teeth. A need to
remove our tongues. I plant
my feet. Fight back with my sheer lack

of movement. Wipe
his face from the slate
with a dirty rag for dirty
lies till he tucks

his cock and tail between his legs. Recedes
into the nightmare that never was

supposed to be.
Bitch man. Who's
the dog now?

We can dissolve in a blanket so blue it's
black. Turn our backs to the white
scroll of his howls. News hammered to a thud.

Kill the media migraine.
Mute the color.

Let us soften the blow in the dim halo of a moonless
night. Sky gives more truth than reality
too unreal to accept. We demand a return
of color that no longer hurts to see.

Nick Norwood

JC

"Don't let anybody try to fool you," Johnny said,
"we all knew cigarette smoking was bad for you."

And now, as Big Guns and Big Oil look up
to Big Tobacco like a kid looking up

to his big brother—sponsoring Big Research
to counter science, history, soul—

we can see forward to a day we'll be telling
our kids Bob Dylan was right all along.

"Johnny's like the north star," he said.
"You can guide your boat by him." And notice

how, in the iconic image of Johnny Cash backstage
at San Quentin, yoked to his own fascist-

killing machine, we know he's raising his big
finger to the whole bought, sellout world,

and how his face is absolutely defiant,
fierce, iron-willed, free.

Achy Obejas

The March[1]

I am about to step outside, I am about to step outside to the elements and my anticipation is a long inhalation that covers the world upon release. This is the beginning of a movement based on facts and not on sentiment or pronouncements, though both sentiment and pronouncements are useful and worthy. As I begin to lift my left foot, my Sartorius muscle allows my knee to move up towards my body. I am joined by others, however they can join with me, others who have suffered, too, and are not afraid to continue suffering. What we seek is a new majority rooted in justice for all whose conscience is committed to ceasing wrongs and doing right. What we want is nothing about us without us. What we want is for each individual to define their own identity and expect that society will respect them. We shift our weight, unlock our knees. Arrange our bodies in the best way for each of us. For an instant, most of us are standing on one foot. We are not in a hurry. We are not dreaming. We are ready to give up everything, even our lives. We shall do it without violence because that is our conviction. What we want is freedom, what we want is the power to determine our destiny. As my left foot comes down, it is coordinated with my right and they match the equivalent movement of those who have joined me, and with whom I am joining. We are firmly rooted. Whenever possible, we let our limbs swing in a natural motion and keep our heads facing forward. What we want is the complete elimination of military forces, not just from this or that territory, but from every corner, every outpost, on earth. What we want is full and meaningful employment. What we want is decent, safe housing. What we want is an education that teaches us our true histories and their consequences on the present. As each of us lifts our right foot (or makes the equivalent movement to ambulate), we are now a perfectly synchronized force, even in our differences and occasional disorder. What we want is an immediate stop to state brutality and the assassination of black people, and native people, and disabled people, and trans people, and women, and children, and mothers and fathers who can only do so much because they are shackled by the very state that seeks to kill them for having foolishly believed they were free. What we want are the doors flung open to Folsom, Riker's, Guantanamo, San Quentin, San Juan de Lurigancho, ADX Florence Supermax, La Sabaneta, Attica, Camp 22, Pollsmoor. It would be fatal to overlook the urgency of the moment. As we advance, we are a thunderous thrum. Some of us will run under the rain in Seattle, and toward traffic to block Lake Shore Drive in Chicago. Others will flood Wall Street and more will storm the port of Oakland. There will be one lonely soul in snowy Bethel, Alaska, and clusters in Little Rock, in sweltering Ferguson, in Tallahassee and Flagstaff, Baltimore, Detroit, Honolulu, Boise, in ancient Salem, Wichita and Northampton, Oklahoma City and Spearfish, South Dakota. And always on the mall in Washington, always on the green, always in the bitter cold that is Pennsylvania Avenue. Nerve and muscle adapt to the rhythmic stimulus of our own noise, the noise we make together. It is true that when in the course of human events, it becomes necessary for one person to connect to another and another and another in order to defend our equality, our difference, our dependence on one another, then

---

1   Much of the text here is adapted from The Black Panthers Ten Point Program, The Delano Manifesto, Equalise It! (a disability manifesto), Martin Luther King Jr.'s "I Have a Dream" Speech, Trail of Broken Treaties, The Transfeminist Manifesto and the Declaration of Independence of the United States of America.

Alicia Ostriker

Veteran's Day, 1968, repeated Veteran's Day 2016

The killing will not stop. A scarlet
hail is always behind my eyes.
The morning paper, shreds of flesh
poisons the bread, the salt, the cheese

Husband, I want to fight the good
battle of hip, and breast, and thigh,
where pleasure, spill of sinew, breeds
outrageous generosity.

I want to see our children spring
Free as this coarse grass. I suppose
the killing will not stop. The killing
will not stop. Who knows. Who knows.

Elise Paschen

Liberty

"You see, the world is in fragments, sir." Paul Auster

Sharing a row beside an older
couple, broken English exchanged,
we are airborne above the clouds.

Sitting beside me, she's so patient
as I rummage through the last-minute
stuffed bag, grabbing *City of Glass*

and vitamins, while right in front
a middle-aged man, his suit jacket
so neatly pressed and flattened

in the compartment, keeps time on
his wrist, refolding today's Business
Section, before he crashes his

seatback down, claiming territory.
In the serpentine TSA
pre-approved lines I tried to read

each person's face as if unraveling
a crime. The well-dressed citizens
on morning flights looking complacent,

while others, walking through the terminal,
avoided any gaze of strangers.
The day after the election, I fumbled

for language as my students broke
into tears, saying they're scared. How
to find words for a friend who's lived

here thirty years without citizenship?
Flying above New York, I picture

enormous letters spelling *Tower*

of Babel across city streets
and blocks, decoded by the sleuth
in this novel. The older man

cradles his wife's shoulder inside
his hand, pointing out the toy Statue
of Liberty – so many miles

below. As we land, the man sneezes.
His wife and I stumble upon
our shared tongue, saying, *Bless you. Bless you.*

Connie Post

Rape Whistle

After the support group
I fidget outside in the
November air

I fear
I have lost my keys again

a small framed woman
catches up to me
hands me the whistle,
forces it, into the palm of my hand
and whispers
"in case"

I put it in my pocket
hold it in place, with one hand

I want to understand the shape
of mercy
how it can narrow itself
through a small silver chamber

I perseverate on how
the same instrument can be used
to coach football or track
or in this case
how to find other ways to run

I want to understand
how to remove a
grease tinged hand
from a sealed mouth

I want to know

how to sleep with out
medication

I am given a list of "emergency contacts"

I want to ask the woman
"what does violation sound like
before it happens"

Susan Power

Our Stories Are Meant To Converge

1

ONE APRIL MORNING I DECIDE TO TAXI TO AWP IN MINNEAPOLIS SINCE
I DON'T HAVE A CAR AND THE BUSES WILL TAKE TWO HOURS TO CARRY
ME FOURTEEN MILES. THIS IS MORE OF A SACRIFICE THAN IT SOUNDS,
THE PRICE OF A MONTH'S ENERGY BILL. THE DRIVER WHO PULLS UP
WITH A SMILE AND SAYS I CAN SIT BESIDE HIM, IS FROM SOMALIA. WE
GET TO TALKING. CAB DRIVERS SEE THE WRITER IN ME, THEY CLAMP
THE STEERING WHEEL WITH ONE HAND, OPEN THE DOOR OF THEIR RIBS
WITH THE OTHER SO THEIR STORIES CAN CLIMB FREE AND BREATHE
AMERICAN AIR. THEY DON'T GET MANY CHANCES. HE TELLS ME ABOUT
BROTHERS AND SISTERS, WHICH ONES ARE HERE, WHICH ONES ARE
BACK HOME, HE TELLS ME HIS MOTHER STILL CALLS HIM A NAME FOR
BABIES. NOT BECAUSE HE ISN'T A MAN, BUT BECAUSE SHE WANTS TO
MOTHER HIM ACROSS UNREASONABLE MILES. HE ASKS ME WHY I'M
HEADED FOR THIS PLACE, THIS CONVENTION PALACE WHERE HE'S
DRIVEN A HUNDRED TIMES, BUT NEVER WITH SOMEONE WHO ACCEPTS
HIS OFFER TO SIT IN FRONT. I TELL HIM ABOUT AWP AND THE THOU-
SANDS OF WRITERS CONVERGING ON OUR CITIES. I TELL HIM ABOUT MY
PANEL, NATIVE WRITERS BREAKING STEREOTYPES. DON'T WE SOUND
LIKE A CHAIN GANG, USING A PICKAXE TO CHIP AT THE LIES WE ARE
WRAPPED IN THE DAY WE ARE BORN? TRUST ME, DISEASED BLANKETS
ARE STILL BEING HANDED OUT BY THE SETTLER CLASS. HE TURNS TO
LOOK AT ME, AND SMILES. A SWEET MAGICIAN WHO CONJURES A STE-
REOTYPE AND DEMOLISHES IT IN SO FEW WORDS HE COULD BE A WRIT-
ER HIMSELF. HE SAYS: I LIKE INDIANS MORE THAN THE OTHER AMERI-
CANS. EVEN WHEN THEY'RE DRUNK THEY TREAT YOU LIKE A PERSON.

2

ANOTHER CAB RIDE TO ANOTHER EVENT, I HAVE PLENTY OF TIME, SO
WHEN THE DRIVER ASKS IF HE CAN SHOW ME HIS PICTURES OF HOME,
I TELL HIM, YES. HE HAS A ROUND SHINY FACE AND WHEN HE SMILES,
HE LOOKS SAD. HE IS FROM NIGERIA, WHERE HIS WIFE AND CHILDREN,
PARENTS AND SIBLINGS, LIVE IN A COMPOUND HE BUILDS FOR THEM
FROM A DISTANCE. HE TURNS OFF THE METER, HIS BOSS AND ARCHI-

TECT, AND PICKS UP A HEAVY ALBUM FROM THE PASSENGER SEAT. HE
BALANCES THE BOOK ON THE DIVIDER BETWEEN US SO HE CAN POINT
OUT EVERYTHING IN HIS WORLD. THIS IS WHERE HE LIVES, NOT MINNE-
SOTA. I SEE GENERATIONS OF FAMILY, AND GENERATIONS OF GOATS,
THE DUSTY ROAD THAT LEADS TO THE THICK WALLS PROTECTING
HIS HEART. WE ARE GIFTING EACH OTHER IN THIS CLOSE SPACE THAT
SMELLS TOO SWEET. A PINE-SHAPED AIR FRESHENER DANGLES FROM
HIS MIRROR AND MAKES US SICK WITH ITS FUNKY ATTEMPT TO COVER
ALL THE UNHAPPY STORIES THAT PASS THROUGH HIS CAR. I'VE NEVER
MET THIS MAN BEFORE, I DOUBT I'LL SEE HIM AGAIN, BUT HE HAS OF-
FERED ME HIS STORY AND I HAVE ACCEPTED IT. THE EXCHANGE IS SOL-
EMN AS A PRAYER. SUDDENLY SHY, HE REPLACES THE ALBUM ON THE
PASSENGER SEAT, RESTS HIS HAND ON ITS COVER. THE PAUSE IS SPA-
TIAL. I SEE US, I SEE EARTH, I SEE THE DISTANCE BETWEEN OUR HOME-
LANDS COLLAPSE AND MEET LIKE THE PALMS OF FRIENDS. HE STARES
AHEAD WHEN HE SAYS, SO QUIETLY I LEAN IN TO HEAR HIM, "I KEEP THIS
HERE, SO I'LL REMEMBER WHY I DO THIS." THAT WAS SEVERAL YEARS
AGO BUT PART OF ME STILL WAITS WITHIN THAT PAUSE, THE MEETING
GROUND OF INTIMATE STRANGERS. I PRAY FOR HIM WHEN I HEAR NEWS
OF NIGERIAN BLOOD, WONDER IF HIS COMPOUND IS STRONG ENOUGH
TO WITHSTAND THE RAGE OF OUR TIME.

3

IN THE DIRTY THIRTIES MY GRANDMOTHER, WANAKCHA WASHTEWIN,
PACKS A PAPER BAG WITH A CHANGE OF CLOTHES, WHAT FOOD SHE
CAN BEAR TO TAKE FROM HER HUNGRY CHILDREN. SHE SETS OFF
DOWN THE DEPRESSION ROAD OF FORT YATES, NORTH DAKOTA, HITCH-
HIKING 1,600 MILES TO WASHINGTON SO SHE CAN APPEAL TO PRES-
IDENT ROOSEVELT TO LET OUR PEOPLE LIVE AS FULL CITIZENS AND
GROWNUPS. MY GRANDMOTHER REFUSES TO HEEL, REFUSES TO ROLL
OVER AND BEG LIKE A DOG, OR A DOMESTIC DEPENDENT NATION. WHY
WOULD SHE? SHE WAS A GIRL WHEN LALA WAS ALIVE, OUR BELOVED
SITTING BULL, WHO KEPT A LITTLE APART ON THE GRAND RIVER SO HE
WOULDN'T BECOME A FORT INDIAN. SHE ISN'T DAKOTA HISTORY, BUT
A WOMAN LIVING IN PRESENT TENSE, A VOICE THAT WILL SPEAK TO
ME FOREVER. SHE'S TECH SAVVY IN THE SPIRIT WORLD, WHISPERS
SOME OF MY FACEBOOK UPDATES THAT I TYPE LATE AT NIGHT WHEN
HER SPIRIT MOVES ME. SHE/WE CONVERT OUR TEARS INTO WORDS
SO WE WILL NOT CRY YOU A RIVER OR TEN-THOUSAND LAKES. SHE/WE
KEEP SCORE, AMERICA, ON BEHALF OF YOUR INDIGENOUS CITIZENS.
WE NOTICE WHEN YOU LEAVE US OUT. OVER AND OVER AND OVER. WE
ARE YOUR FOREBEARS. YOU WOULD NEVER HAVE SURVIVED WITHOUT
US. WE AREN'T JUST YOUR FORGOTTEN PAST. WE ARE YOUR FUTURE.
YOU'VE RUN US INTO THE GROUND WITH THE STEAM-ROLLING TER-

MINATOR THEY CALL MANIFEST DESTINY. YOU DECIMATED OUR NUM-
BERS WITH CARELESS SNEEZES AND AIRBORNE DISEASES, AND SERI-
AL-KILLER-LIKE STEALTH INITIATIVES THAT FELLED US AS EFFICIENTLY
AS YOUR ASSAULT ON OUR ANCIENT FORESTS. BUT YOU'VE CUT OFF
YOUR NOSE TO SPITE YOUR FACE. YOU'VE FOULED YOUR OWN NEST.
WHO WILL LEAD YOU FROM THIS NIGHTMARE? WHAT POLITICIAN OR
ECONOMIST OR COPPER-TONGUED PUNDIT WILL KNOW HOW TO SAVE
THE THIN SKIN THAT STANDS BETWEEN YOU AND THE END TO WATER?
WE'RE AMERICA'S MOST PROLIFIC SURVIVORS AND WE'RE STILL QUIET-
LY SHARING THE STORIES YOU THOUGHT WERE RIDICULOUS BUT WILL
TURN OUT TO BE THE MOST VALUABLE TREASURE NEVER LISTED ON
THE NEW YORK STOCK EXCHANGE. WE NOTICE EVERYTHING, AMERICA,
AND WHY WOULDN'T WE? THIS IS OUR HEART-TRAVELED, STORM-CEN-
TERED, SPIRIT-FILLED TERRITORY OF ORIGINAL ABUNDANCE. THIS IS
OUR NATIONAL RELATIVE. YOU NEED US TO OFFER THE RIGHT GIFTS,
PROVIDE TRANSLATION. YOU WALK ON OUR EARTH BUT YOUR TREAD IS
A NOISY DEATH. IF I WERE YOU I'D REMEMBER US MORE THAN YOU DO.
IF I WERE YOU, I'D SHOW A LITTLE RESPECT.

4

ELDERS SAID MY STORY DOESN'T BEGIN WITH ME, OR MY MOTHER, OR
HER MOTHER, OR HER FATHER. THEY SAID THAT'S WHAT AMERICANS
DO, BEGIN CHAPTER ONE WITH "I AM BORN." ELDERS TAUGHT ME TO
TAKE EVERY OPPORTUNITY I HAD TO HONOR THOSE WHOSE SHOUL-
DERS AND TERRITORY WE STAND UPON BECAUSE AMERICA WORKED
SO HARD TO STAMP THEM DEEP UNDER THE GROUND, IN GRAVES
BENEATH GRAVES. WE ARE HERE BECAUSE THEY GAVE US LIFE, RE-
SOURCES THEY PRESERVED FOR US. THEY DIDN'T WANT TO DRAIN THE
LAST DROP. THEIR STORIES LIE BENEATH OUR STORIES. THEY INSPIRE
US, THOUGH WE MIGHT NOT WANT TO GIVE THEM CREDIT. AMERICA
TELLS US TO BUILD RESUMÉS, AND RESUMÉS DON'T HAVE A SLOT FOR
ANCESTORS. THE INDIGENOUS PEOPLE WHO WALKED THESE TRAILS
AND HILLS AND PADDLED THROUGH CENTURIES OF RIVERS WERE
SUPPOSED TO BURN THEIR STORIES IN FACTORY FLAMES, HAND THEM
OVER IN CONFESSION AND SAY A LIFETIME OF OUR FATHERS TO MAKE
UP FOR THE SIN OF SPEAKING DIRECTLY TO GOD. WHEN I WAS YOUNG
I WANTED A LITTLE CREDIT FOR MY WORK. WANTED SOMEONE TO AC-
KNOWLEDGE THE HOURS I SPENT READING AND WRITING AND HONING
MY SENTENCES WITH LITTLE GIRL SWEAT THAT BLURRED THE INK OF
MY BLOOD. NOW I GIVE CREDIT WHERE CREDIT IS DUE, AND STACK UP
MY NOTEBOOKS WITH GRATITUDE THAT SOMEONE WHO CAME BEFORE
ME SPEAKS TO MY HEART. I KNOW NOW HOW MUCH MY VOICE COMES
FROM THIS GROUND, AND THE DEAD. AND IT IS MY HONOR TO LIFT THEM
OUT OF THEIR GRAVES.

Melissa Pritchard

December 17, 2016

I am thinking of my two year old granddaughter, Juniper Skye, of her wondrous engagement with the world, her joy in each new day, her purity of spirit. Her funny little laugh, and the way she only likes to wear a lavender ballerina tutu and glittery sneakers with lights that flash as she twirls, falls, jumps up again.

I am thinking of the children of Aleppo.

I am thinking of the children I recently mentored at Path to Shine in Columbus, Georgia, some of whom have family members in jail, all of whom struggle with the stigma of poverty.

I am thinking of the children of Flint, Michigan, whose water remains contaminated.

I am thinking of the children on the prisons of poverty we call reservations.

I am thinking of Barron Trump, of the bizarre and badly distorted world he is growing up in, one made of false gold and fool's gold. A poor boy in a gold tower.

I am thinking of my yoga teacher's little girl, who had a role as one of the mice in the Nutcracker last week, of my former students, bearing babies now, raising children of their own.

I am thinking of children whose mothers are in prison, of children in the Phoenix Children's Hospital, a short distance from my house, of the children of migrants and refugees.

How, I wonder, can we respond to the privilege of our lives with anything other than compassion, generosity, kindness and joy?

Have the saints, those recognized and those who quietly and directly touch our own lives, taught us nothing?

Has St. Francis taught us nothing? Mother Teresa? Pope Francis? Martin Luther King? Gandhi? There is an endless list of saints, of course, known and little known. And we all know those who by a word or an act saved our lives, whether they know it or not.

Has art taught us nothing if not to cherish self-expression and be tender with the expression of others?

Have the animals, trees and plants, the constellations, taught us nothing? Trees communicate, nurture one another through their root systems, give of themselves for the good of the community. In the balance between self and selflessness lies survival.

The elephant is a wondrous being, deep with memory, emotion, attachment to other elephants. My dog is a wondrous being as is yours.

I look with immense sadness at our nation, at what has become of the idea of democracy, of justice and liberty for all. I never was one for national patriotism, but now, as our nation is under threat as never before, from within and without, from those who care only for corrupt wealth and power's abuse, I feel a fierce desire to protect our Bill of Rights, our Constitution, our Supreme Court, our Declaration of Independence, the rights of women, of refugees, of the poor, of all genders and ethnicities. I feel a fierce desire to defend the earth, our planet and home, its animals, trees, waters, skies.

I seek inspiration in Walt Whitman, Henry David Thoreau, Gloria Steinem, Elizabeth Warren, in poets, painters, musicians, teachers, doctors, mothers and fathers, in countless, measureless others. In a high tide of others.

"I still believe people are really good at heart." wrote Ann Frank.

I copied her words onto the first page of my first journal when I was fourteen. I still believe it. I see love stories around me every single day, acts of kindness, selflessness, bravery, all indicating the profound goodness of hearts.

A few unscrupulous people, by unfair and conscienceless means, have seized political power, financial power, educational power, environmental power, judicial power – and I am angry.

A therapist once asked me, as I told him of my life, why I never got angry. He would be furious, given my life. I didn't know, I said, quietly priding myself on my inability to rage at what was unjust or unfair, at what at happened to me to put me in a chair, mildly tranquilized, sitting across from that kind man who was my therapist.

I know now that I had only buried my rage, out of fear of its power. I believed it was a negative force, destructive, cruel. I no longer believe that.

Rage, properly directed, given the eloquence of honest language, can be a transformative power, a power with all the force of the goddess Kali or Buddha or Jesus or Indra.

When I am deeply moved, I tend to go silent, I need to ferment what has moved me, go mute. Eventually, and I rarely know when, I find the words I need. The truest, most passionate ones.

So forgive the clumsiness, inadequacy and oversights of this piece. I am enraged at what has happened and is happening since November 8, 2016, the day, some are saying, when Democracy died. I will not say that, not yet, for there is work to be done to address what is happening to this nation, to us, the people of this nation, and I am, by temperament, a stubborn optimist. I will do the work, show up, despite every foul bit of daily news.

I am thinking of Juniper Skye making me soup out of plastic ice cream, plastic peas and water. Of how she feeds me with a little blue spoon, of how good her soup tastes.

I am thinking of the children of Aleppo.

Of the children we all once were.

I will fight for the children, resist without violence or vulgarity. I will be strengthened by the courage and grace of my companions, by those beside me, those still living and by those turned to dust and memory who are, in spirit, ever nearest me.

Lucyna Prostko

What Belongs to Him

*"One may lay violent hands on his own being,
or what belongs to himself..."*
Dante, Canto XI (Transl. Robert Pinsky)

A rock opens its narrow slanting jaw
where yellow foam spits sulfur
and death, until your wrinkled hand

dips into the stream. I know who you are,
with your softening arm on which a bruise
flowers and disappears, and then the purple

black absence of your eye. But now you
belong to this man, who
strangely voracious and sane raises to eat

the purple dust of your dreams. Inexplicable, even now
dozing on a bench in a water-green park, warming the bottle
with both his hands, as if it were a lamp

possessed by a ghost, but you feel for him,
even though your eye won't open for days,
and I cover you with a blanket as if it were an impenetrable wall

against him, and he listens, pokes against the newly grown
skin, wills a door for himself, screams and hits with his fists,
then pleads, but I tell you remember the fairy tale

about the rooster and the fox; if you let him in,
he will not leave you, marking your body
like a map of himself,

the conquest of his creation, brush
painted with the colors of his rage,
as if it were an abstract painting.

You rage, too, drink more than he does,
and cry to my answering machine on New Year's Eve, voices inside you
whimpering rather than weeping.

Why do you insist on running
toward the underground river, as if it were
a holy stream?

                         Holy Mary darkens her brows
and creases over your bed until all that's left
is a black hole, plaster torn around it, as if something

has been tearing at the center of your life, and I see
a new mark, still darker, deeper
inside your breast. You whisper, disappearing like incense

through a window, and he walks away to come back,
not so big this time, but cunning toward the thing he owns.
I shake your hands up in the air, watch how they dangle,

like small mute bells, touch your foot
while you sleep, and you quiver,
a bow stretched to its limit.

                         As a woman over sixty
who has never been sixteen, you are fierce
in love, even when you are cornered

into the last circle.
You are, of course, your own
hell, but I want to reach you, I keep spinning

toward you. I watch
how he blows into his hands
folded as if in a prayer,

or as if about to whistle on the blade
of grass, and how ready he is to bite into
what's left of your succulent lips.

Lucyna Prostko

Layers of a Dream

In a dream, a strange family welcomes me
to this land where I am a mere visitor,
a pebble in a deep stream of history.

They call me their daughter-in-law,
and I give thanks,
stretch my hands to earn my worthiness,

to be beloved of pines and forest spirits.
A granddaughter of a different vision –
my ancestors dragging their trunks

filled with linen shirts and sunlit wishes
through Ellis Island and into Detroit
where they work for many years, blending

into the patchwork of poverty, spilling Polish folk songs
through narrow windows. I am tucked into their dream,
a blanket of stars punctuated

by blue silence.

                    How would I know
I would be walking on this lake shore,
still harboring water lilies, their

yellow eyes guiding dragonflies and loons?
Here I am -- sitting on this rock, tracing its circular patterns with my fingertips –
a history of fissures, scars

through which granite spills into slate, rifts and semi-circles
where the earth contemplates its fate over
and over again.

       When the history turns darker,
I recall my grandmother's struggles, her passage
through deep hells of war, her plea for

another kind of journey. I let the fears
subside, thinking of other beginnings, always
beginnings.

       And I think of my students
the record of their young struggles, their grandparents' wishes
for them, made plain in this hour.

When threatened
by hate, they bow over books, they greet
each other with kindness.

Can they stop violence at its core --
when they speak of fairness and love,
when they comfort one another?

Dean Rader

America I Do Not Call Your Name Without Hope

After Neruda

America I do not call your name without hope
not even when you lay your knife
against my throat or lace my hands
behind my back, the cuffs connecting
us like two outlaws trying to escape
history's white horse, its heavy whip
a pistol shot in the ear. Lost land,
this is a song for the scars on your back,
for your blistered feet and beautiful
watch, it is for your windmills, your
leavened machines, for your fists. It
is for your wagon of blood, for your dogs
and their teeth of fire, for your sons
and the smoke in their hearts. This is for
your verbs, your long lurk, your whir.
This is for you and your fear, your tar,
for the white heat in your skin andfor your blue bones that one day may sing.
This is for your singing. This is for the past,
but not for what's passed. This is for daybreak
and backbreak, for dreams and for darkness.
This song is not for your fight, but it is a song
for fighting. It is a song of flame but not for burning.
It is a song out of breath but a plea for breathing.
It is the song I will sing when you knock
on my door, my son's name in your mouth.

From Dean Rader's forthcoming poetry collection "*Self-Portrait as Wikipedia Entry*" **(Copper Canyon Press; February 2017)**

Major Ragain

The Brief Life of Honeysuckle

That evening in Illinois
on Vernor lake down by the dam,
we were fishing the last light.
The spring sky had cleared
after an hour of hard rain.

For a week, the wild honeysuckle
had been in full boom, a quarter
mile spangle along the dam, gold and white blossoms,
the sweet musky scent lifting us
out of the boat, out of our hard shells.

The sunset kissed clouds had turned
A pale ostrich pink, before fading.
Then, a burst of sound. I looked up
just as they flashed overhead,
a great horned owl pursued by one
red winged blackbird, colors flared,
and led by another redwing.

A few seconds, and they wheeled around
a stand of trees. Gone. Sixteen year old
Bradley spoke with his Cherokee blood tongue,
It's an omen. The opening and closing of a door.

On the way back to the dock,
the words of the prophet Muhammad
came back to me: *God has made a polish*
for everything that tarnishes.
And the polish for the heart is remembrance.

What brushed past me this evening?
That dark wing polishes my
heart, even now.

Margaret Randall

Words. Numbers. Pictures. Distance.

Words felled by backlog stagger off tongues,
break from mouths
into an empty space now numbed to shock.
Words like *terror, loss, why,*
forfeit their ability
to stand where we feel.

Words like *gay, Hispanic* and *Muslim*
only get in the way.
Orlando and *Ataturk*
stretch our map
but place us beyond its crumbling edge.

In the wake of this failure, numbers take a shot:
41 at the airport, 49 in the dance club,
20 school children, 6 teachers, 43
who would have been teachers,
their bodies burned
by men in suited power.

Five unarmed black boys, 5 white police: do these fives
hold a different weight in us,
their wives' bereavement
or children's loss
a different pain?

Pictures step in to try their hand
—worth a thousand—
those final minutes
on a dying cell phone,
last message tweeted home,
notes, flowers, and teddy bears
swelling the newest memorial.

Color crouches beyond the mind's borders,
memorizing itself
upon a future
that may not arrive in time,
memorials barely visible
in rained out distance.

Words, numbers, pictures no longer work
and color only consoles in future tense.
Safe from the viscous stench of death
we are at a fatal remove.
Imminent threat fades to worn rhetoric.
Life at the edge goes on.
Them and *us* is not an answer
that can stop the madness, loss,
descent into post-history.

Margaret Randall

The Morning After

—to the children

It's the morning after and the polar bear
licks blood
from his foot's white fur.
Ice is jagged and cuts, its islands recede
to the beat of human denial.
Far to the south: a dying parrot's heart cries.

It's the morning after and beneath the wall
long scarring our southern border
tunnels carry *coyotes* and their human cargo
while real coyotes and smaller animals
burrow for daily bread, unaware
of a madman's ravings, pompous threat.

It's the morning after. I wish there was a pill.
So many hard-won battles tremble
on this map redrawn by hatred's hand.
The Bully in Chief stands before us:
triumphant, tricked by the deceptive weave
of his own New Clothes.

It's the morning after and emergency rooms
fill with attempted suicides:
queer teenager, black youth, young girl
who hoped her ceiling would begin to crack,
boy whose brother was murdered by the cop
still riding his neighborhood patrol.

Six-year-old Maia tells her mother *Wake me
when Hillary wins.* The next morning
she is afraid to go to school:
If we speak Spanish in the street,
she wants to know,
will they send us away?

It's the morning after. Shock subsides
to fear and rage
throughout the world.
But beware of an elite
still measuring loss by lies and votes,
unable to hear the real stories:

It's the morning after, one of many. Listen
to the heartland's threatened factory,
another child who wakes up hungry,
love too afraid to speak its name
or the single mother of three
without a home.

Trust me rings hollow on the liar's lips.
I will fix it isn't the answer.
Only together can we resist:
by loving, creating,
and embracing the vulnerable among us
four more years.

Margaret Randall

You Cannot Kill Our Spirits

for Standing Rock, Ayotzinapa, and for all those who in our world, struggle against all the dirty wars . . .

it is not only because we dream
to live in a world that battles with ideas
instead of bullets and bombs
of a world that believes
in humans thriving
instead of those
who aspire only dollars

you are afraid of us
and have been for so long
of our beautiful voices
of our Cuahtemocs and Goyathlays
our Crazy Horses, and Sitting Bulls
our Zapatas, Villas, and Sandinos
our Ches, Celias, Fridas, and Fidels
our Ho Chi Minhs, and Arafats
our Malcolms, and Martins
our Russell's, and so many many more
Voices
Ours

but you'll never silence us   no
more of us are born everyday
no matter how many you kill
or how much you distract us
how many you trap
with your shiny things
or that self-medication
still we know in our souls
there is a better way to live
a better way to love
to honor this earth

of which we are all
but a small part

your wanton murder
all that senseless mayhem
the disappearance of our women
our youth our leaders
will not stop us
you cannot kill our spirits
you cannot stop our earth-seeds
from growing up   no
no matter how much you try
our ideas of life and love
will continue to bloom
in the blood of our children
and their children's children

Odilia Galván Rodríguez

Spider Woman

Spider woman weaves
weaves and heals
the holes
in the web
of life
daily torn
by scorn and
disregard
for life
for the living
power

Spider woman weaves
weaves dreams
of the people
to change
the world
spinning
in a new direction
away from
ignorance
away from hate
and greed

Spider woman sees
sees the seeds and
the wheel
of fortune turning
turning out of control
while Mother Earth is
churning all that chaos
and jerking it off her back
she wonders
who will keep their balance
and who will be left
                    Standing

William Pitt Root

"The Only El Dorado That Is Real": Retranslating Neruda

We must open America's matrix to
bring out her glorious light.
Pablo Neruda

1.
Sometimes while sitting with you wide open
      --con diccionarios y café,
            local ravens and sirens
      just outside
            under sun or among stars—
                  from everywhere I still feel again

that stark darkness pressing in
      as I descend in the iron cage
            through a shaft blasted

deep into earth
      with all the others I cannot see
            who cannot see each other.

2.
Near here, for money, years ago,
I worked in that big mine
            below these hills of chaparral
helping to render solid earth
            treacherous
with the hive of hollowed domes and shafts
            inhabited by laborers
who've known this life forever.
                  Down here
only the young talk of love.
Those a little older boast of
"strange" and GTO's.
             By thirty
they will talk lovingly of
their aging cars
      but payments
on the double-wide and doctors
for the wife and kids
      occupy their minds by then,
take their dreams hostage.

3.
The eldest, having learned
to take a certain delight
          from such darkness,
pride themselves on their skills
splitting stones with huge hammers
          in a single blow

while we newcomers with younger muscles
pounding   pounding   pounding
          end our first shifts
half finished but done in.
While oldtimers under hot showers whistle
          we hoist our mud-caked gear

creaking up to the ceiling on
great treble hooks gleaming
                    where, hung like
          so many gutted miners,
      by the next day everything's

          dried hard as bone.

4.
I remember at the end of each shift
that feeling
          as the man-train
brought us over dark rails through firedoor
          after firedoor, brought us in
          from the lines farthest out,
the places where no one would reach us if there was a fire

back to the lift-cage rattling its half mile
                    up the mainshaft, often in silence,
          as everyone prayed the cable would hold yet again
and suddenly
there was the world:
                    desert bleached by blind sunlight,
               night sky opened wide by stars.

5.
Men die in such places,
as you well know:
               Some unbent, some broken,
falling into holes
they don't see
               and the holes they do.

And it was just such a place
          you came to,
                    summoned
from the labyrinths

of the written word
　　　　by men black-faced,
black-lunged,
　　　eyes still
　　　　　fierce as fire.

And it was there,
　　　　at the Lota coal mine,
　　　　　　that you found

among the miners emerging
　　　　　that one-- face disfigured by fatigue,
　　　　　　　eyes blinking dust—
"rising as if out of hell"
　　　onto the fiery nitrate field,
　　　　　who extended his hand to you,

proclaiming
　　　"I have known you
　　　　my brother, for a long time."

6.
When you were killed, Don Pablo, fearful for their own lives
the people braved machine guns, clubs, defying
　　　　visors black as insect eyes to march forbidden
through streets crying out your name, shouting
and calling out lines from your poems, singing
　　　　down into the darkness of death to you,
hero of their love, hero of love's courage, you
who mined their hearts tirelessly your whole life,
　　　　refining that ore into the airy gold of hope,
the only El Dorado real for them,
the only El Dorado that is real.

Appeared first in the author's *STRANGE ANGELS: New Poems* (Wings Press, 2013)

Joseph Ross

Choice

My ballot blocks my throat,
making it painful

to sing, speak, even cough.
I always thought

it would be enough. Now
the torn skin must

speak. The wet wound
must sing its protest.

We must find the streets
again, our human chants.

We must insist, with our throats
raw, our lips unsure.

Our neighbor-citizens
have eaten a rotten fruit.

We did not love them
out of it. We did not listen

with our hands. We did
not confront our deepest

sin when they spoke it.
We have swallowed

a page from a discredited
book. A lie revealed

as a lie, hundreds of times

over. This page of fear,

this invitation to hate
our neighbors. These

words live now,
because somehow,

we chose them.

Lindsey Royce

Bus Ride With Potluck and Apathy

i.

A chorale of stories and shallow slicks
leave me weighing the impact
the oncoming truck
might have on this bus.

This Coca Cola semi,
nostalgic logo passing,
whose ad agency teaches
the world to sing in perfect harmony.

People pass time jawing trivialities,
yarns scrubbed for seatmates
and limp as wet newsprint.

while my mind spins out
like a pamphlet-crazed mimeograph
and trees brown by the highway
bend from exhaust.

ii.

Talk of Thanksgiving
weeps down the windshield,
rain more urgent
than Natives being forced from their land,
even cheers for the big game.

Those who want love and compassion
for themselves
hiccup gossip with no sense of urgency
that since the election

a gang yanked a noose
around a Black boy's neck,
another went wilding in a tricked-out pickup
and hospitalized two men for holding hands,

yet another Black man was murdered
for singing.

Bright neon eyes
watch savagery, calm as stars,
and I ask the night,
Please open our hearts and mouths,

but silence those who would die for nothing,
who gripe when a player takes a knee
as if the flag now symbolized something human.

Abel Salas

I Stand

For my nephew Tayo [TA-YO]

I stand with the student Dreamers
I stand with Black Lives Matter
I stand with Tatanka Yotanka
And the great-grandfather
Buffalo who gave Sitting Bull
His vision and his name
I stand with the families
Of the 43 in Ayotzinapa
Of Trayvon and all those
Merely guilty of colored skin
I stand in the skin I'm in
I stand with the skins at
Standing Rock to protect
The water with prayer and
A hope, a belief born in the
Blood of ancestors who fought
To protect the herds of buffalo
A sacred relative who gave
Them food, warmth and life
I stand with the stampede
Of one-thousand bison come
To say they hear our cries of
Pain and how they, too, will
Stand beside the two-legged
Warrior women and men in
Defense of our mother, for we
Have no other, say our buffalo
Brothers, and her rivers carry
The memories of all our dead
To a final place of peaceful rest
Upon the sea where our relatives
In skies above with feathered skin
Watch over them, even as cousins
Dressed in scales and dancing fins
Sing them to sleep with lullabies
Dreaming of what once had been

Metta Sáma

& on the fifth day God created

the whales later destroyed in a novel
about the unbearable whiteness of being
a white whale in foamy white waters prodded
at by white men upon a ship with white sails
God's awe we like to call them Jonah we say
to add shock to his story was swallowed by a whale
but really it was just a big fish unsignified
& frankly merciful three days + three nights
Jonah squatted in the *belly of hell* safe & sound
from all sorrow except his own I reckon
I should make some allusion to ships and slavery
the middle passage but all I can think about is
#wypipo and Jonah's un violent story and the great
white whale's violent one you see can't you
one story begins and ends with brown people
seeking justice forsaking God to return to the goodness
of Genesis and one story begins and ends with white people
plotting the slaughter of something greater than them
a dream of superiority   perhaps I should back off
from talking race in these times of post postracial mythology
and pre truth and pre trump and post dupe & God
said it was all good it was all good it was all supposed to be good

Metta Sáma

It's hard to imagine loving God

of the Bible such an impossible
figure floating and yes ethereal
& lodged too firmly in our minds
oh god we lament why hast thou
forsaken us oh god isn't that just
the funniest thing ever oh god
I'm coming I'm coming oh god at
other times we ask if god is alive if god is
listening if god loves us why tsunami
why drought why wildfires why flood
why hurricane why tornado why typhoon
why is the arctic melting why is the great
barrier reef stressed out why did mount
nevado del ruiz wake after two decades
of slumber where is this God of the bible
oh god oh god oh god are you there
it's me it's me it's me

Lauren Schmidt

The Social Worker's Advice

The Haven House for Homeless Women and Children

Jabbing a finger at my face, you say, *You can't have*
empathy. Empathy will eat you alive, as if empathy
were a beast with feathers, fur, and hair, with hind legs
and deft feet, wings and claws, a beast that soars,
stalks, lunges, springs, a beast that chases, a beast
that screams instead of sings, with giant jaws
and a tongue budded with a rapacious taste for fools
like me, fools who don't believe the beast exists to eat,
who let it burrow its snout between our legs, fingers,
up to our armpits—the spaces of our common human stink.

But you see a beast that sniffs and snarls for a thick blue vein
to sic, and when I look at you I understand the beast more plainly—
I see that its skin collects pock marks each time you dock
merit points to teach the mothers not to "talk Black,"
I see that its forehead sprouts a thousand of your scornful eyes,
its claws slash as swift and deep as your condescension—

because what you mean is that I can't have empathy
for these girls, for times like these, for a place like this,
for Nicole who tallies the number of days it's been
since she last flushed her veins with a spoon-cooked mix,
twenty-eight days and counting. No empathy
for Nicole because she can never seem to find
matching socks for her four-year-old son, or because
she folds flowers from twice-used computer paper
to calm her nerves. Bouquets of paper daisies
sprout from vases on all four tables in the dining room.

What you mean is that I can't have empathy for Takina,
 who was told to go by Tina because her white, adoptive
mother—middle-aged, middle-classed—prefers it.
Her birth-mother is five years gone and Tina-Takina
thinks she might be pregnant again. I can't have empathy
for Denice who is pregnant with her third, but didn't know
until she was too far in, for Angelica who fell down the stairs

while holding her infant son, too spent from pre-sun
feedings and weeping in the wee hours as minutes lurch by.
Each tick-tock is the sound of the dead-locked door
of the nighttime aide who snores in the small room
near the exit like a beast at the gates, preventing escape
from this place, this time, from lives like these
without signing a release form for the Division of Youth
and Family Services, like Dionna, who took her two kids
to a hotel where, alone, at night, she stares at ceiling holes
in the red glow of the word VACANCY flashing through
windows with no curtains. I can't have empathy for La Quita,
so thin that when she aims her breast at her baby's lips,
she prays she has something wet and real to give.

When you say, with your wagging finger, *You can't have
empathy. Empathy will eat you alive*, what you mean
is that I can't have empathy for these girls, and when I look
at you, I cannot help but wonder when you first believed
empathy would do more than sniff and lick your palms.

So, I say, let it take me, then, this beast of your invention,
let it slip its fangs into my skin and tear through my throat,
let it suck all the fat and blood from off my solid bones.

Reprinted with the author's permission from *Filthy Labors*, Northwestern University Press, 2017

Susan Scheid

Breaking News (dateline Washington, DC)

We interrupt this program to let you know that Racism is alive and well despite reports of its death earlier this century. R not only managed to survive what seemed like its imminent demise, but seems to be thriving and strong. R had hidden from the public view and many speculated that it was not going to live much longer. Spokespersons for R deny that R was ill, stating only that R was staying out of the public eye for "personal reasons". However, thanks to a long-shot quack, and some miracle incantations, R began to slowly re-emerge this year. Spokespersons for R said, in interviews over the summer, that R would "tell it like it is" and "openly speak [its] mind," although no details were forthcoming immediately. However, by late summer it was obvious that R had gained much strength and when R's full recovery was announced in the beginning of November, our reporters had a chance to speak with R. In private interviews, R disclosed, when we asked about future plans now that the public knew of R's struggle and full recovery, R simply stated, "Why, make America great again, of course."

Lee Sharkey

Tyrannus

—Leonard Baskin (1982)

Insistent blank colossal male afflatus, inexorable graphic engine in dire sem-
blance to ourselves. Sniggling the threads of our being. I brood him out of an old
black book, densities of white and blackness speaking to the eyes. As he repels
me so he compels me, smelling like ink and reading like triumph, the blind bulk of
him, the microcephalic terror. The forest of his vacant pride. I cover my head and
am visited by angels slathered in oil and ash. I Am Who I Am, his circumscribe,
bent over him, scoring code into every crossing, rendering his primate hand as
an overhang of branches. I nest a blackbird in his thigh. Turn your head, look
closely—his tiny scrotum becomes an egg.   ◆

Lee Sharkey

On history

The big trees gone, and the bulls, gone to slaughter
To survive here requires iron labor
All night the rain slaps down on a stone

♦

After years of buying food for the dead
we have something coming for their gold crowns

♦

To arrive at the placid face of the woman
bending and lifting, sliding an iron over cotton
I have sold 500,000 to slavery
crossed the bottomless sea on my fingertips

♦

Look how the fathers adore their children
slinging them over their shoulders
their limbs limp, silk

Kim Shuck

War Song

If you've dreamed of invisibility as a quiet space with
No edges if you've
Practiced invisibility
At the supermarket and in the
Streets if you
Built your own worlds
Gradually opened the windows
Added mirrors one by one and
Sometimes were surprised that you
Cast a reflection at all if you had to
Teach yourself to speak
Word by word in a language that
Excluded you then
Gradually
Created yourself there from each
Coaxed letter from each
Sound invented in your
Moments of transparency
If you are one of the
Translucent if you create worlds out of your own
Flesh
Meditate on the pavement
Fade steadily in your birth home
If you sing
Songs from outcast cultures
Rejected identities if you are
Illegal on streets in
Toilets or in
Schools if you still build lay
Strong words
Words that can support the weight of a person
Words that can be nailed over windows the
Storm is now and
Maybe the storm is always we can
See you we can see you still

Peggy Shumaker

Parenthood, Unplanned

When a jasmine-scented
teenager (not yet my mother)

came up pregnant
with me, my father

stepped up.
They did what teenagers did

in 1951. Married.
Mismatched

spectacularly--
fifteen years of yelling and beer.

Four kids and two
miscarriages

before she turned
twenty-four.

No education
past high school.

So after the divorce,
crap jobs,

crappier men,
government cheese,

no sleep.
Haunted, her eyes.

There are men
making decisions

right now
about lives of girls

and women.
Some do not want

children to know
how their bodies work.

Some do not trust
women to make

decisions. As if
women were people,

as if women
know what's best

for their lives,
for the lives

of their children.
That broken teen

who carried me, who
pushed me out

into this world,
that brilliant

ragged girl
died young, worn down

in her thirties.
One small life,

I know. The only life
she had. I speak for her

when I say
Let women live.

Let women be.

Aisha Sabatini Sloan

Dear America,

Once, after a bad breakup, I made myself do yoga every day for two weeks. I dedicated myself to some limitations for this daily routine: I ad libbed from a sequence in the practice manual we used when I completed yoga teacher training and listened to an hour-long episode of the radio show *On Being*. I tried to let Krista Tippett determine the duration of my practice but usually after a half hour of stretching and some super abbreviated sun salutations I was up and googling the Beatles song about the weepy guitar and writing the lyric on facebook and crooning "I don't know why nobody told you how to unfold your love" into the computer screen while snot ran down my face.

Settling into savasana took in what Joanna Macy said in her interview with Krista about how pain, when faced, turns. I brought my knees into my chest as I sobbed while she read her translation of Rilke, "Let everything happen to you. Beauty and terror. Just keep going. No feeling is final. Don't let yourself lose me." I don't know that this practice hastened or lightened the mourning process but it felt important to harness my grief and shove it into something potentially transformative.

Last week, my girlfriend and I flew to New York for a visit. Even though I had lived in Brooklyn for a couple of years once upon a time, I felt nervous to go back, ride the train and be in a big city after being so used to a small one. Almost immediately we traded in our big world anxieties for the excitement of the everyday. Late one night we were led into a room where Ocean Vuong and Juan Felipe Herrera and Natalie Diaz and Saeed Jones and Rigoberto Gonzalez were eating dinner. It didn't feel so delusional to believe, for a spell, in magic. We decided that everything was going to be ok, president wise, in order to get through the trip. Toward the end we noticed that we were starting to float away into a kind of delusional paradise, using the term "dissociation" a lot when someone brought up politics. When we got home we found the fear waiting for us in the living room. I realized at that we seemed to be moving beautifully through the real live stages of grief—depression, denial.

I entered into "bargaining" the other day when somebody on facebook mentioned writing letters to the electors. I decided to throw myself into it the way I tried to get really effective when called upon to write letters to the staff of a prison that held my nephew in solitary confinement for over a year. I am mostly an ethos pathos kind of girl, so these letters had the tone of Oliver Twist cowering with a bowl in his hands.

With the electors I tried to think of the fastest trick to their heart-guts. I peered at their names and chose from a list of heroes on a Wikipedia page for action adventure movie heroes/villains and wrote in big, bold letters: **"This moment in time is like the end of an action adventure film. You are Matt Damon. You are the hero. Be the hero. Please."** I also tried Will Smith, The Girl with the Dragon Tattoo, Julia Roberts, Russell Crowe and Liam Neeson. I never did Catherine Zeta Jones for some reason. Quick question: is it just me or are most of those electors white?

A day after I sent that batch of letters, I decided to reach out to another set of electors with a different approach: watercolors. I put on Issa Rae's show, *Insecure*, and tore watercolor paper that I'd meant to use for Christmas cards last year into post card sized sheets. I addressed them first and then painted on them using a very dried out watercolor set running low on blue and yellow. I brought out my acrylics. I got abstract for a few hours. There were some, how do you call it, pink *washes*. Some dots. I like to do a red line across the page sometimes. A Diebenkornish gesture. There were a couple of good ones. I had had half bottle of wine by the time I wrote, "I emplore you. No, I implore you," to somebody in Texas or Arkansas, followed by a message that conveyed my very specific hopes for their electoral vote decision.

I woke up feeling dehydrated and exhausted from hours of the kind of non-sleep you get when you drank too much bad red wine and kept the salt lamp on while *Frasier* played for several hours into the night and you didn't even bother to brush your teeth until two am after eating Karamel Sutra ice cream and you never asked your dog to move over so your back is sore. And then to be faced with this fiasco: your girlfriend is out of town with the car. You have a bike, an empty stomach, lots of caffeine in your system, and no stamps. How do you buy stamps without going all the way to the post office?

After I put a bunch of abstract art in the mail for twenty nine strangers I got back on my bike and felt so empowered that I entered swiftly into the "I need to jog and clean the house" phase that I usually require if I'm going to stop spinning out into a destructive mess. So I had my dog drag me half a mile up the road and back and I mopped to Pop Culture Happy Hour and eventually I realized that it was time to start doing yoga again. And that it might be necessary to do yoga and meditate every day now, and not drink so much, and feel my fear more. And clean up the dog shit from the back yard. And listen to music that might let my soul maneuver itself around all those feelings. Feelings like: an orphanage of children in Aleppo asking to live.

In a recent article for The Guardian, Rebecca Solnit asked all of us to take re-sponsibility for coming up with the big idea that could keep him out of office: "It's up to us, which means it's up to you. Think big. And act." Inspired, I quoted her to some friends over dinner. We sat under a lamp made from deer antlers. We were talking about what we could do. Every time we had an idea that made my heart beat faster, the light dimmed or surged. We looked at each other like kids in a movie hovering hands over a ouija board, baffled by the possibility of our own power.

Every few days, I realize that I have the responsibility to clear a path for better ideas, as Solnit has pleaded. Less wine, more meditation. As this year comes to a close I hope we can all use the tools we have cultivated, whatever they are, in order to make the space for the idea that could save us.

Love,

Aisha Sabatini Sloan

Patricia Smith

Excerpt from Saga of the Accidental Saint

March 3, 2014, Iberia Parish, LA—
Police say that Victor White III, 22,
shot himself while handcuffed
in the back of a police cruiser.

November 19, 2013, Durham, NC—
Police say that Jesus Huerta, 17,
shot himself while handcuffed
in the back of a police cruiser.

July 29, 2012, Jonesboro, AR—
Police say that Chavis Carter, 21,
shot himself while handcuffed
in the back of a police cruiser.

He reached back and found
his own hands with his own
hands, worked his bound
fingers to set his free fingers
loose, then used that shackled
hand to free the other shackled
hand, and the freed shackled
hand, still shackled, was still
bound to the other hand once
both were freed. Once free
in the shackles, the shackled
hands turned to the matter
of the gun, which couldn't be
there because they'd searched
my baby twice and a gun is
a pretty big thing unless it isn't,
unless it is dreamed alive by
hands that believe they are no
longer shackled. Stunned in

cuffs, but free and searching,
the left and right hands found
a gun with a stink like voodoo,
a gun that couldn't have been
there, wasn't there, but was.
The left-handed him used
a cuffed hand, which could
have been either left or right
(since both were free), to root
around for a trigger and fire
a bullet into the right of his left-
handed head, impossible but
not really, since the preferred
killing hand may have preferred
its shackles. The policemen,
who had searched my baby
twice and cuffed both his free
and unfree hands behind his
back before his hands found
his own hands and pulled,
heard no human sound at all
during all that frantic magic,
no *fuck!* as my boy struggled
to get his left shackled hand
to do what his right shackled
hand wouldn't do, no frenzied
pound of one bracing foot
against the door, no grunt
or whoop of glee to mark all
all those times he slipped out
of custody and in again. But
what they did hear the bang
of the gun that wasn't there
(but was) just when it sent
that bullet into the right side
of his left-handed head. *Sounds
like sacrifice,* they thought.
Slumped, eyes cocked and
undone, my child was amazed
at the sweet hoodoo he had
managed. Both left and right
hands were shackled and free
behind him, there was an eerie
perfect circle of smoke in his
hair. *Suicide,* they both said at

the very same time, and since
it was odd how they had reached
the same conclusion, they smiled
and shook their heads. Noting
the shackles, they praised their
God in the light of miracle while
the boy who couldn't have done
what he did, but did, bled down
to zero. *Guess he couldn't take it,*
one of the alive said to the other.
He didn't mean wearing the shackles.
He meant not wearing them.

Patricia Smith

When the rock

is split, the operative noun is resurrection—
the ragged skin of soldiers softens as compromised light
ekes across their jawlines and the backs of their hands.
Guns reconsider their blooded smoke, go limp with orchard.

When the rock is split, the bladed wind of the ax swing
cools the brow of a father in Baltimore,
a man angry with his own color.
He is pressed flat to the floor with factory,

beneath the confounded squeals of his children
and a refrigerator begging for cheap cuts of eat.
When the rock is split, he remembers to stand.
When the rock is split, black boys who have

succumbed to various phases of murder
flip their hoods down from exploded crowns
and claw for the ghost of their gone mothers.
When the rock is split, those mother stop short

of that tragic bend over fresh tombs. They no
longer loop endlessly through that necessary line,
their hair sweated flat beneath bandanas,
their bellies tight and writhing with the next

victims of war. Before the ax is swung, forgive
them for crying out at the sight of the blade.

When the rock is split, war is relegated to backdrop,
the staticky crackle of cliche on the grayed face
of a 1950s television screen. John Wayne ambles
through the smoke to tell us how wildly and wrongly

we have been dreaming. When the rock is split,
a single language will burst with bound fury from
the new throat. We will all speak in the backslap
of music threaded with jazz measure and trumpet.

Though yes, there will still be heartache's thin
thread. We will still scream we will still weep, we
will still be so remarkably us. When the rock is split,
we will not succumb to the lies history has told us.

We will not join hands, to warble new alliance toward
the heavens. That lyric misled us. We are not the world.
Instead we will lift the single hand of the man or woman
beside us and we will study its lines, its history of dawns

and plummeting suns. When the rock is split, nothing
changes at all except everything. Refugees rise from dust,
borders waver and whip, a son in Chicago comes home.
The son is once again the overwhelm, the expletive that

dies in the mouth of the hater and who doesn't hear?

Melissa Studdard

Last Dance

I wanted to take a selfie with the world
but her black eye could not be covered

nor the midnight in her gait so I asked
her to dance instead. Two moons in her

feet, two stars, two phosphorescent fish—
how they swam across her strange islands,

dragging behind them lines of tackle and bait.
Protruding from her side, an arrow fletched

with mottled turkey feathers bled splinters
and dust around her own scarred-over wound.

She did not cry as she lifted her broken
and bangled arm to drape across my shoulder

but it was then I saw she was bleeding from
her nose and breathing shallow, arrhythmic

waves of pain. On her banks, squid and starfish
washed up dead and slicked in black. *Who did*

this to you? I asked, thinking of revenge. She
pointed, then, at me, rewrapped her arms around

my neck, and we began our next dance as one
bold shadow against the petrochemical glow.

Melissa Studdard

he

loosened the pussy bow
& grabbed the pussy
& fattened the country
on split and enriched
meal & led all the dicks
to the booth to breed
hate & miscounted
the ratio of pig to stall
& mishandled the chick
ens who are so depressed
they no longer make eggs
& everyone eats sawdust
off the barn house floor
& some of us are dying
while others are convin-
ced that sawdust is gold

Carmen Tafolla

Floricanto Al Agua

Prayer from San Antonio 2016 to Standing Rock

Agua, Agua Dulce
Waterfall of Life transforming
Rainshower Bloom of Promise
Blessed Bloodflow of our Planet
Agua, Agua Dulce

These Guardians of the Water speak to her with
respeto for the joy-drenched miracle of life
walk filled with courage to protect the future
con cariño for the children yet to come
Stand tall against the teargas
and the bullets slammed into their faces
the freezing hoses stabbing icicles into their skin
facing sharp-toothed dogs and well-paid,
well-armed guards. They stand tall
and vow to save the water

And we, Cousins from the Corners of the World,
echo their song, sing strength, pray action, fight
For THIS is the hour
for sense and ceremony
respeto rippling into our blood
For WE are the water
and when the water is poisoned
so are we
And when the hour is past
so are
we

Listen with your soul. Here ring the ripping breaths
of a woman spirit trying to birth this planet
and its offspring into life
Through a labor hard, outcome uncertain
There is no longer time to turn away
for her voice has gone dry as cracked leaves
from trees already drinking death
and her water

has broken

Carmen Tafolla

United States December 2016, when the Cabinet-Elect is headed by Exxon & Banking CEOs

The Indians of Standing Rock stand guard,
some with their VietNam Vet baseball caps,
some with their Medals of Honor,
protecting water on their land
from companies sold rights
that were not owned.
Against the jailings and the beatings, they stand firm,
armed only with their love of mother earth
as the oil pipelines cut through tender bellies
of their land and slap the rivers with knuckled
pipe sealed with a tar-based
glue....

The City of Corpus Christi has just advised
its residents that city water is not safe
Neither to eat nor wash nor bathe
and that not even boiling it will help.
Perhaps some leakage from a nearby pipe
Perhaps some odd occurrence underground.
Corpus Christi, Body of Christ,
Body of Christ... This is my
body...

Fracking Companies in South Texas
rape the earth and crack her core
tap the hidden poisons of the underworlds
and cloud these pristine ranchos with odd fumes
that bring strange coughs that do not seem
to leave the lungs for months, then *just forget*
to seal the holes where stank dark gasses
keep on pouring up, *just pack*
their bags and profits with a tip of
their new cowboy hat, *just say*
Frack You...

Doctors report the cases of black lung disease
multiplied at such a magnitude it makes no sense
not even to the coalminers who for generations
breathed these fumes sent leaking through
fragmented cracks now soured and changed
from something rotten at the core. *Something is
happening, something new, they plead. These men
now die much younger, rate ten times higher than
ten years ago. Something new must be in what they
breathe…*

The new head of the D. of Energy,
the same one who forgot its name
and once believed it was a useless place,
says there's no need to clutter us with rules
and no need to protect an earth that's doing
fine. And all the "experts" He appoints
are oddly amused when all these letters cross their
desks from people who should have better things to
do. They scratch their heads at repetitious
patterns of complaints and oddities of nature
happening now and wonder what in the *world*
could be causing all this mess. Then ride on home
in their new car, and turn the set on to Reality TV,
where crazy mean indignities are being piled
on losers who just laugh. *Just
laugh.*

Jon Tribble

Testimony Bed

I know the faces of hate that curl
around our passing like shell casings
hickory nuts shed each autumn twist
back into a hard knot of useless wrapping.

Wrecked-car, tar-paper neighborhood
where every other fence held back
a "white dog" nurtured on fury waiting
to unleash on any passing dark face.

Side by side we cannot pass out of sight
in enough of a hurry without these
small Southern towns turning sinister
as our past and present history—

classmates beside me in first grade asked
to pass along notes "encouraging"
their parents to consider "majority-minority
schools" less than a decade after Central High.

The Midwest was a heavy white blanket
we smothered beneath as an invisible novelty,
but in Little Rock the battle lines are as clear
as the faces of the children we pass by,

their small hands clinging to the dark or light
hand of the parent on watch, a mother
or father whose glance passing our direction
carries more knowing than either of us has.

It is not political nor politic, not temporary
nor ever likely to simply pass without some
notice, but when we intertwine our fingers
and walk together we give witness to lives

and a nation where so much depends upon
who you pass each night beside, what truth
lingers each morning in promises that dress
the bed tighter than any white sheet ever could.

(Published previously in *Natural State*, Glass Lyre Press, 2016).

Jon Tribble

Declaration

The white supremacists next door are feeding the squirrels again—
the plywood lean-to they set up against the oak's trunk
during last December's flattening cold and heavy ice now
a springtime fixture with a dish of birdseed out front
which never seems to empty. When I first noticed their effort
to shelter the bushytail bandits from the freezing air,
Darwinian indignation rose within me, the question boiling out,
Who saves squirrels in a town ratty with them?
But I've never asked. I let this family—a mother
and two adult sons as best as I can tell—live in peace.

Let me be blunt: my wife is black and I am white,
though neither of us resembles the colors
these monochromatic labels usually signify.
We walk together in this world in an always obvious fashion
and we know where not to be and when.
These are the lessons of our particular time and place.

Still, a house is not merely brick and wood;
it is often also illusion. The safety of neighborhood
watches, of smiles and waves, all the comfortable familiarities
can crumble like a wormy foundation when a flag
announces its allegiance in the night.
                                        Our neighbors have three—
two Confederate battle flags positioned for careful effect:
the largest, the centerpiece of the living room,
proclaiming their picture-window "heritage"
to every car driving down our street;
the smaller stars and bars scrimmed behind the beige curtain
in the bedroom facing *our* house, so that each night
when the lights come on this reminder of segregationist pride
greets our returning home.

These two would be enough,
statements from garden-variety White Citizens Councils
and their poorer relations in the Klan, remembrances of things
not long past. The third flag concerns me more,
a red banner on the other window of the same corner bedroom
that reminds me of reports on White Aryan Resistance
brutalities, Christian Identity rallies, militarized camps
of the Cross, the Sword, and the Arm of the Lord type,
the public and scary private aggression
from internet-fostered marketing of hate.
I haven't sneaked close enough to be sure whose particular pride
this accent of interior decorating means to celebrate,
haven't crept past the sleeping squirrels at night—
the only time the flag shines through for the outer world—
to examine the details of the cloth's design
like it was a cell section of a biopsy, a tumor
either benign or malignant.

I am afraid of stepping across
that invisible fence between our properties, or, if "afraid"
is not entirely accurate, I am cautious.
Hunteresque scenarios (the white supremacist fantasy
of a lone wolf executing interracial couples by the author
of the *Turner Diaries*), bullet-in-the-back scenes
from the Medgar Evers-Alan Berg history of cowardly
intimidation—I grew up in the Little Rock of post-Central High,
a place where *niggerlover* was surer fighting words
than even *cocksucker*—I know the animal as sure as I knew
Marlon Perkins and Jim would never harm the tiger
they trapped in the net-and-spring snare on *Mutual of Omaha's
Wild Kingdom*—if you recognize the danger
in a thing you can live with it, carefully.

We do owe the squirrels so much. My wife and I
joke about them training on their new obstacle course,
mobilizing a furry first-strike brigade, their blitzkrieg
through the neighborhood driving out the chipmunks
and the bunnies, not to mention wreaking havoc
on the strategies of our other neighbor's cats.
When I saw the mother planting pansies in their back yard,
I imagined *Mein Kampf* ice cream socials,
goosestepping barbecues going on all summer long
in her blossoming victory garden. Our dark humor
is not funny, but it sustains us. It is in bad taste—like hate.

In the Law School in our university town,
a stern face joins the field of smiles and frowns
on the plaques commemorating past graduating classes.
But this student was not only a would-be lawyer;
he named himself Pontifex Maximus of the World Church
of Creativity, a racial superiority religion preaching
separatism, extermination, and war.
When Morris Dees of the Southern Poverty Law Center
came to speak here, he asked that this man and his followers
be seated closest to the stage, and Morris told the audience
early and often, "I'm not here for you, I'm here for them,"
motioning to the front row. I doubt they were listening,
but he kept speaking.

        The next summer, over the Fourth of July
weekend, one of the Pontifex's former acolytes apparently
loaded up a light blue Taurus with a small arsenal
and proceeded to target Orthodox Jews leaving Sabbath
services in Rogers Park—six were shot—
before fatally wounding Ricky Byrdsong while he was walking
with two of his children in front of his house in Skokie, Illinois.
Before leaving the Chicago area, the suspect shot at
an Asian-American couple in a vehicle in Northbrook.
A series of shootings took place across central Illinois—
two incidents targeting African Americans in Springfield;
a minister was shot twice in Decatur; and an Asian student
from the University of Illinois was shot
as he walked with friends in Champaign-Urbana.
On Independence Day, Won-Joon Yoon, a 26-year-old
graduate student, was shot twice in the back and killed
outside a Korean United Methodist church in Bloomington, Indiana.
Later that night, following a reported carjacking of a van
and a high-speed chase by police, the suspect
was fatally wounded when he shot himself. He died
in a hospital just up the interstate from where we live.

Over thirty states in the U.S. elected Klan leaders at one time
or another—it's not class or gender or ethnicity or upbringing,
though any of these can be the switch that first turns off the light.
Bad ideas are boils festering on the skin of our collective body—
leave them alone or merely pick at them, they infect and grow.

I struggle to tolerate the intolerant,
the ACLU's absolutes on free speech are intellectually right
and eminently defensible, but when in high school

I stumbled upon "Custer's Revenge," a video game
that rewarded the player who killed the most Indians,
burned the most teepees, with a squaw
to rip the clothes off of at the end, when I first heard
the Holocaust jokes about a Volkswagen and its ashtray,
I felt as if my hand were slammed in a car door
by someone who wanted to watch how much I would scream.
So I must think of the squirrels before I think of my neighbors
because the squirrels are not drilling in military formations
as they roll and fall over their ramp of plywood—
they are merely playing, loving, if squirrels can love,
this different moment in the world's shape than the trees and branches,
the grass and rocks of their usual existence.
And the squirrels are the best reminder that my neighbors
have within the capacity to cherish something simple,
vulnerable, starving, and dying in the cold.

I am not forgiving them, which is not my place.
My life and my wife's life do not allow me to forget
that they are there: but I also know they are everywhere.
We hold these Truths to be self-evident, that neighbors all
are people nearby, with rooms or apartments or houses—
slow-moving vehicles accumulating damage,
a friend once told me—and that good neighbors
help out and bump into one another
no more than they want or need to. So if their presence
sometimes causes me to crank up the volume
when I'm listening to Bob Marley singing
"Get Up, Stand Up," or War inviting "Why Can't We
Be Friends?," or Parliament Funkadelic celebrating
"One Nation Under a Groove"—I'll try to keep it down
to a respectable level, but I did want them to know
there is other music, better songs to dance to.

Melissa Tuckey

Truck Fump Manifesto

I want to live in a country where my black and brown friends have time to create art, save the economy, heal the planet, cure cancer, bake cookies, and enjoy their children, instead of mourning, mourning, mourning the death of everyone and everything. I want to live in a country where my white friends share the grief of every needless death. Love so fierce it cracks us open. I want us not to forget who we are.

I want the fireflies in the late night trees behind your house to be the only sparks flying tonight. I want a cacophony of birds faithfully singing the world awake to be the only legislators.

I want sleep. I want you to have sleep. If you can't have sleep, I want your waking hours to be illuminated books reminding you that beauty will outlive us. I want dragonflies with metallic painted wings. A darkness of shining eyes – all of us breathing in this mystery together.

I want all children to know they are brilliant and safe. I want no spirit to have to grow up at four years old. I want no locked and loaded, no hallway patrol, no armed guards on the playground, no hiding place for sharpshooters. I want people of conscience to return to their work dreaming the world.

I want the blessing of rain--the movement of water-- the communal nature of nurture, the shared cup. I want no more reduction, no more language that doesn't recognize the sanctity in every being. I want laughter at the family barbecue. I want a fourth of July that celebrates kindness instead of guns. I want a sanctuary for bees. A country for the beautiful multiplicity that is us.

Melissa Tuckey

Dear mother,

I forgive you for giving birth to me, just as
you have forgiven me for being born—some births
are easier than others, at nineteen, you followed
a man across state lines to be his bride, with me
in utero. No mother mothered you as you tried
to figure out how to suckle, how to calm—
how to do all these things without sleep or money.

We lived together in clouds of cigarette smoke,
as you worked your way through college.
Thank goodness you chose the right man—
he did not run from us—but stayed
all of these years. And when it was time for us
to both grow up, you taught me how to fight
and I taught you how to let go.

But now at 50, I am not sure I can return your calls.
There's something difficult we must discuss.
I think you know what it is. Please tell me how
you plan to keep me safe from the man that you elected
because I do not intend to stay out of harm's way
when everything I love is being destroyed.

Yrs. Truly,

Luis Alberto Urrea

Hymns to the Broken: my manifesto

(Written and Presented at Tin House, July 2016. Portland, Oregon.)
I am stripped,
but not afraid.
-- Rick Elias

Dearly Beloved--

you know why we're gathered here.

My family and I are given to epic journeys. We ramble on, in love with poking around. This career of mine has afforded us the freedom to go. Pretty much at will. Jess Walter knows it was not always this way for many of us. Except in our minds. Except when we were reading books.

Some years ago, we were driving through Navajo lands. We stopped at a road-side store, and the indigenous man working inside suddenly cried, "I can't take this shit no more!" An unseen woman in back shouted, "I can't take this shit no more me too!" Their accents reminded me of my own ancestors' accents in Mexico. And *not taking this shit no more me too* seemed like an excellent place to be when it's time to finally write something with purpose.

I come from a formerly rock-clogged dirt road called Rampa Independencia. Independence Ramp. On the western edge of an outhouse-rich barrio called Colonia Independencia. Independence Colony. On a hill above the Great Walled City of Tijuana, Baja California, Mexico.

This is a good place to come from if you're strong enough, and you're funky enough. If you want to become a writer. Everyone around me is vaguely embarrassed when I bring it up, which is why I start every reading by saying, "Tijuana in the house." Tijuana's so uncouth. Own it.

The orange-faced power-cowboys want us to be ashamed. Shame keeps us silent. Silence keeps us invisible. The meek shall inherit the earth--once they vanquish shame with their songs. Shame is the enemy.

All I have is what I carry. What I brought. Nothing fancy. This walk across the desert has been long, thirsty. And often without hope. What has sustained me is you--you writers, my tribe. Your joy. Your love. Your rage. Spilled out right on those pages. You, my writers, are water for we who die of thirst.

I have come here to sing hymns to the broken.

I have come here to offer bread to the disrespected.

I have come here to rhapsodize over the forgotten.

For the children of that forgotten place that gave me story have no bread and do not sing.

Why do you write?

Do you write because you cannot not write? I am talking to you. Do you write because your beauty and pain choke you and shake you and make you weep from your own sacred strength? I see you. Do you hoist a heavy bag of human shadow onto your weary back each morning, put on your bravest face, and walk into another dizzying day hoping only to connect? I am singing to you.

Listen: A. R. Ammons said,

> I write for those who have
>
> no comfort now and will never have any.

Listen: Sharon Olds once wrote a poem called "Love in Blood Time." I was so broke I could only afford used books, and I bought the book with that poem in it. At the foot of that lovely sexual poem, the woman who had owned the book before me had written the only marginalia she left behind. In purple ink. It said:

I was happy once.

I'm not posing as a saint here, though my wife says I have a Jesus complex. I am greedy. For I never had that comfort, nor expected it. Yet I longed for it. And it suddenly came--when I had a book in my hands.

So, if you want to be rich and powerful, I can't help you. Man, I used to scrub public toilets on the graveyard shift. Glamour and I are not on intimate terms. However, if you get it figured out, feel free to contact me right away and tell me how.

#

In spite of the very excellent really good very tall huge wall that's allegedly coming to the Mexican border, the reality is that we writers are all citizens of a borderless nation. It's called Story. Story doesn't build walls--it knocks those bastards down and builds bridges with them. Just walking to the bakery, you are writing a novel. Your shadows on the lawn are poets.

What are you writing?

My first writing teachers were probably the liars and yarn-spinners of the Urrea family. A word-drunk lot, they were. But the shamans of story, my first medicine women, were the six indigenous women sweating over the relentlessly hot comal in the colonia's tortilla shop. Women from far mountain villages where, if they wanted to survive, they'd listen for the engines of government trucks late at night and early in the morning. Women from non-binary cultures, some of whom recognized three human genders, some four, some even six normal genders. Can you imagine such a world? Women from cultures more ancient than all the Conquistadores in their iron trucks. Invisible women. Women who were disrespected, even while they fed us all.

They used their hands to shape the maiz dough into round pages where they wrote our story. Disks the same shape as the sun. (Annie Dillard says, "I love with my hands, not my heart.") Their own sweat went into the tortillas, flavoring them, and their breath and their laughter. Hands going pit-pat-pit-pat. They knew what I could not know: the ancestors called corn the flesh of the sun and the goddesses. Pit-pat-pit-pat. And we were but the flesh on the earth itself. Growing in the sun. Pit-pat-pit-pat.

That same food, invented in jungle empires 10,000 years ago, has never changed. Called tlaxcalli in the mother-tongue, passed down through the millennia from woman to woman. Pit-pat-pit-pat. Forever perfect. And I was in love. I was a big player--even if I was seven or eight. I looked upon them and thought, "Sultry vixens, you will be mine. I shall marry you all. Just wait for me. I'll catch up with you!" And they, delighted that a blue-eyed changeling was among them, fed me hot tortillas. Oh yeah. Salt in a fresh tortilla? Or better, butter? I practiced my stage persona, and their attention and tortillas were my applause.

How many women, in those 10,000 years? And how many men joined them? Ten million? One hundred million? And each time those hands met, pit-pat-pit-pat, they were saying a prayer of hope for us.

Like our gatherings where we talk about our stories, it was true communion.

Why do we write?

I think of an old western movie by Sam Peckinpah. Ride the High Country. In it, Joel McCrea says to Randolph Scott: "I just want to enter my house justified,"

That always seemed like a good reason to me.

#

II.

Interviewers often ask me, "Luis, how come your books are so funny?" The easy answer is, "Because I'm a freakin' genius." I never tell them the truth. I'm funny because I'm so deeply sad and angry.

You writers are a bonnie clan of crafty lasses and strapping young lads. I see you carouse and drink and sing karaoke. But I also know that you wouldn't be in such places as writing conferences, of all places, listening to craft talks on a summer afternoon if your lives had been a non-stop party-time laff riot.

Scarred much?

Listen: the great Korean poet, Ko Un, said: "By the pain of your darkness the moon rose."

Do we write to escape? Do we write to afflict the guilty? Do we write to comfort the wounded and the betrayed? Or do we take the hardest step? Do we take a machete to that thicket of overgrown shame, hack our way to ourselves and take our own hands and lead ourselves back to the light? Do we honor ourselves because try as they might, those who tried could not break us? Stories and songs don't have bones.

#

Allow me to tell you a bad story. Take what you need and leave the rest.

Imagine a child who was awkward. A man-child. One who could not play sports and was picked last for every schoolyard team. A mama's boy who was seen to be embracing his male friends once too often for the taste of his male guardians.

Who spent hypnotized hours among women. Now, imagine those male guardians driven to rage by his imagined pre-adolescent failure to be a man, according to their dank fantasies of manhood. And, if you would, imagine those guardians taking that boy to a crooked dentist, a man, let's say in Tijuana where these things happen.

And imagine these men taking dental drills to this boy's mouth, with no pain killer. And every time that boy writhed, cried, raised a hand in self defense, or begged for mercy, these male guardians answered him with insults and shouts, called him "Pussy" and told him to be a man.

And these sessions took place more than once.

Why do I write?

You know. I'm not telling you anything you don't know. I was that boy.

I am trying to write for him. I am trying to get back in there and grab him. He's still in the chair. And I cannot yet take his hand. Because I am ashamed of him. Can you help me?

Shame. Shame, they teach it to you. Fat children are not ashamed. Physically challenged children are not ashamed. Little girls are not ashamed of being girls. Black children, immigrant children, gay children, Mexican children are not ashamed. Even Tijuana children are not ashamed. We teach them to be ashamed. And we tell them it is for their own good.

We are brainwashed by big power people who put us in those chairs. We are assailed by those who love drills more than humans. It's a filthy lie. You help erase it for me. Erase it. Burn it every day with your beauty, with your strength.

I know you have been in that chair. Some of you are still there. And God bless you, my sisters and my brothers, if you have not been there, you will. Everyone feels the chair. Even rich people. Even beautiful people. Even your mother. Even Prince sat in that chair.
Here's what's sick. Not the chair. Not the drill. Not even that our guardians betrayed us. What's sick is that your sacred personal essence was found wanting by people who thought in some inconceivable way that the drill was...love.

For your own good. Anyone who says that to you is the serial killer of your beauty. Anyone who finds you too shrill, too fat, too skinny, too flat-chested, too awkward, too ambitious, too embarrassing, is an asshole. Anyone who left you because you weren't good enough for them--asshole.

Manhood? Are you kidding? I am the definition of manhood. In my own way. You too, are man and woman--it's yours. You set the agenda, not the assholes. I thank God David Bowie came along and even the guardians finally threw up their hands in despair and left me alone.

#

Why do I write?

Because I'm a hypocrite. I'm preaching love, and I want to break those bastards who insulted you. Who looked down on you. Eudora Welty said: "Out of love you can speak with straight fury." I hate the shooters. I hate the tasers. I hate the loud-mouthed power-cowboys on TV who teach our children to be ashamed of themselves. I want to be King Henry the VIII because I want to see heads on spikes. (But free Anne Boleyn, you jerk.)

And I also write because it's the best job in the world. I cry "Tijuana in the House" because it's bad-ass.

I own this. I write because Richard Hugo said: "An act of imagination is an act of self-acceptance."

Writing is a big sandbox full of Tonka trucks and Godzilla toys.

 We get to sleep in late.

We wear fabulous slippers.

We're caffeinated.

We have the chocolate.

We have Curtis Mayfield on the stereo.

And we get to go to work naked whenever we feel like it!   #

III.

Some final thoughts.

I was lucky to be led by life to the poetry of Etheridge Knight. I was fortunate to be young enough to sit at the feet of his wise art so I could still learn something. And Saint Etheridge spoke my dearest writing rule, the one I clutch in the dark, the one I tell myself when I want to break things. He knew bad things. He lived the racist hell America so generously offers its people of color. He lived hard old days and lonesome nights. He survived a bid in the penitentiary. What I'm saying is Etheridge Knight was not some wealthy hot-yoga chai-tea sipping surfer feeling New Agey in his BMW. Still, he said this brave, tender thing, and he meant it:

"You have to be telling people essentially 'I love you' or else you have no basis for your art."

Ponder it. When it hit me, I could only bow my head and say, "Yes, Sir."

Yes. Fill your pen with love, or don't bother picking it up.

#

In closing, another small story. Don't worry. It's your happy ending. You don't have to flinch. No drillers. Maybe a bluebird will even fly into your heart and sing.

Those who have been with me have heard this before. But it bears repeating. I wrote a novel called *The Hummingbird's Daughter*. Took up twenty-six years of my life, and a lot of it was spent with medicine people and curanderas. Twenty-six years is a long time to wrestle with God and writing. Well, anyway, there came a time when I was invited to visit a small community of healer women in the Mexican city of Cuernavaca.

As we sat there, eating green jell-o , an old healer woman came to the door and asked for water. Those of you who enjoy mysterious underpinnings of imagery like I do, like that detail. The ancient woman of secrets comes out of the sun seeking shelter and water. And she got jell-o, too.

This is what she told me: "You are one of us." No, I said. I wish. "You are," she said. I would give anything to be able to heal people, I said. To be able to take away pain. I would give up everything and do that. "You could," she said. "Because you are one of us. You are just lazy. You don't want to study." I was over ten years into the project at this point and didn't feel lazy. But I laughed. Dismissively, she said, "You can do it by *writing*." What? "Didn't anybody teach you anything? Literature is one of the healing arts. It's a shamanic act. You can heal people with words." This was from a woman who did not read.

And this is the image she put in my mind. It has never left me. I tell it often. I think about it at least once a week. Like the drill story: take what you need and leave the rest.

When you're an artist, any kind of artist, something happens when you make your art. You could be writing your novel, writing a poem, or cooking breakfast for your family. It doesn't matter. When you are making your art, with your heart and soul, you ignite a small signal fire. It can be seen in the spirit world. On the other side. As you work, it grows. And the fires of the other artists are lit all across the plain.

There are souls out there who are lost. Souls who are afraid, Alone. Confused. Perhaps they died suddenly, or violently. Perhaps they were drunk, or too ill to know what happened. But they are wandering in the gloom. And they see the light of your art. They come toward it. You give the broken a chance to huddle in its warmth.

And then they go to the next artist's light. And the next. They follow your signal fires until they have found their way all the way home.

That's it.

My Baptist friend thought that was in league with Satan. Jesuits dug it. You can make up your own mind.

Why, then, write?

Pit-pat, pit-pat. The tortilla makers say, "Child, we're all broken. That's what makes us holy." The tortilla makers say, "Everybody knows Leonard Cohen sang *There is a crack in everything, that's how the light gets in.*" Those ladies of the corn say, "The Psalms said God has special love for broken people and broken places." They say, "We peek through the cracks and see each other in the dark." They know those men in their trucks wield their drills and remember where we are scarred so they can re-wound us.

The tortilla makers say, "We kiss you on your scars to remind you that you're beautiful."

Listen: Kim Stafford said,

> I pledge allegiance to the
>
> doomed building, clumsy
>
> person, old salmon struggling
>
> up a shallow stream

I pledge allegiance to you. My tribe. You writers. You readers.

Sisters, brothers, let us stop fooling around. We are necessary. Now. Let us light our fires. Let us do the work of witness. Let us fly the colors of our joy. Let us take heart, take comfort, take pleasure in what we do. Can you hear me calling you? Can you see me out here? I am alone before you. I am stripped, but not afraid. The trucks are coming. And I am still stuck in this broken chair. I need you. I am reaching out to you. Help me get up. Help me get to that house and enter justified. Would you touch my scars with grace? Would you take my hand?

There is something I need to tell you. Are you ready for it? Here it is. I love you.

I love you.

I love you.

I love you.

I love you.

I love you.

I love you.

Amen.

Pamela Uschuk

After The Election We Watch The Super Moon Rise over The Rincon Mountains

for Terry Acevedo

The mountains are burning and we cannot sleep.

We light candles at the Grotto where daughters toss the dark braids of sick mothers at Guadelupe's feet, where fathers pin photos of the stricken for slivers of miracle, uphill from the Mission's dome, White Dove catching sunset's irridescent wishes in sky bioluminescent as plankton in the Sea of Cortez.

We breathe the dust of conquistadors who must applaud these election results caught in the tyrant's clenched teeth calling hate from under the cracked sidewalks of the despised poor who believe in promises thin as light disappearing at our feet.

The mountains are burning out of control, flames higher than our dreams of peace, eating pine trees, the hearts of deer, flames higher than the orange-faced despot's fiery rhetoric of fear.

At hill crest, we sit on concrete losing heat to stark dark taking desert in its irrevocable mouth, sit stunned despite the stinging bites of the fire ant colony skittering up our invading calves.

Unsheltered, we cannot sleep, see the huge yellow corona crowning, the birth of our moon closer to earth than its been since our own births more than half a century past.

We wait, women holding tight our arms against news that darkens daily, against the crisp flap of white sheets, the sneering narcissist chorus recounting rapes on TV. There is nothing else to do but lean against one another's sorrow, our disbelief.

We've left our candles of hope burning in the maw of the Grotto below to witness the balm of moon rise while mountain slopes turn inferno sending contrails of smoke to choke twilight's last blue song.

Oh, Moon, you are so late, grinding up slow behind jagged Rincon peaks, backlit with enough gleaming milk to feed thousands of refugee children hunted like rabbits by our border guards. Have you heard their small bones cry sleepless in detention cells?

We watch wildfires more immense than our nightmares consume miles of ridges, burning past our history as the super hunter's moon blesses supplicant cacti offering thorns to heaven.

Closer we lean into our shivering until a blizzard of crushed diamond light breaks screaming white, striking us blind, cauterizing our battered hearts, rejecting the nuclear wasps of power and revenge hissing from the tyrant's tongue.

The moon's perfect snow glows sharp as an arctic blade slicing open our hopeless arms, baptizing our faces with reflected light, and we know no tyranny can long last under such scrutiny.

Even in darkness, doves breathe, nestled in sparse mesquite leaves. We recall the canyon wren displaced roosting in the mission's adobe eaves with angels that have flown for centuries, moon-dazzled, drizzled by light bouncing from solar storms translated in their genes.

Moon's ice white chin lifts for Venus. Mica glitters each of our steps over volcanic rock past the Grotto's knotted prayers for compassion, past our long burning candles, navigating treacherous gravel the color of winter fields, taking us home, beyond any terror or grief.

Richard Vargas

11/24/16
thanksgiving; a rebirth

no family meal
no friends and drink
laughter or lounging listless
on soft sofa watching meaningless
football games

i walked to the edge of the Rock River
lit dried sage bundled and wrapped
in scarlet twine

faced south as smoke
encircled me under gray sky
and cold air embraced my bones
closed my eyes and prayed
asked that my brothers and sisters
protecting our water and lands
be safe from rubber bullets and grenades
water cannons and tear gas
asked the spirit of the river
to come between them and
the corporate enforcer's intent

faced west and felt the sacred smoke
wash over me as i asked for strength
of heart and resolve of spirit to face the rising evil before us
to be worthy of the pain that awaits in the days ahead
asked for a shield of butterfly wings and a sword of feathers
arrows made of poems and song
sharp and straight

turned and faced north
thoughts and prayers sent to
comrades in arms
fellow veterans deploying to meet

the serpent of greed head on
plunging into combat with
the will of the warrior and the
heart of the peacemaker

finally i faced the east
grateful for this moment
this renewal of self
inhaled the surrounding smoke
and felt one with the calm
flow of the river
embracing me
bonding me to this land
and its people

i dropped the burning sage into the water
my gratitude acknowledged
by the soft sound of water
meeting flame

Richard Vargas

doing laundry the saturday after the election

wondering if the numbing sensation
i wear these days like a second skin
will ever slough off
will i ever feel again

when on cue
as if she could read my thoughts
a stout and voluptuous black woman
standing at the table behind me
breaks out into song while folding
garments of all sizes from the several
piles of clothes rising up before her

her sultry voice honed from a people's
hanging from the wrong end of a rope
sings of being a motherless child
needing guidance from heaven
and a strong shoulder to lean on
during the dark days ahead

so it happens here
in the most unexpected of places
gospel and blues wrapping around
the cold dead space in my chest
transforming it into a warm shelter
for my anger to lie down and sleep

this is the part of the poem
where i'm supposed to praise
our ability to take a hard sucker punch
and carry on the good fight
but the reality is this pool
of sewage and shit we made
for ourselves is sucking me down

i'm choking on tears
yet to be formed

the words on the page of the book

i hold in my hands begin to blur
and slide off the paper

my cheeks are hot and wet
i pretend to continue reading

Eddie Vega

Asoleado

The Mexica believed in a cycle of
birth – death – rebirth
that the world where we live is a product of this cycle
where four suns previously shone, each dying
A new world was reborn from a new sun, rising

Today we live in the age of the Fifth Sun
a sun born from the sacrifice of a humble god that couldn't move
so it required a sacrifice of blood to get it going

My blood boils in sacrifice every day as I stand by
watching my people insulted by pale-faced, dark-minded politicians
who have not come to terms with their own racist identities

Asoleado,
means Sun-drenched
My mother's reasoning for why my head hurt after being outside so long
but I suspect the headache was a metaphysical growing pain
as the distant European in me struggled to mingle with my indigenous blood

The sun pushes back the pale veil revealing my identity as
descendant of Nezahualcoyotl – warrior-prince and poet

Or so I hope

The Hispanic in me can see only half of my family tree
genealogy is reserved for the Spanish-speaking lines
of poets and playwrights of an assumed nobility
To say I am *Hispanic*
only emphasizes a language I speak,
nothing of a dialecto that's been long lost
The tongues of my people were ripped out by conquistadors and missionaries
A cruel twist of fate - I can write poetry in two languages
each of which belongs to those who conquered my savage blood
I can express myself best in the tongues of those that oppressed

The Mexica believed that the monarch butterflies that return to their Valley every year
were the souls of their ancestors come back to visit
Those butterflies – endangered these days
die in North America because their roosts have been ignored, destroyed
When my current homeland has literally become inhospitable to my ancestors,
what hope is there for me?
Would I even recognize my ancestors if I saw them in my mirror?

Soy *mestizo* -
spanish for the racial make-up of a Spaniard
plus a tribe of people they didn't bother to write down
I could be Aztec or Maya
or maybe Chichimeca, Chinanteco, or Coahuiltecan
Zoque, Huasteco, Tarahumara, or Kikapu
but I'll never know which one
just like I'll never know if it was the conquistador who took a liking to the native
girl
or the dark-skinned warrior that went up to the daughter of the alcalde
with a wink and a smile, an eyebrow and a spear
each raised with further intention –
"Quióvole, chula?"

(And I'd like to say "screw you!"
to whichever side it was that put male-pattern baldness into the gene pool)

My family tree is a mesquite
and those limbs were long chopped off
dried in the sun, and burned
Everyone appreciates the aroma
No one asks how the branches made it to the fire

So here I stand before you a Mexican mutt
Mestizo
Chicano
Tejano
Sun-drenched
Asoleado
descended from
warriors that worshipped the sun
builders of temples that still climb to the sky, and
poets that sang of this precious world

Proud to be
Son
of the Fifth Sun

Hijo
del Quinto Sol

Dan Vera

November 9: Because Love Remains Dear

Let grief be grief.
Let sorrow be sorrow.
Let rage be rage.
Let all truths inhabit their places.
But here at the coldest hour,
Let hope be hope.
Let us remember we are the children
Of those who suffered before us.
Terror is in our bloodlines
and so is resistance.

Here in the garden we planted,
the earth is now shaking
as something breaks forth.

Jesse Waters

Confession of the Number Crunchers

After the shock and the grieving, a law
was passed which made it illegal
to write the number zero in a counter-clockwise circle.

A few scientists and a marketing systems analyst had determined
the country's ills would be reversed if all citizens agreed
upon only writing proper clockwise zeros. Not everyone agreed.

Not all of us thought that way about nothing, so a new
law was introduced:
                              The number one will now represent

what the number zero has always stood for. The number zero
will no longer be kept in circulation. There is nothing

to be further gained from nothing. No one
seemed shocked, and as there was nothing
tangible to grieve for, we voted, and got
on with our business of emptying this universe.

Jesse Waters

Friendly Fire

To make matters worse, someone built
an escalator eleven stories high
that went nowhere. Every day people
step on at the bottom, rise slowly

above the filled streets, and higher still above buildings
until they fall to a screaming death. At dawn,
each body is mysteriously buried before the great
escalator opens that morning. Soon, a warning is posted.
Flyers go out, town meetings fill, but all the proper forms

have been filed with the city long ago.
At night, a thick chain prevents unauthorized use.
The town kids hang out there in the parking lot.
Sometimes they duck under that chain, and sit and drink
on the first few steps of the dark.

Jesse Waters

Red And Return

Jolek, young, and stupid, did not die
in the Nazi death camps. Instead, he cut
off his own left hand around January 19
40, at Birkenau, or Sosnowiec. Three feet
from an infirmary, or a cafeteria,
with a hatchet, across an Oak tree stump
or a make-shift plyboard bench like an overgrown
root come due, Jolek cut off his own left hand.
True, he was still right-handed – with that good
right hand Jolek banged through the clinic (mess hall) doors,
"My hand, my hand!" he cried, and they staunched
the wound closed, but no one would touch
Jolek's lost left hand back out in the cold.
The Polish kapo who'd seen the whole thing
forbade anyone to go near it, the story goes, and in hopes

of buttering up told the sergeant
(after losing in cards the night before), who told
his captain, who thought the story unusual,
a Jew cutting off his own left hand. This captain
went first to Jolek in the infirmary and asked,
 "Why? Why would you cut off your own left hand?"
but Jolek had no answer, would not tell why,
and the captain was so taken by the (lack of) story
that once Jolek's arm had "healed" he was given
the kapo position over ninety-five older prisoners,
and Jolek beat them with his good right hand,
beat them as he clutched his stump to his chest,
and made them jump and dance til they passed out.

                    But before all this,
as that captain left the infirmary he stopped
to stoop at the still-bleeding, still-shivering left hand,
"Look," he gestured to the sergeant – actually a friend
from Dachau, or Wiesloch, from before the war –
there in the web of Jolek's left thumb and forefinger,
in prison ink blue, was a dime-sized tatoo

of the Star of David, lots of Jews had them –
in different body places – and as they looked,

in January's cold fist, the story goes, Jolek's hand
turned blue and the tattoo disappeared.
It was an amazing thing to watch, I imagine,
and that captain and the sergeant talked about it
over the years and stayed friends, and thought a lot
about being called upon to do something bad –

called upon by your country to do something
bad, because they were not animals, or demons,
but workaday men and not sure about that even, I found out:
I met them both on the way to Dachau, by coincidence,
absolute luck at a tram stop near the Munich airport (moving through
after a funeral for the one's brother, or wife) and we just struck
up a chat, in English, and talked about the war
because I asked. Compelled, I think, by Jolek's hand, by memory,
like breaking open, they cut each other off
telling me how this Jewish man named Jolek
chopped off his own left hand with a hatchet, Jolek
who wouldn't take the hand back, Jolek with his left arm
clutched to his chest the rest of the year – how
they'd watched the Jew in Jolek disappear from his body.

Jolek, Jolek, Jolek, until I just had to tell them –
had to tell them about my Great-Uncle Jolek,
young and mean and stupid, who did not die
in the Nazi death camps but rather cut off his own left hand
and that no one in our family ever knew why, and it's true,
it's true, I said I wouldn't lie to you, sir, and we
sat quiet for a moment. We embraced then, I hugged
him hard like I would my good father, and he hugged back hard,
I don't know why, but it's how my story goes.
In his eyeglasses lay everything cracked – forgiveness, pride
and clean anger – or maybe it was my reflection in those lenses,
but I knew then that losing a hand, even cutting
off another man's hand means only half
what it takes to cross the human heart.

Michael Waters

The Book Of Constellations

Dominican Republic

We'd forgotten, again, *The Book of Constellations,*
so stretched on sand, unable
to finger even one winter warrior, to sketch one
creature lumbering shaggily
past muted heroes assembled star by star by God.
Or by man who squints below,
imposing myth in fearful murk upon far heavens.
No brilliance here. One hand stalks
crabwise into yours as husked coconuts plunge earthward.
We attempt slight revisions:
naming constellations after less mythical beings
who ruined our half-century
by harming helpless creatures left briefly in their charge:
Idi Amin, Ceauşescu,
Marcos, Pinochet, the Papa Docs and Baby Docs,
that hypocritical fool
Strom Thurmond dragged to hell fifty-three years past his time,
Pope John Paul—but then we stop.
When did human love mutate into this reptilian
seething that makes us despise
ourselves? *Whose hand in mine?* So we revise: Noguchi,
Miles, Allen Ginsberg, Balthus,
Joe Strummer, Raymond Carver, Muriel Rukeyser,
Bob Marley and Audre Lorde!—
heroic trespassers thrumming heaven's negative
spaces, prodding the icy
stars to wheel once more and assume fierce grandeur with each
invocation of their names,
who kindle such generative, indelible fires
across the universe, *yes,*
our only universe, dear God, belovèd, amen.

Donley Watt

Writing in Winter

Perhaps now, except for the echo in our tortured brains, we will hear "Lying Hillary" no more, and (not soon enough) the sickening "Killary" bumper stickers will fade and tatter away. Small consolation, for Trump's target has simply changed from Hillary to the continuing overt denial of truth and the suppression of dissent. This is no longer about defeating a talented, yet vulnerable opposition candidate, but an extension of how our now President-elect grouped journalists in a corner at his rallies where he could egg on his deluded, absurdly self-named Christian crowds to verbally accost and harass them. And now, if his history teaches lessons, his standard message will continue: when anything negative is written or reported about him, his predictable response will be, "The media lies, the media can't be trusted. Listen only to me to hear the truth." Blatant and threatening demagoguery, alive in America,

This is not Venezuela, where an arrogant authoritarian President Maduro silenced many of that country's major newspapers, and *El Nacional,* one of the handful remaining, publishes only under extreme duress and unveiled threats. And in Caracas, when the people protest graft and waste, theft and deceit by those in power, with the economy now crippled, and they take to the streets en masse to protest, the military and government-armed brutal gangs, divide, assault and disperse those brave enough to march.

Will this be our fate? Will our press and journalists, our community of writers be belittled and bullied into silence? Unimaginable until now, a time unmatched in recent history when we seem leaderless, suddenly lacking a strong woman or man to step forward and challenge this President-to-be, a man strange and dangerous, ego-driven and lacking a moral center; deaf to all appeals to reason.

But we will write, we will speak out. We will not be silenced, even if our words are mocked or ignored, even if they seem no more than dead leaves swirling in this dark winter's wind. They are our words, connected to our lives and to those we love, and we write these words for to us they matter.

Patricia Jabbeh Wesley

The Unbuckling:
An African Dirge

Nov. 9, 2016

Does anyone else feel like they've lost a loved one, lost
their mother, the other end of their umbilical cord?

Lost their blood root, their link to tubers that have
forcefully stretched underground for years, their

crisscrossing roots of underground family part, like
losing their childhood friend, their sister-kin, that

hard loss, like the dashing against a hard thing?
That loss of freedom, a tragedy of some sort, an

undoing of many decades of freedom, the unfolding
of a great hold, an unbuckling of tired steel knuckles

against steel, the loosening of what was, this freedom
that in the palm of a refugee is fine diamonds, sparkling,

after the dark of war? Oh, I can't bring myself to shake
off this mourning. My friends, come, freedom died

last night. Lay out the mourning cloths, lay out many
mourning *lappas,* lay them out in the dark morning dew.

Even the sun will not come out to meet us this morning.
The sun does not want to look us in the face after

this election oh, give me a piece of cloth, a large towel
so I can wail my pain, oh, my people, who will help me

grieve this grief? Lay out many black *lappas* end to end,
lay them out in the early morning dew until the night

rescues this reluctant sun. Lay them out so the mourning
women can sit and cry dirges for this great loss, oh, how

did we stumble so hard? Oh, did they go out and sell
our hopes for thirty pieces of silver, ah-ah? But they say

this is a free country-o, home of the free, where other
tens of millions looked into the eye of a piece of paper

and darkened it with their hate, but is that what they call
voting, and did they paint it so they didn't have to see

the dark of my skin, their scratching that made all that
evil of the man seem so good? Did we lose our way

into the long ago past, oh, how my blood ripples within
my dark blood. Maybe I'll wake up to hating people

someday, like staring at the white woman or the man
at the red light, and going, *I wonder if she/he was among*

the percentage of those. I'm glad I know you know I know
you voted for him, but it's all the other millions, like

the man tailgating me yesterday, his Drump flag flying
above one side of his truck, and on the other,

the Confederate flag. The good news is the bad news
of our common loss. The bad news is the good news

of our awakening. I think I'm writing a poem. I can see
the lines on my page, long lines across our cities, people

of all shades, marching, lines of the undoing of this
injustice, lines in protest because we are not a people

void of strength. We will unbuckle each biting pain
of such a woeful day. We will unshackle each shackle.

Patricia Jabbeh Wesley

Too Many Chickens Are Coming Home to Roost

Let us open the doors. Let us lift the shutters
over the thresholds of the doors, let us
remove the bars from the door posts,
too many chickens are coming home to roost,

and it is not the storm. It is not the August
or September Hurricane. It is not the storm
that's driving home all the angry of heart,
all the hate that, like aged tar on broken

pavement, has lifted onto the roads, and now,
too many chickens are coming home to roost.
Let us open the doors, not to let them in.
Let us open the doors to let us out.

Do not turn down your lights. Do not go to
bed with your eyes closed. Do not let out your
young sons. Do not wander into unknown places.
Do not listen to the wind. Too many roosters

have come home to drive us away from town.
We who came running from the fires of our
homelands are now being told to flee again?
Too many roosters have come home to roost

because hate is not a thing we can hold
in a sift. Hate is not a thing we can place a finger
upon to soothe away hurt. Hate is as hard
as a burning stone, as hard as pain, as an open sore.

Patricia Jabbeh Wesley

After the Election

After the election, we will hold hands again
and be black and white, again, and lie together
in bed without the world banging at us, banging
the brains of our bodies into us not being us.

After the election, we can go back again into
the world, where an earthquake killed hundreds,
and yet we didn't want to know it, and we don't care
after all, there is the election news, bigger than

the world, where we have turned into a faraway
Island of us and us. After the election, we can
call up the friend we lost in the pile of rubble
when the earthquake of hate dug deep scars

like graves, where we buried love and peace.
And now, all around us are enemies we cannot
know. After the election, we shall walk upright,
lift our heads, say hi, without a heavy heart

or maybe, with a heavy heart. We shall become
not white or black or dark or even not a Muslim
or maybe not, maybe not, I say. Maybe, after
the election, we shall need boats with ropes

to pull us out of the flooding of dark rivers
of hate, maybe, we shall now carry not just a
rifle, not only an automatic bullet spitting gun,
but machetes and bombs since the election

was not about a leader, but about something
like a storm that uproots not only the trees, but a
whole town. After the election, maybe, maybe,
we will put away our bile of speech, our anger,

our lies about the swamp that was not a swamp.
Maybe, we shall go out and see our neighbor again,
maybe, a picnic, maybe again, we shall hold hands
with someone of the other, maybe, maybe, not.

Bill Wetzel

One Drop

This speech was the opening segment for a panel named "Protecting the Sacred: Panel on Indigenous Environmental Issues" held on November 28, 2016 at Revolutionary Grounds Books & Coffee in Tucson, Arizona.

One drop.

I want to talk about one drop of water.

But first, I will tell you a story.

Nearly 80 years ago, in a little reservation house that no longer stands today, a young man would wake up every morning in the dead of winter to go to work on a state highway road crew. Not long before this, during the Great Depression, his own father would work one day a week for the Bureau of Indian Affairs. His father would get "paid" one pouch of tobacco, some potatoes and rice, and one dollar for his efforts. So, like his father, this young man knew what it was like to live & support a family through hard times. He would wake every morning, walk to a neighbor's house, and haul water from the well back home for the use of his young wife and seven children. He would then walk four miles of dirt road to a highway, where he would hitchhike 6 miles to work, then back later on that evening. As the highway project continued, his trip eventually grew to over 30 miles one way and back. This was often done in weather as cold as -40 below zero. This man was my grandfather.

From that point, he saved his money and got a car. Soon he was elected to the Blackfeet Tribal Council. A few years later, he was made tribal chairman. And eventually, he was elected the President of the National Congress of American Indians, where he became personal friends with President John F. Kennedy and his brothers.

I tell that story for three reasons.

First, this was a dark time in our nation's history. We were devastated by the Great Depression. Then World War 2. We endured national trauma. Including the shameful internment of our fellow citizens, Japanese-Americans. In many ways we are going through a similarly dark time. 15 years of war in the Middle East. An economy which hasn't fully recovered from the Great Recession of 2008. And we face a threat from an authoritarian president-elect, who openly spews hate and bigotry against Muslims, people of color, and many of our most vulnerable citizens.

However, reason number two, we persevered. Just like my grandfather who worked hard and survived through tough times, our country did too. At the end of World War 2, the United States had 6 percent of the world's population, and 50 percent of the world's wealth. We were a superpower almost without historical precedent. And we spent decades building a robust middle class. We are a strong people, and we will get through this darkness.

And third, this brings me back to water. Every single day my grandfather started his day hauling water for his family. Water is essential to life. It is the base for everything. So it is no wonder, why our brothers and sisters in Standing Rock, North Dakota are fighting so hard to protect their water source, in what should be considered one of the greatest civil rights issues of our time. If not the greatest.

But there is something else about water. Water is powerful. It is a force of nature.

Think back to that one single drop.

It reminds me of the beginning of my friend, the great Dine' poet, Sherwin Bitsui's award winning book "Flood Song." The book starts with one word.

To'.

Descending down a page.

Like droplets.

To'

To'

To'

To' is the Dine' word for water.

Those droplets become a torrential storm. Then they become a flood. Together they are a force of nature that cannot be stopped until it runs its natural course. And after the flood, as my friend writes, there is a rebirth. The flood comes and cleanses the earth. Then it grows back beautiful again.

Now I am just one man.

To'

These panelists are each one person.

To'

To'

To'

And all of you are individuals.

To'

To'

To'

But like water, when we all get together we are a force of nature. We are a force for change that nothing or nobody can stop. And after we are done fighting our fights, and changing the world, preserving Oak Flat, shutting down the fracking of Chief Mountain, and now stopping the Dakota Pipeline, then there will be a rebirth.

And the world will be more beautiful than ever.

Eleanor Wilner

Parable of the Eyes

Somewhere in America, on the plains,
is a silo full of eyes.
                    They are closed,
shut tight, though, now and then, a few
tears run, and a rivulet of salty water
shudders the piles in the murk
of those great bins, like storage lockers
people put things in they can't re-
member why they bought, once
valued things that got in the way
as they moved from here to there,
and there to here:
                    here, where the bells toll
day and night—deep bronze the sound,
its slow decay goes on and on,
and the eyeless try to drown the sound,
sit down to watch the news, when
the knock of the fist comes on the door,
and you can hear the grinding of gears
as the trucks pull up outside,
                    and the eyes, locked in
the heartland silos, suddenly blink
and open wide, and all they see
is other eyes
in all that darkness
staring back.

Eleanor Wilner

The Photographer on Assignment

Midnight, night sounds--owl scream, restless sleep,
Alaskan summer, high noon all night, unnatural
to the body's mind. The camera falters
in my hand. And I am cold, observing here
so near the pole, though the sun is sleepless
all summer, still the night is cold, even the shutter
sticks from the cold, stutters, deep disquiet
in the veins, as I watch the she-owl
guarding her open-mouthed young, beaks a Y
of hunger. No cover in this tundra but low shrub,
too long a winter has kept life close
to the ground, where the lemmings thrive,
plentiful in the stunted grass. I watch
the male owl soar on opened wings, hunting
while the female guards the nest; again
and again, he strikes—lemming after lemming,
and since the sun stays up, the lemmings
stand revealed; they don't conceal themselves
but hope to warn their predators away
with their small, fanged aggression--
to their grief. Easy targets, all.
In the unforgiving light, the owl
spins overhead, talons open as he dives--
the lemmings pile up, the nestlings can eat no more,
stuffed and sleepy, but, in all this light,
the owl keeps hunting, dropping lemming after
lemming from his claws. The sun burns, the owl hunts,
the lemmings are a bleeding pile of useless flesh
and fur that grows and grows beside the sated nest.
That is the photo I bring home: a monument
to the harvest of that white night.

William Yellow Robe

Breathe Deeper

Just but a moment,
brother,
sister,
a moment,
a small breath,
less than a splinter of a fear,
less than a moment of hate,

that breath,
that courage,
rushing into you,
feel it,
enjoy it,
now,
breathe deeper,
slowly,
not out of panic,
but with the motion, of a mother,

your eyes dropping fear from you in tears,
clearing and seeing truth,
the reality that is yours,
the reality you can change,
discard the hate and fear others refuse to own,
replace it with this breath,
your own heart beat,
and begin,
change is not an end,
but a moment,
to create life,
create yours...

CONTRIBUTOR NOTES

Elmaz Abinader's recent poetry collection *This House, My Bones*, was the Editor's Selection 2014 from Willow Books. She has a memoir: *Children of the Roojme, A Family's Journey from Lebanon*, and book of poetry, *In the Country of My Dreams…* Elmaz is co-founder of The Voices of Our Nations Arts Foundation (VONA/Voices). She teaches at Mills College. www.elmazabinader.com

Samuel Ace is the author of *Normal Sex, Home in three days. Don't wash.*, and *Stealth*, with Maureen Seaton. He has received the Astraea Lesbian Writers Fund Award, the Firecracker Alternative Book Award and is a two-time finalist for a Lambda Literary Award. His work has appeared in or is forthcoming from *Poetry, Fence, Posit, Vinyl, Troubling the Line: Genderqueer Poetry and Poetics, Best American Experimental Poetry 2016*. www.samuelace.com

Jack Agüeros (1934-2014) published three collections of poems: *Correspondence Between the Stonehaulers* (1991); *Sonnets from the Puerto Rican* (1996); and *Lord, Is This a Psalm?* (2002). He also translated *Song of the Simple Truth: The Complete Poems of Julia de Burgos* (1997). He served for more than ten years as the director of El Museo del Barrio in East Harlem.

Warren Alexander's kindergarten teacher claimed he was the first five-year-old cynic she ever encountered. He took this as a compliment and honed that trait into a somewhat useful skill. Some years later, he received an M.A. in Creative Writing from NYU, where he studied with Thomas Keneally, Peter Carey, and E.L. Doctorow, among others. He also eceived Honorable Mention on six or seven occasions from the *New York Times* Caption Contest, but denies he was responsible for the paper discontinuing the feature.

Andrew Allport is the author of *the body | of space | in the shape of a human* as well as a chapbook, *The Ice Ship & Other Vessels*. His work has appeared in *Orion, Boston Review, Colorado Review*, and many other journals. He lives, writes and teaches in Durango, Colorado. Visit andrewallport.wordpress.com for more information.

Beth Alvarado is the author of two books, *Not a Matter of Love* and *Anthropologies*. Recent work has appeared in *Guernica, The Sun*, and *The Southern Review*. She teaches prose at Oregon State University-Cascades low residency MFA program and is the fiction editor of *Cutthroat*.

Doug Anderson's first book of poems, *The Moon Reflected Fire*, won the Kate Tufts Discovery Award and his second, *Blues for Unemployed Secret Police* a grant from the Academy of American Poets. His memoir, *Keep Your Head Down: Vietnam, the Sixties and a Journey of Self-Discovery*, was published by W. W. Norton in 2009. His most recent book of poems is *Horse Medicine*. He has taught in the MFA programs at the Pacific University of Oregon and Bennington College, Smith College, and the University of Massachusetts.

Tara Ballard has spent the last seven years in the Middle East and West Africa, where she and her husband teach at local area schools. She holds an MFA from the University of Alaska, Anchorage, and her poems have been published by *The Southampton Review; Salamander; Wasafiri; Spoon River Poetry Review; War, Literature and the Arts;* and other literary magazines.

Aliki Barnstone is a poet, translator, critic, editor, and visual artist. She is the author of eight poetry collections, including *Dwelling* (Sheep Meadow, 2016) and *Bright Body* (White Pine, 2011). She translated of *The Collected Poems of C.P. Cavafy: A New Translation* (W.W. Norton, 2006). Her first collection, *The Real Tin Flower* (Crowell-Collier, 1968), was published when she was 12 years old, with a forward by Anne Sexton. Her poems have appeared in such journals as *New Letters, Los Angeles Times, Prairie Schooner,* and others. Her awards include a Senior Fulbright Fellowship in Greece and the Silver Pen Award from the Nevada Writers Hall of Fame. Professor of English and Creative Writing at the University of Missouri, she serves as poet laureate of Missouri.

Rick Bass is the author of over 30 books of fiction and nonfiction, including, most recently, *FOR A LITTLE WHILE: NEW AND SELECTED STORIES*. He is writer-in-residence at Montana State University, teach in the Stonecoast MFA program, and am a board member of the Yaak Valley Forest Council (www.yaak-valley.org)

Kate Bell's poems have appeared in *The Artful Mind, Turning Wheel*, and the *Manzanita Quarterly*. She lives in Eagle County Colorado where she teaches reading and writing to middle schools and takes long walks in the mountains with her wolf dog.

Marvin Bell's recent books are *Vertigo: The Living Dead Man Poems* (Copper Canyon) and, with Christopher Merrill, a lyrical nonfiction dialogue, *After the Fact: Scripts & Postscripts* (White Pine).

Wendell Berry's scores of books—poetry and prose—have for decades observed and wisely appraised the effects of how we as a nation have "lived our lives by the assumption that what was good for us would be good for the world. We have been wrong. We must change our lives so that it will be possible to live by the contrary assumption, that what is good for the world will be good for us. And that requires that we make the effort to know the world and learn what is good for it." It is this sensibiity that can make America authentically great by educating us in the true nature of thrift, which is a global generousity. [Enjoy him now on You Tube.]

Sherwin Bitsui is originally from Baa'oogeedí on the Navajo Nation. His collection of poems, *FLOODSONG*, won the American Book Award and the PEN Open Book Award. Since 2013, he has served on the faculty of the Institute of American Indian Arts in the low residency MFA Creative Writing Program.

Roger Bonair-Agard is a native of Trinidad & Tobago and Brooklyn, and author of four collections of poems including the Nat'l Book Award long listed, Bury My Clothes (Haymarket Books, 2013) and the most recent Where Brooklyn At?! (Willow Books, 2016). He is co-founder of NYC's louder ARTS Project and the founder of The Baldwin Protocols Reading Series. He fronts the Brooklyn based band Miyamoto is Black Enough, and is Program Director at Free Write Arts & Literacy at Cook County Juvenile Temporary Detention Center. He lives in Chicago, IL.

Christopher Boucher is the author of the novels *Golden Delicious* and *How to Keep Your Volkswagen Alive* and the managing editor of *Post Road Magazine*. He lives with his wife and two children in Watertown, Massachusetts, and teaches writing and literature at Boston College and Oregon State University Cascades.

Karen Brennan is the author of seven books of varying genres, including new fiction, *Monsters*, Four Way Books (2016). Her fiction, poetry and nonfiction have appeared in anthologies from *Norton, Penguin, Graywolf, Spuytin Duyvil, Michigan* and *Georgia*, to name a few. A National Endowment of the Arts recipient, she is Professor Emerita at the University of Utah and teaches at the Warren Wilson MFA Program for Writers. She holds a Ph.D. from University of Arizona.

Nickole Brown's books include *Sister* (Red Hen) and *Fanny Says* (BOA Editions). She was the editorial assistant for the late Hunter S. Thompson, worked at Sarabande Books for ten years, and was an Assistant Professor at the University of Arkansas at Little Rock. She is the Editor for the Marie Alexander Poetry Series and lives with her wife, poet Jessica Jacobs, in Asheville, NC. Her poem "Trump's Tic Tacs" was published in the *Assaracus* issue "If You Can Hear This: Poems of Protest and Resistance to an Inauguration."

Sarah Browning is Co-Founder and Executive Director of Split This Rock: Poetry of Provocation & Witness. Author of *Killing Summer* (forthcoming) and *Whiskey in the Garden of Eden* and co-editor of *DC Poets Against the War* and special issues of *POETRY* magazine, she is an Institute for Policy Studies Associate Fellow and winner of the People Before Profits Poetry Prize. "Drinking as a Political Act" first appeared in *The Volta: Evening Will Come* and "In Guantanamo" first appeared in *Big Bridge*.

Christopher Buckley's *STAR JOURNAL: SELECTED POEMS* is published by the Univ. of Pittsburgh Press, 2016. Among several critical collections and anthologies he has edited: *Bear Flag Republic: Prose Poems and Poetics from California*, 2008, and *ONE FOR THE MONEY: THE SENTENCE AS A POETIC FORM*, from Lynx House Press, 2012, both with Gary Young. He has also edited *On the Poetry of Philip Levine: Stranger to Nothing*, Univ. of Michigan Press 1991, and *Messenger to the Stars: a Luis Omar Salinas New Selected Poems & Reader* for Tebot Bach's Ash Tree Poetry Series.

Chuck Calabreze may sound like a fake name; however that may be, he is surely among our most genuine poets. He is rumored to live in the southwest among eagles who keep him around for laughs and his leftovers.

Carmen Calatayud was born to a Spanish father and Irish mother. Her book *In the Company of Spirits* was a runner-up for the Walt Whitman Award and a finalist for the Andrés Montoya Book Prize. For five years, Carmen was a moderator for Poets Responding to SB 1070, a Facebook group created by poet Francisco X. Alarcón after Arizona passed its 2010 racial profiling law.

Work by 2013 Texas Poet Laureate **Rosemary Catacalos** has twice appeared in *The Best American Poetry*, and she has held NEA, Stanford Stegner, and Dobie-Paisano fellowships. A fine press chapbook, *Begin Here*, appeared from Wings Press in 2013. She currently serves on the Texas Commission on the Arts touring roster and lives in her hometown of San Antonio, Texas.

Teresa Mei Chuc was born in Saigon and immigrated to the U.S. under political asylum with her mother and brother shortly after the Vietnam War. She is author of two poetry collections, *Red Thread* (Fithian Press, 2012) and *Keeper of the Winds* (FootHills Publishing, 2014). Her newest chapbook is *How One Loses Notes and Sounds* (Word Palace Press, 2016). She is editing the poetry anthology, *Nuclear Impact: Broken Atoms in Our Hands*. Founder and Editor-in-Chief of Shabda Press, a member of Coast to Coast Poetry Press Collective, Teresa teaches at a public high school in Los Angeles.

Alfred Corn is the author of eleven books of poems, two novels, and three collections of criticism. He has received fellowships from the Guggenheim Foundation, the NEA, the American Academy of Arts and Letters, and the Academy of American Poets. He has taught at Oklahoma State University, Yale, U.C.L.A., the University of Cincinnati and Tulsa University. In 2013 he was made a Life Fellow of Clare Hall, Cambridge. He lives in Rhode Island.

Glover Davis is Professor Emeritus of Creative Writing at San Diego State University. He has published six collections of poetry: *Bandaging Bread, August Fires, Legend, Separate Lives, Spring Drive*, and *My Cap of Darkness*. Davis' work has appeared in many journals, including *The Southern Review, Poetry, Yale Review, Crazy Horse, Prairie Schooner,* and *The New England Review.*

Alison Hawthorne Deming's most recent books are *Stairway to Heaven* (Penguin Poets 2016), *Zoologies: On Animals and the Human Spirit*, and *Death Valley: Painted Light*, a collaboration with photographer Stephen Strom. A 2015 Guggenheim Fellow, Deming is Agnese Nelms Haury Chair in Environment and Social Justice at the University of Arizona. "Letter to America" was first published in terrain.org.

Chard deNiord is the Poet Laureate of Vermont and author of five books of poetry, including *Interstate, The Double Truth,* and *Night Mowing*. He lives in Westminster West, Vermont.

Natalie Diaz was born and raised in the Fort Mojave Indian Village in Needles, California, on the banks of the Colorado River. She is Mojave and an enrolled member of the Gila River Indian Tribe. Diaz teaches at Arizona State University and the Institute of American Indian Arts Low Rez MFA program. Her first poetry collection is *When My Brother Was an Aztec.*

Sean Thomas Dougherty is the author or editor of 15 books including the forthcoming *The Second O of Sorrow* (2018 BOA Editions), and *All You Ask for Is Longing: Poems 1994- 2014* (2014 BOA Editions). Recent poems in *North American Review*, and *Best American Poetry 2014*. His website is seanthomasdoughertypoet.com. He works in a pool hall in Erie, PA.

Pulitzer Prize winner and former U.S. Poet Laureate **Rita Dove** has published numerous books, most recently *Sonata Mulattica* and *Collected Poems 1974-2004*; she also edited *The Penguin Anthology of Twentieth-Century American Poetry*. Among her many awards are the National Medal of Arts and the National Humanities Medal. She is Commonwealth Professor of English at the University of Virginia.

Alexander Drummond is the former publications director at the National Center for Atmospheric Research which does cutting edge climate research, and is the author of the biography *Enos Mills: Citizen of Nature*, which deals with conservation history in the early twentieth century and which laid the ground work for today's land preservation and wilderness initiatives.

Heid E. Erdrich is the author of five collections of poetry, most recently *Curator of Ephemera at the New Museum for Archaic Media* from Michigan State University Press. Heid is Ojibwe, enrolled in the Turtle Mountain band in North Dakota. She has collaborated on interdisciplinary artworks and curated visual arts exhibits for the past 10 years. Heid teaches in the low-residency MFA Creative Writing program of Augsburg College.

Martín Espada has published numerous books as a poet, editor, essayist and translator. His latest collection of poems is called *Vivas to Those Who Have Failed* (2016). He has received the Shelley Memorial Award and a Guggenheim Fellowship. His book of essays, *Zapata's Disciple* (1998), was banned in Tucson as part of the Mexican-American Studies Program outlawed by the state of Arizona.

Shangyang Fang grew up in Chengdu, China. He is currently a Civil Engineering student at the University of Illinois, Champaign, Urbana. He writes poetry in both English and Chinese.

Howie Faerstein's *Dreaming of the Rain in Brooklyn*, a selection of the Silver Concho Poetry Series, was published by Press 53 and a second book is in the works. His poetry can be found in numerous journals. He lives in Florence, Massachusetts...*The military-corporate state will be opposed at every point!*

Blas Falconer is the author of *The Foundling Wheel* and *A Question of Gravity and Light*. He teaches at San Diego State University and in the low-residency MFA at Murray State University. His third book-length collection of poems, *Forgive the Body This Failure* (Four Way Book) is forthcoming in 2018.

Annie Finch is the author of numerous books of poetry, including *Eve, Calendars,* and *Spells: New and Selected Poems.* Her poems have appeared in the *Penguin Book of Twentieth-Century American Poetry* and onstage at Carnegie Hall. Annie has performed her poetry and taught workshops at conferences, schools, and universities around the world. Her pussy grabs back. More at anniefinch.com

Ann Fisher-Wirth's fourth book of poems, *Dream Cabinet*, was published by Wings Press in 2012. Her other books are *Carta Marina, Five Terraces*, and *Blue Window.* She is coeditor of the groundbreaking *The Ecopoetry Anthology*, which appeared from Trinity University Press in 2013. Her work has been published widely and has received numerous awards and prizes. She teaches at the University of Misssisippi, where she also directs the Environmental Studies program, and she teaches yoga at Southern Star in Oxford, MS.

Carolyn Forché is the author of four books of poems, including the most recent *Blue Hour.* Her fifth and forthcoming collection is titled In the *Lateness of the World.* She is also the editor of two anthologies: *Against Forgetting: Twentieth Century Poetry of Witness* and *Poetry of Witness: The Tradition in English, 1500-2001* (with Duncan Wu). She is a 2017 recipient of the Windham Campbell Prize in Literature. She is a University Professor at Georgetown University, where she also directs Lannan Center for Poetics and Social Practice.

Keith Flynn (www.keithflynn.net) is the author of seven books, including five collections of poetry and two works of non-fiction. His most recent titles include *The Golden Ratio* (2007), *Colony Collapse Disorder* (Wings Press, 2013), and a collection of essays, entitled *The Rhythm Method, Razzmatazz and Memory: How To Make Your Poetry Swing* (Writer's Digest Books, 2007). Flynn is founder and managing editor of *The Asheville Poetry Review*, which was established in 1994. For more info: ashevillepoetryreview.com.

Since **Manasseh Franklin** had her first glacier encounter in Alaska during summer 2013, she's made it her mission to make the incredible experience of diminishing ice more visible to the general public. Her writing can be found in *Alpinist, Western Confluence, Trail Runner, Rock and Ice* magazines and more. She holds an MFA in Creative Nonfiction Writing and Environment and Natural Resources from the University of Wyoming.

Yahya Frederickson's books include *In a Homeland Not Far: New & Selected Poems* (Press 53, 2017), *The Gold Shop of Ba-'Ali* (Lost Horse Press, 2014), and *The Birds of al-Merjeh Square* (Finishing Line Press, 2014). A former Peace Corps Volunteer in Yemen and Fulbright Scholar in Syria, Saudi Arabia, and Kyrgyzstan, he teaches at Minnesota State University Moorhead.

CMarie Fuhrman is an Indigenous daughter of the Rocky Mountains. Passionate about the wild and sacred, CMarie concentrates her writing and poetry on protecting cultural heritage, preserving open places and remembering Native peoples. She has won the Burns Award for Poetry from the University of Idaho, published in *Metaphor, Juxtaprose, Cutthroat*, and *Taos Journal of Poetry*. CMarie is currently enrolled in the MFA Program at the University of Idaho and lives in the high mountains of west central Idaho with her companion Caleb and their two dogs Cisco and Carhartt.

Christian Anton Gerard is the author of *Holdfast* (C&R Press, early 2018) and *Wilmot Here, Collect For Stella*. He's received Pushcart Prize nominations and Bread Loaf Writers' Conference scholarships. His poems and essays appear widely. Gerard is Assistant Professor of English, Rhetoric and Writing at the University of Arkansas-Fort Smith. Find Christian on the web at www.christianantongerard.com

Greg Glazner's books of poetry are *From the Iron Chair* and *Singularity*, both with W.W. Norton. His awards include The Bess Hokin Award from *Poetry*, The Walt Whitman Award, and an NEA Fellowship. An electric guitarist as well, he performs with bands in California, Colorado, and Washington. His collaboration with composer Garrett Shatzer premiered in 2014. He teaches at UC Davis and in the Rainier Writers Workshop.

Dr. Richard Grossman is a retired obstetrician-gynecologist who has practiced in Durango, Colorado for almost 40 years, and used to perform abortions. About half of pregnancies conceived in the U.S.A. are unplanned, and many women choose to abort an unwanted pregnancy. Access to safe and legal abortion services are important for two reasons: Nothing can change a woman's life so much as being forced to raise an undesired child; and our world is already overpopulated. This piece originally appeared in the Durango (Colorado) Herald. You can find past Population Matters! columns at: www.population-matters.org"

Hedy Habra has authored two poetry collections, *Under Brushstrokes*, finalist for the USA Best Book Award and the International Book Award, and *Tea in Heliopolis*, winner of the USA Best Book Award. Her story collection, *Flying Carpets*, won the Arab American National Book Award's Honorable Mention. "Even the Sun has its Dark Side" was first published by *Inclined to Speak: An Anthology of Contemporary Arab American Poetry* (2008) and, later, collected in *Tea in Heliopolis*. More at hedyhabra.com

Teri Hairston is a poet and fiction writer. She was the 2005 winner of the Salem College Rondthaler Award in both Poetry and Fiction as well as the winner of a John Woods Scholarship in writing to study abroad in Prague. In February 2013 her poem "A Love Song" was featured in *Poetry in Plain Sight Winston-Salem*. "An Indiscretion" was the winner of the 2013 Women's Writing Award in *Firefly Ridge*. Several poems have been published in *Cutthroat: A Journal of the Arts*.

Sam Hamill has published more than 40 volumes of poetry, essays, and translations from ancient Greek, Latin, Chinese, Japanese and Estonian. He is Founding Editor of Copper Canyon Press and the founder of Poets Against The War. His collected poems, *Habitation*, was published by Lost Horse Press.

Joy Harjo has written eight books of poetry, including her most recent, *Conflict Resolution for Holy Beings*, which was shortlisted for the Griffin Prize and named the American Library Association as a Notable Book of the Year, a memoir Crazy Brave, which was awarded the PEN USA Literary Award in Creative Nonfiction, and many others. She was recently awarded the Academy of American Poets Wallace Stevens Award.

Robert Davis Hoffmann and his wife Kris live in Sitka, Alaska. While being raised in the Tlingit village of Kake, Alaska, he learned his tribal art form from his father. He uses art and writing to describe the protracted effects of colonialism on his people, addressing universal themes of trauma, grief and loss. In poetry, he journeys toward healing and restoration.

Linda Hogan's (Chickasaw Nation) latest collection is *Dark. Sweet. New and Selected Poems*. Her novel *Mean Spirit* was a finalist for the Pulitzer Prize. Other novels include *Power, Solar Storms*, and *People of the Whale*. Her poetry includes *The Book of Medicines*, finalist for the Book Critics Award, and *Rounding the Human Corners*. Her nonfiction includes *Dwellings:A Spiritual History of the Natural World* and *Woman Who Watches Over the World*. Hogan has received a Guggenheim Fellowship, an NEA Award, a Lannan Fellowship, and the prestigious PEN Thoreau Prize for 2016.

Cynthia Hogue has nine collections of poetry, most recently the about-to-be-published *In June the Labyrinth*. She has two collections of translations (with Sylvain Gallais), including *Joan Darc* by Nathalie Quintane (La Presse, 2017). Her work has appeared recently in *Field, Poetry International, Crazyhorse, Prairie Schooner, Kestrel,* and *Best American Poetry 2016*. She teaches at Arizona State University.

Garrett Hongo was born in Hawai`i and grew up in Los Angeles. He attended Pomona College, the University of Michigan, and UC Irvine, where he received an M.F.A. His latest book of poetry, *Coral Road*, was published by Knopf in 2011. Among his honors are the Guggenheim Fellowship, two NEA grants, a Fulbright Fellowship, and the Lamont Poetry Prize from the Academy of American Poets. He teaches poetry at the University of Oregon and is working on a book of non-fiction entitled *The Perfect Sound*.

Pam Houston is the author of five books of fiction and nonfiction including *Cowboys Are My Weakness* and *Contents May Have Shifted*. She is the director of the literary non profit, *Writing By Writers*, and teaches at the Institute of American Indian Arts and UC Davis, and many other places. She has a memoir of place forthcoming in 2017 from W.W. Norton called *The Ranch*.

LeAnne Howe (enrolled citizen of the Choctaw Nation) author of *Choctalking on Other Realities* (2013) is the winner of the inaugural 2014 MLA Prize for Studies in Native American Literatures, Cultures, and Languages. She writes poetry, fiction, and plays. In 2015, Howe received the Western Literature Association's 2015 Distinguished Achievement Award. She's the Eidson Distinguished Professor of American Literature in English at UGA.

Richard Jackson is the author of nearly 25 books, 13 of poetry, and winner of Fulbright, Guggenheim, Nea, NEH, Witter-Bynner and 5 Pushcarts. He was awarded the Slovene Order of Freedom for his humanitarian and literary work in the Balkans, and most recently the Dane Zajc Residency in Ljubljana.

Patricia Spears Jones is an African-American poet, playwright, editor and activist who resides in Brooklyn. She is author of *A Lucent Fire: New and Selected Poems* (White Pine Press) and seven other collections. Her plays were commissioned by Mabou Mines. She is editor of *Think: Poems for Aretha Franklin Inauguration Day Hat* and *Ordinary Women: Poetry of New York City Women*. She is a recipient of grants from the NEA, NYFA and awards from The Foundation of Contemporary Art and The Barbara Deming Fund.

Marilyn Kallet is the author of 17 books, including *The Love That Moves Me*, poetry from Black Widow Press. She has translated Paul Eluard's *Last Love Poems*, Péret's *The Big Game*, and co-translated Chantal Bizzini's *Disenchanted City*. Dr. Kallet is Nancy Moore Goslee Professor of English at the University of Tennessee. She also leads poetry workshops for VCCA-France in Auvillar. She has performed her poems on campuses and in theaters across the United States as well as in France and Poland, as a guest of the U.S. Embassy's "America Presents" program. The University of Tennessee lists her as an expert on poetry's role in times of crisis.

Willie James King, a native of Orrville, AL, writes and dwells in Montgomery, AL. His poems appear widely. Regarding the two poems contained here: "You Can Go Back, If you want," was first published in *Mudfish*, and later reprinted in *Malpais Review. To Console Them, Urthona* (UK). His work has been nominated nominated for several Pushcarts.

Yahia Lababidi, Egyptian-American, is the author of 6 collections of poetry and prose. His most recent, *Balancing Acts: New & Selected Poems* (Press 53, The Silver Concho Series, 2016) debuted at #1 on Amazon's Hot New Releases, under Middle Eastern Poetry. He is, currently, putting finishing touches to a new collection of aphorisms on art, morality and the life of the spirit.

William Luvaas is the author of 6 books, including *Ashes Rain Down*, Huffington Post's 2013 book of the year. His stories & essays have appeared in dozens of publications. Honors include an NEA fellowship in fiction and first place in Glimmer Train's fiction open contest. He is online fiction editor for *Cutthroat*. www. williamluvaas.com twitter: @williamluvaas

Clarence Major's most recent book is *Chicago Heat and Other Stories* (Green Writers Press, 2016). He was award the 26th Annual 2016 PEN Oakland Lifetime Achievement Award for Excellence in Literature in December 2016. His most recent book of poem, *From Now On: New and Selected Poems*, was published by the University of Georgia Press in 2014.

Fiona Martin is a sophomore at the University of Tennessee, Knoxville where she is double majoring in Women, Gender, and Sexuality Studies and English. She serves on the executive board for Sexuality Empowerment and Awareness at Tennessee. Her work "the future is queer" is her first published poem.

Michael Martone was born in Fort Wayne, Indiana. His most recent books are Winesburg, Indiana, and Memoranda, a book of hint fictions about the purpose of the federal government of the United States.

Tim McBride works at SAS Institute in Cary, NC. He has also worked for US-AID, NC State University, and the Centro Internacional de Mejoramiento de Maíz y Trigo in El Batán, Mexico. He has published one book of poems, *The Manageable Cold*, with TriQuarterly Press at Northwestern University. He won the 2014 MacGuffin Award, selected by Carl Dennis.

Megan McNamer's essays have appeared in *Salon, Sports Illustrated*, and *The Sun*, and she has won awards for her fiction from *New Millennium, Glimmer Train, Carve Magazine*, and the *Travelers' Tales Best Travel Writing Solas Awards for 2016*. Her debut novel *Children and Lunatics* (Black Lawrence Press, 2016)—which Rick DeMarinis called "strange and subtly frightening" —won the Big Moose Prize. She lives in Missoula, Montana.
Leslie McGrath is the author of two books of poetry. Her poems and interviews have been published in *Agni, Poetry magazine, The Academy of American Poets, The Writer's Chronicle*, and *The Yale Review*. McGrath teaches creative writing at Central CT State University and is series editor of The Tenth Gate, a poetry imprint of The Word Works Press.

Tyler Meier's poetry and prose have appeared in *Poetry, Boston Review, Indiana Review, At Length, jubilat, Washington Square*, and *Bat City Review*. He works in Tucson at the University of Arizona Poetry Center.

E. Ethelbert Miller is a writer and literary activist. He is the author of several collections of poems and two memoirs and the former board chair of the Institute for Policy Studies. For fourteen years Miller has been the editor of *Poet Lore*, the oldest poetry magazine published in the United States. He was awarded an honorary degree of Doctor of Literature in 1996 by Emory and Henry College. In April 2015, Miller was inducted into the Washington, DC Hall of Fame. In 2016, Miller received the AWP *George Garrett Award for Outstanding Community Service in Literature and the DC Mayor's Arts Award for Distinguished Honor*. His most recent book is *The Collected Poems of E. Ethelbert Miller*, edited by Kirsten Porter and published by Willow Books.

Bryce Milligan is a recipient of the TLA Lone Star Award, "Best of the Year" picks by Bank Street College and *Publishers Weekly*, Gemini Ink's "Award for Literary Excellence" et al. *Bloomsbury Review* called him a "literary wizard." Milligan is the publisher of Wings Press. His most recent book is *Take to the Highway: Arabesques for Travelers* (West End, 2016), which Jane Hirshfield calls a work of "distinction and evocative power."

Darlin' Neal is the author of the story collections *Rattlesnakes and the Moon* and *Elegant Punk* (Press 53). A recipient of the D.H. Lawrence, Frank Waters, and Mississippi Arts Commission Fiction Fellowships and a Henfield Transatlantic Review Award, she is associate professor in the University of Central Florida's MFA Program for Writers."On The Road to Money, Mississippi" first appeared in *Crux: A conversation in words and images South Africa to South USA.*

Kim Nicolini's art and writing have appeared in *CounterPunch, Bad Subjects, Punk Planet, Souciant, La Furia Umana*, and *Berkeley Poetry Review*. Her memoir in letters with original artwork titled *Dead Rock Stars* was published in conjunction with a solo show at Beyond Baroque Literary Arts Center. Her first book of original art and writing is titled *Mapping the Inside Out.*

Nick Norwood's third book of poems, *Gravel and Hawk,* was published in 2012. His poems have appeared widely in such places as *The Paris Review, The Oxford American, Shenandoah, Poetry Daily,* and elsewhere. He teaches at Columbus State University, where he also directs the Carson McCullers Center for Writers and Musicians in Columbus, Georgia, and Nyack, New York.

Achy Obejas is the author of *The Tower of The Antilles & Other Stories* as well as *Ruins, Days of Awe* and three other books of fiction. In 2014, she was awarded a USA Ford Fellowship for her writing and translation. In summer 2016, Mills College debuted its low-residency MFA in translation, conceived by Achy. For more information, go to http://www.mills.edu/mfa-translation. For more about Achy, visit www.achyobejas.com.

Alicia Ostriker's most recent book of poems is *Waiting for the Light,* a collection that focuses on the world and the cities we live in. Ostriker teaches in the low-residence MFA Program in Poetry and Poetry in Translation at Drew University.

Elise Paschen's new book of poetry, *The Nightlife,* will be published in spring 2017. She is the author of *Bestiary* and *Infidelities* (winner of the Nicholas Roerich Poetry Prize), and her poems have appeared in numerous anthologies and magazines, including *The New Yorker* and *Poetry.* Paschen teaches in the MFA Writing Program at the School of the Art Institute of Chicago.

Connie Post served as Poet Laureate of Livermore, California (2005 to 2009). Her work has appeared in *Calyx, Comstock Review, Slipstream, Spoon River Poetry Review, Valparaiso Poetry Review* and *Verse Daily.* Her first full length Book "Floodwater" (Glass Lyre Press 2014) won the Lyrebird Award. She is the winner of the 2016 Crab Creek Review Poetry Award.

Susan Power is an enrolled member of the Standing Rock Sioux and a native Chicagoan. She's the author of *The Grass Dancer* (PEN/Hemingway prizewinner), *Roofwalker,* and *Sacred Wilderness.* Her most recent fellowships include a Loft McKnight Fellowship for 2015-16, and Native Arts and Cultures Fellowship for 2016-17. She lives in Saint Paul, Minnesota.

Author of ten books, **Melissa Pritchard**'s award-winning fiction appeared most recently in *Ploughshares, Ecotone* and *Agni* and is forthcoming in *The Georgia Review.* A 2017 *Pushcart Prize* recipient and the 2016 Marguerite and Lamar Smith Fellow at the Carson McCullers Center in Columbus, Georgia, Melissa is currently at work on both a novel and a story collection.

Lucyna Prostko was born in Poland. From an early age, she has been immersed in the stories of her grandparents whose lives had been tragically affected by the outbreak of World War II. She graduated from the M.F.A. program at New York University, where she was awarded the New York Times Fellowship. Her poetry has appeared in various literary journals, including *Fugue, Washington Square, Ellipsis, Salamander, Cutthroat* and *Five Points*. Her first book of poems *Infinite Beginnings*, published in 2009, won the Bright Hill Press Poetry Book Competition. She is currently pursuing Ph.D. in English at SUNY Albany.

Dean Rader's *Works & Days*, won the 2010 T. S. Eliot Prize, and *Landscape Portrait Figure Form* (2014) was a Barnes & Noble Review Best Poetry Book. He edited *99 Poems for the 99 Percent: An Anthology of Poetry* and won the 2015 George Bogin Award from the Poetry Society of America. *Self-Portrait as Wikipedia Entry*, will appear in 2017 from Copper Canyon.

Maj Ragain has for decades taught writing at Kent State while hosting the annual Jawbone Spring Poetry Festival, monthly readings at Last Exit Books, as well as a writer's circle for veterans. "Poetry" he says, "is an ongoing conversation, yoking solitude and community." Among his titles are *A Hungry Ghost Surrenders His Tackle Box* (2006), *Twist the Axe: A Horseplayer's Story* (2001), and *Burley Dark One Sucker Fired* (1998). He is finishing a new and selected collection to be called *Gravy*, in honor of the late, great Ray Carver's poem.

Margaret Randall (New York, 1936) is a poet, essayist, oral historian, translator, photographer and social activist. She lived in Latin America for 23 years. Her most recent titles are *She Becomes Time* (poetry, Wings Press) and *Only the Road / Solo el camino* (a bilingual anthology of eight decades of Cuban poetry, Duke University Press).

Odilia Galván Rodríguez, poet, writer, editor, and activist, is the author of five volumes of poetry. Her latest book, from Merced College Press, is a collaboration with photographer Richard Loya, entitled, *The Nature of Things*. She is also co-editor, along with the late Francisco X. Alarcón, of the award-winning anthology *Poetry of Resistance: Voices for Social Justice*, The University of Arizona Press. She has worked as the editor for several magazines, most recently at Tricontinental Magazine in Havana, Cuba and Cloud Women's Quarterly Journal online.

William Pitt Root's dozen plus collections include *Strange Angels* and his translations *Sublime Blue: Selected Early Odes of Pablo Neruda* (2013). Translated into 20 languages, his work appears in hundreds of litmags and anthologies including *NEW YORKER, THE ATLANTIC, APR, NATION, POETRY*. Recipient of Guggenheim and Rockefeller, N.E.A. and Stanford University grants/fellowships, Root served as United States/United Kingdom Exchange Artist. Poery Editor for *Cutthroat, A Journal of the Arts*, he is finishing various mss., hiking with Pam, her Zazu, and his affable werewolf Mojo Buffalo Buddy.

Joseph Ross is the author of three books of poetry: *Ache* (2017), *Gospel of Dust* (2013) and *Meeting Bone Man* (2012). His work appears in many anthologies and journals. He won the 2012 Pratt Library/ Little Patuxent Review Poetry Prize. He teaches English and Creative Writing at Gonzaga College High School in Washington, D.C. and writes regularly at www.JosephRoss.net

Lindsey Royce holds a Ph.D. in Creative Writing and Literature from the University of Houston, an M.A. from New York University, and an M.F.A. from Brooklyn College. Her first book, *Bare Hands*, was released in October of 2016. Royce's poems have appeared in numerous American periodicals. She currently lives and teaches in Steamboat Springs, Colorado.

Christin Rzasa is a graduate of the University of Montana, where she was fortunate to have studied poetry with Richard Hugo. She has been a veterinary technician in western Montana for thirty years and lives on a small farm, in her spare time writing poetry as well as creative non-fiction based on my experiences in the field of veterinary medicine.

Based in Los Angeles, journalist and poet **Abel Salas** has written for *The Austin Chronicle, Los Angeles Times Magazine, Los Angeles Magazine, LA Weekly* and the *New York Times,* among others. His poems have appeared in *Zyzzyva, Washington D.C.'s Beltway Poetry Quarterly, Cipactli, In Motion Magazine, Kuikatl* and *Huizache* as well as in the anthologies *Poetry of Resistance: Voices for Social Change* (University of Arizona Press, 2016) and *The Coiled Serpent: Poets Arising from the Cultural Quakes and Shifts of Los Angeles* (Tia Chucha Press, 2016).

Metta Sáma is author of the chapbooks *the year we turned dragon* (Portable Press @ Yo-Yo Books), *le animal & other creatures* (Miel), *After "Sleeping to Dream"/After After* (Nous-Zōt-Press) and *Nocturne Trio* (YesYes Books). A fellow of Black Earth Institute, Metta is currently on the Advisory Board of Black Radish & is co-founder of Artists Against Police Brutality/Cultures of Violence.

Lauren Marie Schmidt is the author of three collections of poetry: *Two Black Eyes and a Patch of Hair Missing, The Voodoo Doll Parade,* and *Psalms of The Dining Room*, a sequence about her volunteer experience at a soup kitchen in Eugene, Oregon. Schmidt's fourth collection, *Filthy Labors*, a series of poems about her work at a transitional housing program for homeless mothers, is forthcoming from Northwestern University Press/Curbstone Press in 2017. www.laurenmarieschmidt.com

Susan Scheid is the author of *After Enchantment*. Her poetry has appeared in *Beltway Quarterly, Little Patuxent Review, The Sligo Journal, Silver Birch Press, Tidal Basin Review,* and other journals. Her work is included in the chapbook anthology, *Poetic Art*. Susan serves on the Board of Directors for Split This Rock. She lives in the Brookland neighborhood of Washington, DC.

Born in Morocco, **Ruth Knafo Setton** is the author of the novel, *The Road to Fez.* Her honors include awards from the NEA and Pennsylvania Council on the Arts, and her poetry, fiction, and creative nonfiction have appeared in many journals. She is working on a screenplay and a novel, and can be reached at: www.ruthknafosetton.com.

Lee Sharkey's *Walking Backwards* just appeared from Tupelo Press. Her earlier collections include *Calendars of Fire* (Tupelo, 2013), *A Darker, Sweeter String* (Off the Grid, 2008), and eight other full-length poetry books and chapbooks. Her work has been published in *Crazyhorse, FIELD, Kenyon Review, Massachusetts Review, Nimrod, Pleiades, Seattle Review,* and other journals.

Kim Shuck has been working on a second childhood for years and is deeply concerned about the soul killing direction in which this country is moving. Kim teaches whimsy under the guise of art and poetry. Shuck is the author of four books, the latest is *Clouds Running In*, Taurean Horn Press.

Peggy Shumaker was chosen as the Rasmuson Foundation's Distinguished Artist. She has served as Alaska State Write Laureate. *Cairn*, her new and selected poems, will be published by Red Hen Press in 2018. Shumaker edits the Alaska Literary Series and the Boreal Books series.

Natasha Singh's writing has appeared in the Modern Love Column of the *New York Times, ThreePenny Review, Crab Orchard Review, South Asian Review* and in numerous anthologies. She has twice been the recipient of the Canada Council Grant for creative nonfiction.

Aisha Sabatini Sloan is the author of *The Fluency of Light* (U. Iowa Press) and *Dreaming of Ramadi in Detroit*, forthcoming from 1913 Press. Her essays can be found in venues like *Guernica, Autostraddle, Ecotone,* and *SUBLEVEL*. When she's not making politically inspired watercolors, she helps coordinate a writing in the schools program that brings local poets to Tucson's public schools.

Patricia Smith is the author of seven books of poetry, including *Incendiary Art*, released in February 2017; *Shoulda Been Jimi Savannah*, winner of the Lenore Marshall Prize, and *Blood Dazzler*, a finalist for the National Book Award. Her work has been published in *Best American Poetry, Best American Essays* and *Best American Mystery Stories*. She is a professor at the College of Staten Island and in the MFA program at Sierra Nevada College, as well a faculty member of VONA and the VCFA Post-Graduate Residency Program.

Melissa Studdard's books include the poetry collection *I Ate the Cosmos for Breakfast* and the novel *Six Weeks to Yehidah*. Her writings have appeared in a wide range of publications, such as *Poets & Writers, Southern Humanities*

Review, Cutthroat, and *Psychology Today.* She is the winner of The Forward National Literature Award and other prizes.

Carmen Tafolla, State Poet Laureate of Texas 2015 and First Poet Laureate of the City of San Antonio 2013-2014, is the author of more than 20 books, including *This River Here, Sonnets & Salsa,* and *The Holy Tortilla and a Pot of Beans.* Recipient of the Américas Award, five International Latino Book Awards, the Art of Peace Award, and many other distinctions, she has been recognized for work which "gives voice to the peoples and cultures of this land."

Jon Tribble is author of two collections of poems: *Natural State* (Glass Lyre Press, 2016), and, *And There Is Many a Good Thing* (Salmon Poetry, 2017). He is managing editor of *Crab Orchard Review* and series editor of the Crab Orchard Series in Poetry published by Southern Illinois University Press. "Testimony Bed" was published in *Natural State.*

Melissa Tuckey is author of *Tenuous Chapel,* selected by Charles Simic for the ABZ First Book Award in 2013. She's a fellow at Black Earth Institute. Tuckey is editor of *Ghost Fishing: An Eco-Justice Poetry Anthology*, forthcoming with University of Georgia Press. She lives in Ithaca, New York.

Luis Alberto Urrea is the author of seventeen books, among them *The Devil's Highway, The Hummingbird's Daughter* and *Into the Beautiful North.* He is a professor at the University of Illinois st Chicago. He did not vote for Trump.

Pamela Uschuk's seven books of poems include *CRAZY LOVE* (American Book Award), and *BLOOD FLOWER* (2015). Translated into a dozen plus languages, Uschuk's awards include Best of the Web and the Dorothy Daniels Writing Award from the National League of American PEN Women. Editor-In-Chief of *CUTTHROAT, A JOURNAL OF THE ARTS*, Uschuk lives in Colorado and Arizona is finishing her blended-genre memoir, *THE BOOK OF HEALERS HEALING; AN ODYSSEY THROUGH OVARIAN CANCER.*

Richard Vargas: Well, we sure stepped in it this time, didn't we? Resist. Create. Persist. Now, more than ever.

Although originally from the Rio Grande Valley of south Texas, **Eduardo Vega** has been living in San Antonio for most of the last twenty years. A graduate of St. Mary's University, Mr. Vega currently works as a high school educator. Most evenings, he can be found at an open mic or slam, sharing his poetry about food, social justice, and Tejano culture.

Dan Vera's a writer, editor, and literary historian living in Washington, DC. He's the author of two poetry collections: *Speaking Wiri Wiri*, inaugural winner of the Letras Latinas/Red Hen Poetry Prize, and *The Space Between Our Danger and Delight.* A 2014 Top Ten "New" Latino Author to Watch (and Read), he has published other poets through Poetry Mutual Press and Souvenir Spoon Books and chairs the board of Split This Rock. www.danvera.com

Runner-up for the 2002 Iowa Review Fiction Prize, and Finalist in the 2013 DIAGRAM Innovative Fiction Prize, The 2012 Starcherone Prize for Fiction and the 2014 Paul Bowles Prize for Fiction, **Jesse Waters** is currently Director of the Bowers Writers House at Elizabethtown College, and a winner of the 2001 River Styx International Poetry Contest. Jesse's fiction, poetry and non-fiction work has been nominated for multiple Pushcart Prizes, and has appeared nationally and internationally in a variety of journals.

Michael Waters' recent books include *Celestial Joyride* (2016), *Gospel Night* (2011), and *Darling Vulgarity* (2006) from BOA Editions. Recipient of five Push-cart Prizes and fellowships from the NEA, Fulbright Foundation and NJ State Council for the Arts, he teaches at Monmouth University and for the Drew University MFA Program.

Donley Watt lives in Santa Fe, NM. His collection of short stories, *"Can You Get There from Here?"* won the Texas Institute of Letters' award for best first book of fiction. Since then he has had four more book-length works of fiction published. His essays recently appeared in *Texas Monthly* and *The Los Angeles Review*.

Patricia Jabbeh Wesley is a Liberian civil war survivor who immigrated to the United States with her family during the Liberian civil war. She is the author of five books of poetry: *When the Wanderers Come Home, Where the Road Turns,, The River is Rising, Becoming Ebony,* and *Before the Palm Could Bloom: Poems of Africa.* She is also the author of a children's book, *In Monrovia, the River Visits the Sea.* Her poem, *"One Day: Love Song for Divorced Women"* was selected by US Poet Laureate, Ted Kooser for American Life in Poetry. Her work has been anthologized and published around the world. She teaches at Penn State Al-toona.

Bill Wetzel's (Amskapi Pikuni aka Blackfeet from Montana) writing has appeared in such journals as the *American Indian Culture & Research Journal, Cutthroat: A Journal of the Arts, Yellow Medicine Review, Studies In Indian Literatures* (SAIL), *Red Ink Magazine, Off The Path: An Anthology of 21st Century American Indian Writers Vol.2.* He is the curator of the Good Oak Bar Reading Series and a 2016 Peripheral Poet. He claims to be the first member of the Blackfeet Tribe to sum-mit Mt. Lemmon. He also can't wait to find out "Who Shot America?" in the first episode of our country's upcoming final season.

Eleanor Wilner's most recent books of poetry are *Tourist in Hell* (University of Chicago) and *The Girl with Bees in Her Hair* (Copper Canyon). Her awards include Fellowships from the MacArthur Foundation and the NEA, the Juniper Prize and Pushcart Prizes. She teaches in the MFA Program for Writers at Warren Wilson College.

William S. Yellow Robe, Jr. is an Assiniboine playwright. His books include: *Grandchildren of the Buffalo Soldiers and Other Untold Stories* and *Where The Pavement Ends: New Native Drama.* He is a published in both poetry and short fiction. He is a member of the Ensemble Studio Theatre of N.Y., N.Y., and the Penumbra Theatre Company of St. Paul, Minnesota.

CPSIA information can be obtained
at www.ICGtesting.com
Printed in the USA
FFOW04n1714300118
44798958-44928FF

9 780998 622002